24 HOURS AT
BALACLAVA

T0386544

24 HOURS AT BALACLAVA

25 OCTOBER 1854

VOICES FROM THE BATTLEFIELD

ROBERT KERSHAW

The History Press

Cover illustration: 'Charge of the Light Brigade, Balaclava, 25 October in 1854' (colour litho) by Richard Canton Woodville Jr (Bridgeman Images)

First published 2019

The History Press
The Mill, Brimscombe Port
Stroud, Gloucestershire, GL5 2QG
www.thehistorypress.co.uk

British Library Cataloguing in Publication Data.
A catalogue record for this book is available from the British Library.

ISBN 978 0 7509 8888 9

Typesetting and origination by The History Press
Maps produced by Geethik Technologies
Printed and bound in Great Britain by TJ International Ltd

CONTENTS

INTRODUCTION

In 1854 Britain and France were fighting to save 'poor little Turkey', the crumbling Ottoman Empire, from the menacing Russian bear. Tsar Nicholas I thought it his holy duty to extend the power of the Empire's Orthodox Church as far as Constantinople and Jerusalem. The Ottomans were ailing, and Imperial Russia, led by Nicholas these past twenty-seven years, knew it, and sensed opportunity. The British, ostensibly defending Turkey against Russian bullying, were actually promoting rivalry against the Tsar in Asia while extracting free trade and preferential religious treatment from a crumbling Ottoman Empire. Revolutionary secularism motivated France, under Napoleon III, ironically promoting the Catholicism that underpinned his reign. He aimed to restore overseas influence and prestige squandered during Napoleon's wars. Russian expansionism was a threat.

Six weeks before, the Allies landed in the Crimea to invest the Russian Black Sea Fleet at Sevastopol. The Battle of Alma, fought six days earlier, was an unexpected defeat for the Russians and resulted in the rapid encirclement of Sevastopol. It was the ninth day of the siege.

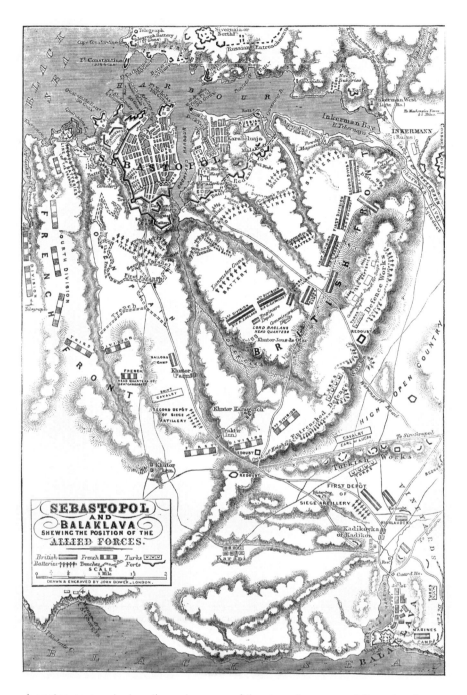

A contemporary nineteenth-century map of the siege lines around Sevastopol. The French were to the left (west) and the British on the right (east).

An intangible Russian menace to the Allied rear had yet to materialise, despite frequent cries of 'wolf' from outlying pickets. So when the first cannon boomed out from the murk, way to the east and rear, senior Allied commanders were jerked into frenetic activity. The unlikely had occurred. A Russian army was knocking on the back door of Sevastopol and on the cusp of severing the British umbilical supply line to its logistics base at 'Little London', Balaclava's harbour, absolutely packed with shipping.

Twenty-four hours of high drama followed. Before mid morning, seven minutes of cut and slash saw 900 British heavy cavalry see off and scatter more than 2,000 Russian horse. At the same time, 400 charging Russian cavalry were deflected by a 'thin red streak' of Scottish infantry from entering Balaclava harbour. Then, within two hours of achieving near victory, the British squandered it by recklessly sending 664 British light cavalry spurring down the 'Valley of Death', as immortalised by Alfred Lord Tennyson's famous poem. Half the British cavalry in the Crimea was destroyed. These epic clashes, which took up less than an hour of fighting, were to occupy a future iconic and reverential place in popular British psyche. The failed charge inspired epic poetry and literature and is still portrayed in Hollywood movie recreations today.

War correspondent William Howard 'Billy' Russell witnessed the events from a grandstand viewpoint on the Sapoune Heights. Writing for the prestigious *Times* newspaper, Russell's dramatic eyewitness coverage moved hearts and souls back home. Russell rode on the back of his influential newspaper in a new era of steamship and telegraph and could get his dispatches back to England in three weeks. There was no censorship, so the facts were as accurate as Russell could see. *Times* readers were electrified by the accounts. Before, all that had been traditionally available to the public were official military dispatches. William Russell was *the* civilian eyewitness on the spot. His electrifying account of the events at Balaclava on 25 October 1854 arrived at Victorian breakfast tables within nineteen days.

Tennyson's famous poem 'The Charge of the Light Brigade' was published in *The Examiner* on 9 December, way ahead of the arrival of the salient facts. Russell subsequently edited this dispatch, but when Tennyson wrote the poem, the *Times* reported 800 cavalry had been engaged and only 200 returned. *The Illustrated London News* claimed only 169 had got back. In fact, between 661 and 664 light cavalry charged, of which 299 fell, 103 of them mortally, but the myth was already set. 'Someone had blunder'd' was Tennyson's not unreasonable assumption on reading the early dispatches, but it was too early to objectively assess recriminations at this stage.

Tennyson wrote classic Victorian poetry, inspired by Russell's heroic prose. 'The whole line of the enemy belched forth, from thirty iron mouths, a flood of smoke and flame,' Russell wrote, echoed by Tennyson's 'storm'd at with shot and shell'. Only with Russell's subsequent edits did it become increasingly apparent that Tennyson's 'cannon to right of them, cannon to left of them, cannon in front of them' had indeed been the case. Russell later wrote that the cavalry 'were exposed to an oblique fire from the batteries on the hills on both sides as well as to a direct fire of musketry'.

When I walked the ground recently with local guide Tanya Zizak, it became apparent that this was probably intermittent fire from three different directions, and unlikely to have been simultaneous. Both men viewed the spectacle at considerable distance: Russell from the Sapoune Heights 2 miles away and Tennyson from his study at Farringford on the Isle of Wight. Clinically removed from the visceral carnage by his position on the Heights, William Russell indulged in a poetic flow as: 'with a halo of flashing steel above their heads, and with a cheer which was many a noble fellow's death cry, they flew into the smoke of the batteries.' This flowery text is replicated by Tennyson, who immersed himself in a dramatic story of knightly figures on horseback. This was the 'noble six hundred', riding into 'the valley of death'. Tennyson's grandson Charles later remembered that the poem was written at a single sitting, after reading Russell's dispatch, barely six weeks after the event.

24 Hours at Balaclava takes the reader down from the Heights, away from a different social perspective, where purchase, rather than meritocracy, determined seniority of rank. Distance sanitised onlookers from the visceral gore, smells and sounds of the moment. The reader will ride alongside the Light Brigade through the valley floor to view, feel and smell fear from the saddle, from the perspective of the contemporary eyewitness letters, diaries and personal accounts that have flowed from the charge. There is a wealth of new material to peruse, much of it from junior officers, NCOs and soldiers. Research has also identified a number of Russian accounts, young artillery and cavalry officers, who offer vivid insights from the opposing side, including French and Turkish accounts.

Today, the sun-dried October grass on the uncultivated land on the Causeway Heights and Fedioukine Hills overlooking the 'Valley of Death' retain considerable historical resonance, but much has changed. It is still difficult to pick one's way across the uneven ground between the Sapoune Heights and the valley below. This was the challenging route taken by Captain Louis Nolan, Raglan's impetuous 'galloper' Aide-de-Camp on horseback, to deliver the fateful order to charge to Lord Lucan.

A petrol station has been built at the 'Y' intersection of the Balaclava and Yalta roads, which overlooks the position where the Light Brigade formed up to charge the Don Cossack Battery at the far end of North Valley. There are now trees, roads, tracks and hillside gardens. The urban areas of Balaclava and Kadikoi have merged, reaching as far as the low hillock upon which the 93rd (Sutherland) Highlanders epically stood as a 'thin red line' to bar Russian horsemen from Balaclava. Balaclava harbour is now a popular Russian tourist destination with many restaurants and apartments. Electric power lines today traverse the area near the site of the charge of the Heavy Brigade, west of the old number 4 redoubt site. Despite the changes, an early morning or dusk walk in late October can still give a vivid perspective of what it looked like in 1854.

This book follows the day through the eyes of the onlookers and the four major instigators of the Light Brigade charge. Lord Raglan, the indecisive leader of an army little changed since Waterloo, gave the garbled order to charge, having never commanded a unit in action. Lord Lucan, who disliked Raglan, received the order, misunderstood it, and gave it to Lord Cardigan. Cardigan was the pompous and arrogant commander of the Light Brigade, more used to ornate parades in London's Regent's Park than the field of battle. He had never been to war and Lucan instructed him to charge. Captain Louis Nolan made it all happen by delivering the written order to trigger the charge.

The day is viewed through the eyes and opinions of ordinary cavalry troopers urged according to Tennyson, 'but to do and die'. 'When can their glory fade?' Tennyson emotionally wrote. *24 Hours at Balaclava* is more about the gritty soldiers' view, the men who saw little, and knew even less about what was actually happening. Letters and diary accounts lift the veil over confusing events. 'It was a most unwise and mad act,' admitted an anonymous Sergeant in the 13th Light Dragoons before the charge of the Light Brigade. 'Every man' felt 'certainly that we must be annihilated'. Private Thomas Dudley with the 17th Lancers described the realities behind Tennyson's 'do and die' stanza. 'Every man's features,' he subsequently recalled, were 'fixed, his teeth clenched, and as rigid as death'. 'When we received the *order*, not a man could seem to believe it,' he claimed. But they charged, nevertheless.

I would like to acknowledge the kind assistance I received from Tanya Zizak, who guided me through the primary landmarks in and around Sevastopol in the Crimea, and Alan Rooney from *The Cultural Experience*, who set up the contact. Tanya showed me the precise spot that Raglan likely stood on the Sapoune Heights as well as offering insightful comments throughout the day we spent exploring the battlefield in 2014. She followed up with useful advice on Russian sources, maps, terrain photographs and interpretations. Her assistance was invaluable. In addition, senior librarian Andrew Orgill and the staff at the Royal Military Academy Sandhurst provided a wealth of original nineteenth-century material and sources.

1

SEVASTAPOL

MIDNIGHT TO 4.30 A.M.

SEVASTOPOL SIEGE LINES

MIDNIGHT TO 3 A.M.

It was a cold, bleak morning on the ninth day of the siege, 25 October 1854. Cannon fire was intermittent. From time to time a flash followed by a sinister thump sent a mortar shell in an iridescent fiery trail across the night sky. Clouds momentarily flickered when the bomb went off, accompanied seconds later by the grumble of an explosion. Further light trails whooshed out of the dark mass of indistinguishable siege lines or spat back from the shadowy silhouette of the city beyond. Occasionally a complete cannonade blasted out; cascading sparkling light reflected across surrounding buildings before dying down again. When such lightning flared, it produced warning cries in the darkness, drowned by the sound of approaching humming projectiles. These climaxed with a howling crescendo into flickering detonations that spewed out showers of earth and stone from the rocky ground.

'It is getting very cold,' Sergeant Timothy Gowing with the Royal Fusiliers recalled in his journal, 'and the sooner we get at the town and take it the better.' Lacking manpower, the Anglo-French Allied army could not completely invest the city of Sevastopol. Russian reinforcements and supplies could still get in from the north. Unable to starve them out, the Allies resolved to batter the defences into submission with artillery. The first land assault had yet to happen. 'It is immensely strong, and looks an ugly place to take,' Gowing admitted, 'but we will manage it some day.' Tonight was Lieutenant General Cathcart's 4th Division's turn of duty in the siege lines, and Gowing 'found the endless trench work very trying, often having to stand up to our ankles and sometimes knees in muddy water, with the enemy pounding at us all the time with heavy ordinance.'

Sergeant Gowing was immensely strong, with a physique to match, and had adapted to the harsh life in the trenches. His party trick was being able to tear a pack of cards in half with his bare hands. Unlike many around him, who sought solace through alcohol, he was abstemious and drank only tea and coffee. Assistant Surgeon Arthur Taylor was also physically worn down. 'I am on duty in the trenches with the siege train every 24 hours,' he complained, 'so that I have one night in bed and the other on the ground.' He had to lie in the open on a regulation blanket, an upgrade from his thin regulation greatcoat that sufficed before. Cholera was rife, an affliction that had accompanied them even after leaving Turkey. 'It was piteous to see poor fellows struck down in two or three hours and carried off to their last abode,' Gowing recalled. Body resistance was reduced by poor diet, overwork and extremes of weather. 'Nearly all of us were suffering more or less from ague, fever or colds, but it was no use complaining – the doctors had little or no medicine to give.' Gowing drew strength from his Christian Evangelist faith, but bleakly observed, 'our poor fellows were dropping off fast with dysentery or diarrhoea; but stuck to it manfully.' Bodies were weaker than spirits, and those fond of the bottled variety had enfeebled themselves through excess.[1]

Sir George Cathcart was irritated by the impasse before Sevastopol, his division needlessly bleeding away in the siege lines each night. Only five weeks before, the Allies had landed 60,000 strong in the Crimea, north of the city. A Russian army of 35,000 was soundly defeated at the River Alma on 20 September and then Sevastopol was outflanked by an unexpected march that enabled the Allies to emerge in front of its undefended south. Partially invested, the city seemed completely at their mercy. Cathcart, the designated successor to Commander-in-Chief Lord Raglan, urged him to attack immediately; they faced only 15,000 Russian defenders, two-thirds of which were sailors. When the French prevaricated, so did Raglan.

General Cathcart could look straight down on the Russian defences from the dominating Sapoune Heights. '20,000 Russians could not disturb me,' he insisted, from this 'strongest and most perfect position' he occupied. The Russians he observed were working on only two or three redoubts at this early stage and 'the place is only enclosed by a thing like a low park wall, not in good repair'. They had surprised the Russians on the landward side of the port city and Cathcart was convinced that he 'could walk into it with scarcely the loss of a man at night or an hour before daybreak'; but Raglan demurred. The ailing French commander St Arnaud, stricken with cholera, was about to be replaced by General Canrobert, and he did not wish to take the risk. Cathcart was incensed and when advised that the siege trains had first to be landed to take on the city walls, he asked, 'but my dear Lord Raglan, what the devil is there to knock down?' Within a few days of indecision, 28,000 Russian soldiers entered the city through the partially invested north. No longer vulnerable to a *coup de main* assault, it could now only be taken by a deliberate coordinated attack.

Sergeant Gowing continued to 'dodge their whistling dicks', huge Russian shells that pitched from the skies, or spat out from the fortress embrasures, standing 'up to our knees in mud and water like a lot of drowned rats, nearly all night'. They longed for the arrival of dawn, which at least brought a rise in temperature. 'We have not one ounce too much to eat,' he recalled, and 'the tents we have to sleep in are full of holes, and there is nothing but mud to lie down in, or scrape it away with our hands the best we can.'

Surgeon Arthur Taylor saw the men were suffering 'and take it in good part'. 'They say they have nothing to do but "eat and fight".' There was little evidence of both but they were under constant fire. 'The ground about,' he recalled, 'and in the rear of our batteries is completely covered with 68 pound shot, shell, and grape, [but] still we have lost few men.' Conditions were bad, 'they seldom seem to wash; soap is hard to get and very dear; no one shaves, they are all too tired to take the trouble.'[2]

At about 3 a.m. observers in the trenches reported that part of the city was on fire. 'The town was on fire with our red-hot shot in three places, and is burning now.' One optimist wrote home: 'They expect in a day or two, if they do not give in, we shall take it at the point of the bayonet, which I hope they will do, for it is pretty near time it was over.'

Lieutenant Henry Clifford, the 28-year-old Rifles Regiment Aide-de-Camp (ADC) to Major General Butler commanding the Light Division, watched hopefully as the fire took hold. But 'the Russians pulled down the houses round it and only about three houses were burnt.' 'The town has been set on fire several times,' he observed, 'and the inhabitants must suffer dreadfully.' Arthur Taylor concurred that the besieging forces were steadily tightening their grip. 'The brave French have pushed their approaches to within 500 yards of the city,' he reported, 'and we are nearly as close.' Despite the hardships, there was fierce resolve to succeed. 'The assault will be made it is hoped,' Taylor recalled, 'as all our men are getting worn out, in three or four days.' Sergeant Gowing had witnessed 'wholesale desertions by Poles from the enemy'. 'We are almost longing to go at the town,' he wrote in his journal, '[to] take it or die in the attempt to hoist our glorious old flag on its walls.' Men instinctively appreciated the attack must happen soon. 'We knew well that the enemy was almost daily receiving reinforcements; we had, as yet, received none.'[3]

Contemporary eyewitness accounts often dwelt on the sheer volume of noise the Sevastopol bombardment generated. 'The air is alive with the boom, the hiss, the whiz of projectiles,' recalled Lieutenant Townsend Wilson in the trenches with the Coldstream Guards. When the British fleet closed in to bombard the harbour and redoubts, 'the noise of the cannonade deafening before, is absolutely stunning now that the ships' broadsides are pelting away at the granite.' Wilson, positioned near a land battery, saw 'a little beyond, or a little short of our works, the earth is ploughed with bounding shot, or indented with deep holes dug by the bursting of shells.' Sevastopol was shrouded in 'dense clouds of smoke' through which he saw 'a round shot, striking the angle of an embrasure, rips out gabions, kills a gunner or two, perhaps dismounts a gun.' Mrs Fanny Duberly, the 25-year-old wife of Captain Henry Duberly, the paymaster of the 8th Hussars, accompanied her husband on campaign. She remained on board a ship in Balaclava harbour. 'I am sick of the siege and the noise of the guns,' she wrote in her journal. William Howard Russell, the perceptive *Times* newspaper correspondent, had written four days before, 'we are all getting tired of this continual "pound-pounding" which makes a great deal of noise,' and more significantly 'wastes much powder and does very little damage'.[4]

Correspondent 'Billy' Russell wore quasi-military clothes and armed himself, but did not fight. He was not originally welcome in the Crimea because Lord Raglan, the Commander-in-Chief, mirrored Wellington's rule of having no truck with journalists. 'Lord Raglan,' Russell later admitted, 'never spoke to me in his life.' He was riding on the back of the *Times*' prestigious newsprint and in the new steamboat and telegraph era could get his dispatches back to England inside three weeks. An experienced correspondent, a droll Irish humour and his cigar-smoking readiness to drink anybody's brandy while able to converse easily with anyone across the social divide paid dividends. He was the civilian eyewitness on the spot. Lieutenant Henry Clifford was quick to spot his shrewd awareness of people, which he recognised as 'a gift'. 'More than one "nob",' he observed, 'had thought it best to give him a shake of the hand rather than a cold shoulder.'

With no censorship, his reportage was as accurate as what he could see and hear, which made uncomfortable reading for Raglan and his staff. 'It is very hard to batter down earthworks,' Russell observed, the only option when only partial investment prevented the ability to starve the enemy out. Russell was picking up what the soldiers in the trenches already appreciated. Nine days before, Lieutenant John Image, out with his first working party with the 21st Fusiliers, wrote in his diary that he was 'surprised to see what little damage was done'. 'The Russians have plenty of labourers,' Russell commented. 'They easily repair at night what we destroy and damage during the day.'[5]

Russell had developed an astute 'feel' for what was going on, based upon his personable conversations with officers and soldiers. 'Our men are worn out with fatigue,' he perceptively reported. 'The daily service exhausts them, and the artillerymen cannot have more than five hours rest in the twenty four,' and conditions were steadily getting worse. 'We found great difficulty in keeping warm with only our regimental greatcoats for covering,' complained Lieutenant John Hume with the 55th Regiment. 'Fleas abounded' and 'all began to find the ground very hard and our bones ached when we got up every morning.' Their only recourse was to chip out hollows to shape hip bones to the rocky ground. Russell wrote:

> Rome was not built in a day nor will Sevastopol be taken in a week. In fact, we have run away with the notion that it was a kind of pasteboard city, which would tumble down at the sound of our cannon as the walls of Jericho fell at the blast of Joshua's trumpet.

The siege was developing features of static warfare that would characterise the experience of British infantry in Flanders sixty years later. Trenches were mud and water channels, and it was cold. 'Our clothing was getting very thin, with as many patches as Joseph's coat,' recalled Sergeant Gowing.

More than one smart Fusilier's back or shoulders was indebted to a piece of black blanket, with hay bound round his legs to cover his rags and keep the biting wind out a little; and boots were nearly worn out, with none to replace them.

Their appearance encapsulated threadbare trench warfare. 'There was nothing about our outward appearance lady killing,' the sergeant recalled. 'We were looking stern duty in the face.' Stoic acceptance of their lot kept morale intact, 'there was no murmuring,' Gowing insisted. 'All went jogging along, cracking all kinds of jokes.' Snipers dominated sectors of the line. One officer on Raglan's staff remembered a Rifle Brigade sharp shooter dropping a Cossack officer from his white horse from 1,300 yards. The new Minié rifle was proving its worth.[6]

The British Army was neither tactically aware nor psychologically prepared for this type of positional warfare. Two days before, Captain Lord Dunkellin with the Coldstream Guards was captured while out at night in the trenches with a work party. The incident verged on Vaudeville comedy, a parody of the philosophy held by many of their lordships that they knew best because of birthright alone. One of Dunkellin's guardsmen had detected the approach of likely enemy in the half-light of dawn. 'There are the Russians!' he warned. 'Nonsense, they're our fellows,' replied his lordship, going toward them peremptorily and demanding, 'Who is in charge of this party?' Sure enough, it was the Russians, who surrounded and spirited him away. 'They are afraid that Dunkellin may have been bayonetted, and have sent in a flag of truce to find out about him,' recalled Lord George Paget with the 4th Dragoons. 'It appears to have been his own fault, or rather his blindness,' he commented on the notoriously short-sighted officer. 'The men told him it was a Russian picket in front of him, and he would not believe them.' Trench work could be hazardous.[7]

The spade was mightier than the sword or rifle in this form of warfare and British soldiers did not find digging trenches congenial work. The Industrial Revolution had transformed British society since 1815 and the average physique of new recruits was hardly the same robust stock as their rustic Napoleonic forbearers. Guards Captain Wilson explained:

> Strange as it may appear to many, English soldiers (with the exception of the Guards, who are almost entirely village born, with an infusion of that most magnificent of physical elements – the navvy) are, to a certain extent, poor hands with the pick and shovel, simply because one half of the men composing our line regiments are town bred – lads of loom and spinning jenny - who possibly never set eyes on a ploughed field before they 'listed'.[8]

By contrast, Wilson saw that the French appeared to regard building earthworks almost as important as musket training. They actually trained their young soldiers to use a pick and shovel. Long hours working in unsanitary conditions with a poor diet had transformed the health and physiques of the British urban working classes. The post-industrial British recruit was shorter, slight, and less physically imposing than the men who had manned Wellington's squares at Waterloo. Many cavalry recruits came from the towns, even though officers said they preferred rural youths. The average Heavy Brigade trooper in the 4th Dragoon Guards was about 5ft 8in tall, weighing just over 11 stone, and had served about five years. Private Albert Mitchell with the 13th Light Dragoons remembered the difficulties 'townies' encountered cutting forage for horses on campaign. 'Some poor fellows had hardly seen a field of corn before they enlisted,' and as a consequence 'these made poor work of it, some cutting themselves badly, and were quite unable to cut the portion allotted to them.'[9]

British soldiers laying siege to Sevastopol may have been less physically imposing than before, but they remained cunningly resourceful. The previous day, Private Maguire with the 33rd Regiment was sniping in the front trenches when he was captured by three Russians. On being marched away he snatched a loaded musket from one of his careless captors and shot him, he then swung the butt and floored the second and the third before beating a hasty retreat. The canny Maguire had realised one of the two men at his side was armed with his own Minié rifle, which he knew to have been discharged. He therefore tackled his companion, hoping the Russian's musket was loaded. All of this was witnessed from the British lines, only about 100 yards away. Maguire escaped and was rewarded by the impressed Lord Raglan with a gratuity of £5, which was immediately spent on grog at one of the many stalls that had mushroomed around Balaclava harbour.

The British expected an all-out infantry assault on Sevastopol at any moment, which would come, they suspected, at no small cost. 'Those Russians must be chained to their cannon,' reasoned Captain Townsend, 'for with them there is no relenting.' The Russians had earned grudging respect. 'The Muscovite never flinches,' Wilson admitted. 'He stands like a man to his guns, both landward and seaward.' Moreover, he seemed to 'be liberally supplied with cannon'. No matter what the damage, the fortifications were swiftly repaired. 'Its embrasures are silent only for a few minutes, and then blaze away hotly as ever.' Nevertheless, optimism remained that the city would soon fall. Lord Raglan had rejected a Russian truce overture the day before to bury the dead in no man's land, suspecting the Russians would simply improve their defences during such a lull. 'He had no dead to bury,' he responded, but the siege was developing an uncanny aura of permanence.[10]

'I rode about three miles up to look at Sevastopol the other day,' Richard Temple Godman with the 5th Dragoon Guards wrote home to his father. 'From the hill above, you can see at about a mile off right into the town and harbour.' Inside the city they could see the inhabitants 'walking up and down' and Russians out busy repairing damage and extending fortifications. It provided an exciting distraction from normal picket routine. Great black fort guns were clearly visible 'looking through the embrasures, and if you show yourself too much, a puff of smoke curls from the walls, and a shell hisses over your head'. Temple Godman had reappeared at the 'splendid view' two days before. The site 'was always crowded with officers off duty, who sit there and smoke and talk all day', he recalled. 'The place is properly called "Gossip Hill".' Insufficient activity had occurred to merit any meaningful discussion. Russian watchfires had been seen only 2,000 yards from the cavalry vedettes at the rear of Sevastopol. Correspondent 'Billy' Russell had reported travellers along the Balaclava road hearing Russian bands playing somewhere in the out-lying villages. Nobody felt this was especially ominous. Mrs Fanny Duberly, accommodated in the stern cabin on the *Star of the South* moored in Balaclava harbour, which at least had a window, had gone to bed early; she was not feeling well. 'Well we knew that they [the Russians] had been busy hanging about among the hills for some days,' she wrote in her journal, 'but we fancied in our folly that they would not attack us.' She decided she would allow herself to sleep in the following morning, 25 October.[11]

CHORGUN VILLAGE, 6 MILES EAST OF SEVASTOPOL

1 A.M. TO 4.30 A.M.

Lieutenant Koribut Kubitovich, a squadron commander with Colonel Vasilii Yeropkin's composite reserve lancer regiment, recalled the atmospheric flickering campfires that spread along the valley of the north bank of the Chernya River near the village of Chorgun. 'Loud sounds of laughter drifted far out in all directions,' he remem-bered. This was the main Russian assembly area for Lieutenant General Liprandi's 12th Infantry Division, 6 miles east of Sevastopol. Kubitovich was a young squadron leader in Colonel Yeropkin's com-posite reserve lancer regiment. His men were young recruits, who had barely served a year. 'Some who were less carefree,' he observed, 'conversed quietly among themselves.' They were preparing for battle. 'They burned letters which they did not want to see in strangers' hands should they die, and wrote last wills and testaments.' A huge social divide existed between officers and the conscripted men and

Kubitovich was wryly amused at the earnest way penniless men obsessed about disposing of possessions that were essentially worthless. 'What do you think of a will,' he was asked by a soldier, 'who has nothing except a shabraque [decorated saddle covering], two uniform coats, and a samovar [cooking pot], but who still earnestly wrote out his bequests?'

Other groups sought solitude near a small patch of woods nearby, while some 'deep in ardent conversation among friends, with memories of the past' were too excited to sleep and talked about their likely prospects in the coming fighting. The fortunate unconcerned or unimaginative were already sleeping in *burka* cloaks or greatcoats 'with no care for tomorrow's business'. Younger men tended to gravitate to the older veterans, who attracted small audiences amid the glow of scattered campfires near the horse lines. They were transfixed 'with animated interest' by war stories describing 'the first impressions when hearing a bullet whistle past, and of much else that each one would come to experience in a few hours'. Russia was at war.

'How unjust it is of the English and French to interfere in this war!' recalled Captain Robert Adolf Hodasevich with the Taroutine Regiment, echoing the prevalent view. 'All of this business is because those Christians stand up for the dog of a Turk, who impales and boils our brethren.' Soldiers were unanimous in their conviction that 'we must all fight for Holy Russia'. Tsar Nicholas I fervently believed it was his holy mission to extend his Orthodox empire as far as Constantinople and Jerusalem. Driven by the inflated pride and arrogance that came with twenty-seven years of unquestioned divine rule, the Tsar sought to profit from Turkey's ailing Ottoman Empire and extend Russian influence into the Eastern Mediterranean. War, as a consequence, had reached the Crimea.

These soldiers had marched a long way to get there. Yeropkin's lancer regiment had ridden from Moldavia west of the Ukraine. Starting initially with alternating march and rest days, they upped the tempo to 30-mile daily forced marches once they reached the Crimea. At first, they were based in the Baider Valley nearby, 'keeping watch over the Tatars and keeping them from driving their herds over to the enemy,' Kubitovich explained, 'and delivering much needed forage to them.' General Pavel Petrovich Liprandi's long-awaited 12th Infantry Division had marched in four days before. 'All of us were sure that offensive operations would begin when they arrived,' Kubitovich remembered. 'Everyone burned with the desire to be in action!' Liprandi's infantry had come from Kishinev west of the Ukraine and had marched for over a month. With no rail links south of Moscow, all movement had been by foot and wagon. 'For a Russian soldier, being on the march is nothing,' Kubitovich grandly declared, because 'the Russian peasant is used to long marches from childhood.' These epic expeditions were exciting. At first, they were cheered through strange towns and villages, and given plentiful supplies of food and drink. Carts were impressed from villages en route, but only within regional boundaries, because Muzhik drivers could not be obliged to drive beyond their borders. Quartermasters then had to round up more in the next region.

Russian soldiers were invariably serfs and because the state rather than private landlords owned most villages, he was a state serf. As such he drew the short straw in life when it came to conscription; 80,000 were selected from age 20 each year to serve twenty-five years in the line or twenty-two in the Guard. Village 'troublemakers' were invariably the first to be selected. Departure was an especially riotous carnival occasion, because once the recruit left his village he rarely came back and if he did, it would be as a stranger. Conscription was exile for life and young recruits were mourned on leaving as if they were already dead. Soldiers surviving service invariably re-enlisted or drifted as vagabonds.

Recruits from the same region were not permitted to serve in the same regiments or near their home area. The first thing that went was his long hair, which indicated serf status; this was immediately cropped to a close haircut. On arrival he was coached by a couple of '*diadkas*' or 'uncles', who were trained soldiers. They were then mercilessly drilled and intimidated in a harsh, unimaginative system that extolled a precision parade-ground posture – carrying arms and goose-stepping – as the guarantee of success in war. Virtually no serving soldier accounts have survived because serfs did not write. 'Stick and fist' imposed total obedience alongside their stoic acceptance of whatever life might bring. Mistakes were rewarded with a 'toothpick', a brutal blow to the face with a cane, drumstick or fist. They could be flogged or made to run the gauntlet, a beating administered during a forced run between regimental lines. Despite forced separation from loved ones and uncompromising discipline and squalor, Russian soldiers were hardy and unquestionably brave. Captain Hodasevich with the Taroutine Regiment remembered. 'The poor fellows suffer in silence their hard fate.' Scores against overzealous officers could always be settled on the anonymous battlefield 'in the heat of the action' Hodasevich maintained. They revered their Father Tsar, the Holy Church and Russia, and did whatever they were told. The active strength of the Russian Army with its reserves was just short of a million men.[12]

As the marching columns moved further south towards the Crimea the vast countryside became thinly populated, desolate and gloomy. There were no carts and less to eat. Native Tatars were paid far more by the foreign invaders and had little regard for the Muscovite Tsar. Artillery Lieutenant Stefan Kozhukhov found the creaking, lurching journey with the 8th Battery of the 12th Artillery Brigade tiresome. 'The north-west corner of the Crimea was not a happy place,' he remembered, 'where ever you look is flat steppe, level, dusty. Nothing to catch your eye.' Something like 75 per cent of the 10,000-square-mile Crimean Peninsula is dry steppe land. 'Even the Kurgan burial mounds which vary the landscape of the New Russia steppe, if only a little,' he explained, 'were only rarely encountered here.' The south-east part of the peninsula is blanketed with the Yayla mountain zone, which soon appeared in silhouette before them.

Kozhukhov noticed the Tatar villages they passed were largely abandoned, their sympathy with the invading allies. 'In the villages of Russian settlers, we only found old women and children, and even they met us with uneasy intimidated eyes,' he recalled. The Crimea was a depressing place. 'Continuously appearing detachments of Cossacks lent an even greater feeling of alienation,' he observed, 'as they gave the country a hostile and unfriendly character.' Tatars were neither liked nor trusted, Captain Hodasevich had disdain for their villages, which were 'neither very clean nor very regular'. His regiment had passed through en route to Sevastopol marching from Novgorod six months earlier and found 'they appeared to look upon us with anything but friendly eyes.' Russians were seen as interlopers. Normally while transiting Russia, 'soldiers were invariably fed by generosity, forced or voluntary' by the locals, 'but in the Crimea we were obliged to depend on our rations,' Hodasevich recalled, 'the same as in an enemy's country.'

Kozhukhov saw an increase in military activity as they approached Simferopol, the capital of the Crimea. 'Tents and smoking campfires scattered in disorder in these bivouacs made the whole region like a vast military encampment,' he remembered. The final approach marches were long and hard. 'We were not led along roads but rather all sorts of paths and tracks.' It was heavy going for the artillery and caissons. As they neared the 5- to 7.5-mile 'Riviera' coastal strip along the Black Sea, where most of the population lived in a synthetic Mediterranean climate, Kozhukhov realised a large military operation was pending. 'Everyone knew that troops were concentrating around Chorgun [village] to begin offensive actions from our side, but no one knew exactly when these would begin.' General Liprandi 'answered our guesses' on arrival: it was to be tomorrow.

Before it got dark 'crowds of the curious went to the nearby heights to observe the enemy positions with spyglasses,' Kozhukhov remembered. They were able to pick out 'four rather large redoubts built on the highest points commanding the surrounding area'. They could see that 'small bushes covered the whole area' – useful perhaps for infantry skirmishers, but not for them – 'since they hindered the free movement of artillery'. They learned the fortifications were not defended by English or French 'but by Turks, who were of course much easier to deal with'. This promoted animated discussion over their likely prospects; 'everyone spoke of difficulties, but no one mentioned failure.' 'Before a battle,' Kozhukhov explained, 'it was somehow not only uncomfortable to speak of defeat, but even to think of it.'[13]

The weather was changing, clouds rolled down off the hills and there was some light rain. Desiring more rest than the fitful sleep they had the night before, the young artillery officer set up a layer of ammunition boxes to make an improvised shelter and spread some straw over the wet ground. He spread his Moldavian horse blanket over the structure and tried to get some sleep.

Lieutenant Yevgenii Arbuzov, serving with the Saxe-Weimar Ingermanland Hussars cavalry regiment, had marched down from Kharkov. Like lancer Kubitovich, he had been preoccupied patrolling the local hostile Tatar villages. They had been encamped 10 miles from Sevastopol when the Allied siege bombardment started nine days before. 'The bombardment was so heavy,' he remembered, 'it was impossible to make out individual cannons firing or even the salvos from whole batteries.' It was that loud 'they could have been thundering from our own position'. That morning they were told 'it was proposed to take four redoubts from the Turks built on the Balaclava heights and drive them out of the village of Kamara.' The objective was to strike a blow at the main British logistics base at Balaclava. Once the redoubts were taken, the cavalry, including Arbuzov's regiment, would sweep down from the occupied Heights and destroy the enemy artillery and siege park at Kadikoi village, near the Woronsov road, just north of Balaclava harbour. 'Once the hussars had put the park's wagons out of order, they were to withdraw,' Arbuzov was briefed. Russian horse artillery would then shell the park to destruction, 'the enemy having been deprived of the means to move it away'. Official Russian reports of the events of this day often contradict Allied accounts and make no mention of what Liprandi's precise objectives were. Detailed planning was not a characteristic of nineteenth-century warfare. Whatever the mission,

Russian soldiers were at least aware there was to be an attack and that there would be a battle.[14]

Initiative in the Russian army came secondary to unquestioning obedience. The main training theatre was the drill square and battle tactics were in a sense performed as parade movements. General Liprandi was not supported by a general staff blessed with a particularly high education or focused intellectual development. Staff officers were little more than ADC messengers with no training or experience of operations, reconnaissance or even an awareness of how topography might influence military courses of action. In 1851 only ten officers had graduated from a staff college tainted by association with the 1825 Decembrist plot against the Tsar. Staff were often held in contempt or seen as a threat; promotion was slower than elsewhere in the army; and the pay was poor, one third poorer than the Prussian army by comparison. Most officers, except in the guard, grenadier corps or prestigious cavalry regiments, were without independent means. Like Allied officers, hardiness and courage were not lacking and despite frugal incomes – Russian colonels were paid only twice that of a lieutenant – honour remained all-important.

Lieutenant Kubitovich's young lancers talked late into the night with the 'old soldiers' by the subdued light of campfires next to the horse lines. Veterans, he acknowledged, 'have a special kind of sense' and were able to 'talk among themselves of a march or battle before the commanders know anything about it'. Men said goodbye to each other. Arbuzov watched when, after prayer services, 'each officer gave his men instructions in case of his death and all his money.' Captain Khitrivo, the 8th Squadron Commander, insisted on paying his 1,600 rouble debt to the regimental fund, because his father would have to pay if he fell in battle. Khitrivo had been gradually repaying since as a young junker (officer candidate) he had been on guard when the regimental cash box was stolen. He would have barely twelve hours to live.

Presently the bivouacs settled down as more men snatched some rest. 'Here or there was only a small candle glowing under a bush, where some officer, lying on a rug, was finishing his letter.' Kubitiovich remarked on how superstitious his men were:

> If the horses neigh and lie down in the daytime it means a long march. If a horse does not eat and stands with its head lowered – it will be killed. If on the eve of battle it keeps nuzzling its owner, then that man will be killed.

He noticed an old respected soldier weeping bitterly over his horse, Yunoa, 'the wildest horse in the whole regiment'. Nobody else could even approach her, apart from him, whom the horse loved and obeyed. 'Truly tomorrow Yunoa will be killed,' the old soldier declared. 'She doesn't eat out of her feed bag and stands here sadly.' They had served eight years together, and nobody else could even groom the horse. 'Tomorrow I'll be left an orphan, with no one to love!' the soldier lamented. The encampment eventually quietened, and 'a profound silence reigned, broken only by horses neighing, the rattle of the sentries' weapons, and the quiet murmur of men asleep.' Yunoa would be dead before the end of the day.[15]

Lieutenant Kozhukhov eventually gave up trying to sleep when rain 'drummed down on my Moldavian horse blanket'. He had been kept awake by his demons in any case. 'Thoughts crowded into my head, each one more unwelcome and malevolent than the one before.' 'What if we fail?' was uppermost in his mind. The Sevastopol army had lost confidence after its beating on the Alma and was relying upon these new reinforcements to get them out of trouble. 'All eyes are upon us; everyone expects us to perform great deeds – but what if we do not fulfil these expectations? … It was said,' Kozhukhov remembered, from 'rumours around the army that General Liprandi had advised Prince Menshikov,' the Commander-in-Chief, 'against initiating the attack' and that they should 'wait for the arrival of the whole of the 4th Corps'. But they were going to attack with what they had. Menshikov was hardly popular after the setback on the Alma. 'He never showed the slightest interest as to the manner in which the men were fed,' complained Captain Hodasevich with the Taroutine Regiment.

Kozhukhov, chilled by the rain, moved to the warmth of the nearest campfire. Two Englishmen were already there, likely civilian sutlers, captured by Cossacks in the Baider Valley. They were unimpressive, speaking no Russian and barely any French and 'were in the most pitiable state'. Soaked through, they plaintively asked for Russian vodka. How did they know the prisoners were English and not French? Kozhukhov asked the sentry. 'In this way, your honour,' replied the soldier, going on to explain: 'With a Frenchman you can converse right away; they are a quick-witted race. But here with these fellows, you wrestle with them for almost an hour and are nowhere close to finding out what in fact they want with all their heart.' They had therefore, he assumed, to be English.

When at 2 a.m. the rain at last eased off, Kozhukhov 'fell into sweet dreams'. But not for long; within an hour the bivouac was stirring: 'Kasha porridge was ready and the soldiers were summoned for their ration of spirits.' His battery commander told him they were in reserve and to start getting ready. By the time they began to harness the horses a mist had descended. Arbuzov's Hussar column was also assembling, 'strung out in the narrow ways between the hills'. Lieutenant Kubitovich's lancers stirred and 'old veterans put on clean underclothes which they always kept in reserve as men ready for death at any moment.' The prevailing wisdom was it reduced wound infections. Commanders busied themselves with the organisation as men prayed, 'and they did so,' Kubitovich observed, 'with all their soul'. Between 4 and 5 a.m. the columns started to march out of the Chorgun bivouac. They were rested, well clothed and fed. Only the odd flicker of light momentarily lighting up the western horizon and the distant crump of heavy mortars showed the direction of Sevastopol.

Their comrades in the city had no idea they were coming.[16]

2

BALACLAVA NIGHT

MIDNIGHT TO 3.30 A.M.

THE CAVALRY, WEST OF KADIKOI VILLAGE

MIDNIGHT TO 3 A.M.

British cavalry soldiers bivouacked on the undulating plain beneath the Sapoune Heights, west of the village of Kadikoi, were wet and cold. They had been exposed to the elements for five weeks. Tents offloaded at Balaclava harbour nearby had arrived only the week before. 'Rain continued at intervals during the night,' reported one Royal Artillery captain, 'but towards morning the clouds broke, and it became starlight.' Autumn was upon them, the third successive day of cloud, showers and rain, another miserable night, the precursor to another monotonous siege day.

Fitfully sleeping soldiers managed only four hours sleep before being roused to continue the punishing routine of saddling up for 'stand-to' one hour before daybreak. Pickets and vedettes had to be relieved followed by interminable stable parades, four times a day.

'The nights were awfully cold and the heavy dews would almost drench us, till the blood felt like ice,' remembered 23-year-old Robert Farquharson with the 4th Light Dragoons. He was an experienced soldier, who had enlisted at 15. 'What with "outlying" and "inlying" pickets, almost always in the saddle, and never undressed, sickness, want of food – and I've gone an entire three days without food,' he complained, 'we were very queer indeed.' Lieutenant Richard Temple Godman with the 5th Dragoon Guards was 22, and considered himself lucky enough to share a small tent with three others, who were all 'obliged to sleep on the ground'. 'There is no room for beds,' he remembered, 'but beyond it being rather hard and cold it does not matter,' because they were always dog-tired. Some of the men had resorted to sleeping inside the large barrels from a nearby wine house and press to achieve some shelter. Sleep was sporadic and intermittent, 'the dews are very heavy at night and we occasionally have a smart shower,' Temple Godman recalled.

The cavalry, unlike their infantry counterparts, manning the more secure siege lines on the Sapoune Heights above them, had pickets facing the rear, covering the eastern avenues of approach to the army siege lines. 'Every day now the Russians loitering or moving in great mass about the Chernya [River nearby] keep us on the alert morning, noon and night,' Farquharson remembered. Duties and alerts were unremitting. 'If we come in from picket fagged, cold and hungry, we might hear the trumpet sound "boots and saddle" at any moment.' 'There are very few things more trying to the dragoon's temper than these sudden turn outs,' complained Private Albert Mitchell with the 13th Light Dragoons, 'often just as he is about to get his meals', which invariably meant 'never seeing it again'. The 24-year-old Mitchell was in the fourth year of his service.[1]

Vedettes consisted of two outriders posted separately ahead of pickets, leaving a dismounted sentry in between, whose task was to warn the pickets about any vedette sightings. The daylight hours were generally quiet. 'After dark we were withdrawn from the top of the hill down into the plain in our rear,' Mitchell explained, 'it being easier at night to discern anyone approaching' because 'you see them the moment they are [silhouetted] at the top.' Cossacks, Mitchell complained, 'manage to turn you out at meal times or at night when you are thinking of getting a little rest'. These rear area security-standing patrols were relentless.

Lieutenant Colonel Lord George Paget, commanding the 4th Light Dragoons, echoed Mitchell's exasperation at the constant and cumulative interruptions of their much-needed rest. 'We are now regularly turned out about midnight, and I shall soon wake at the regular time, but we always turn in again in half an hour,' he remembered. Darkness fell by 7 p.m. and soldiers generally managed to rest by 9 p.m., but had to be in the saddle again an hour before the 5 a.m. daylight alert. 'Every fool at the outposts, who fancies he hears something, has only to make a row, and there we all are, generals and all,' Paget lamented. Twenty-nine-year-old Captain Michael Stocks with the 1st Dragoons called the interruptions 'the poorest fun I know of,' describing 'lots of Cossacks who retired when we approached and approached when we retired'. 'They remind you of rabbits,' he observed, 'but not quite so harmless.'

Four nights before, on the 21st, a report that 20,000 Russian foot and 5,000 horse were marching on them resulted in both cavalry brigades being called out, and the 4th Infantry Division was marched down to the plain from the Sapoune Heights. This was the third callout in four days. Paget's light dragoons were the only troops engaged in a light brush with the enemy before the Russians withdrew. He phlegmatically remarked, 'Well, I suppose 500 false alarms are better than one surprise, so there is no help for it.' Paget was a reluctant participant. Four months before departing England he had married his beautiful cousin, against the express wishes of his father. The intention had been to sell his commission to raise the money, but the advent of war meant it would be dishonourable to resign.

There was yet another alarm the following afternoon on the 22nd, which kept the cavalry saddled the entire cold night. 'If a heavy dragoon or any other thick-headed individual sees a Cossack,' wrote

22-year-old Cornet Wombwell with the 17th Lancers to his father, 'he comes galloping into camp and instantly magnifies the Cossack to 500. So of course out we all go and by the time we get there, not a soul is to be seen.'

Every alert resulted in the encampment being packed up, in expectation of a move, another punishing routine on top of prevailing tensions accruing from the stand-off. The British Heavy and Light Brigades screened the logistics hub at Balaclava as well as the approaches to the rear of besieged Sevastopol. Essentially, they were encamped on the front line. On return to camp after one such alert, Albert Mitchell saw 'sure enough everything was packed … Our kettle had been emptied in a ditch, and looking there we found our dinner. We picked out the best of it and after all made a tolerable meal, only it was cold, dirty and late.'

'We are now in rather a ticklish position,' explained Cornet Fiennes Wykeham Martin to his stepmother, 'having Sevastopol before us, and a large army behind us.' Everyone was becoming increasingly exasperated at the involuntary stalemate. 'Them Rooshans is too ugly to show their faces by day,' remarked a Highland soldier with the 93rd; 'I wish the brutes would come on and take their licking without too much bother.'[2]

Not everyone was cold and uncomfortable this night. Private 'Butcher Jack' Vahey was blind drunk and under close arrest in the 17th Lancers guard tent, on the hillside near Kadikoi village. He was a typical 'jack the lad' character: married, 5ft 9in tall, and in the 17th 'Deaths Head and Cross Bones', as the regiment was called. His nickname stemmed from his resourceful ability to pass himself off as a butcher, for which he received payment, as well as extra money digging graves.

> I never was backward [in] coming forward when there was any work to do, and when some fellows were moping helplessly in the tents, or going sick to the hospital, every morning I was knocking about as jolly as a sand boy, doing a job here and one there.

Vahey's commendable enthusiasm for odd jobs was about 'contriving to get more or less tipsy before nightfall'. This resulted in his arrest on the evening of 24 October, 'on slaughtering day'. His butchering had been required 'and there was a lot of rum knocking about'. 'The Commissary guard knew how to get at the grog, and were free enough with it among the butchers, for the sake of a nice tender steak.'

Working with Private Paddy Heffernan from the Royals, they were 'as drunk as lords' when it came to wash-up time. One of the Commissary officers stumbled across them 'while in this state and clapped us in the guard tent before you could say *knife*'. Fortunately for him, Vahey was a popular 'rough and tumble' type with officers and men alike. 'Indeed, had it not been for my inordinate fondness for the drink, I might have got promotion over and over again,' he claimed. He was still a private soldier at 31, after sixteen years' service. 'I used to find my way shoulder high into the guard tent pretty regularly once a week, and more than once I only saved the skin of my back by being known as a willing, useful fellow when sober.'

'One place was as good as another to us,' the incorrigible Vahey recalled. At least they were not outside freezing with a vedette, or enduring the cold showers that intermittently drummed down on their guard tent. 'We lay there contented enough all night, taking an occasional tot out of a bottle which Paddy managed to smuggle into the tent where we were confined.' They caroused until 'it was getting on for morning before we dropped off into a heavy, drunken sleep, out of which the Commander-in-Chief himself would have had a tough job to have roused us.' Retribution would come with the morning.[3]

Lieutenant Temple Godman as adjutant with the 5th Dragoon Guards had to stand at arm's length and count the strokes at the last flogging he oversaw, en route to the Crimea. 'I have the full benefit,' he recalled, overseeing fifty lashes: 'It is a very disgusting sight; a few strokes properly administered makes a man's back the colour of a half ripe plum, blue and red, and towards fifty every stroke draws blood.' It was his duty to ensure 'the farriers lay it in as hard as they can'.

The other ranks found such punishments equally unsettling. Albert Mitchell saw four young men in the 13th Light Dragoons faint as 'the flesh changed colour, and the blood began to flow' when Private William Doyle received fifty lashes. He agreed with their French allies, who employed the guilty at the most degrading and laborious work to 'make the defaulters useful to their well-behaved comrades'. Flogging victims were rarely the same men afterwards. 'They have lost all self respect,' Mitchell commented, 'and very naturally think they have lost the respect of their comrades also.' This was sometimes the case, he accepted, 'but as a rule, I believe they came in for a certain amount of pity and sympathy.'

Vahey would be at the mercy of this system the following morning. Drunkenness was hardly a unique occurrence. When the invasion fleet arrived at Scutari, Constantinople in late April, 2,400 of 14,000 men were declared drunk at watch-setting, the end of the day, according to Lord Raglan's nephew and ADC, Lieutenant Colonel Calthorpe. Desertion of a post merited a flogging and Vahey's fate would depend upon Captain Morris, his newly joined Commanding Officer. It was at the regiment's whim.[4]

Vahey belonged to an army essentially unchanged since Waterloo. It dressed similarly and its discipline was the same. A private soldier could only be punished by hanging or flogging, there was nothing in between, so Vahey was playing a dangerous game. 'Honour' and 'grit' differentiated officers from soldiers. Officers were not paternal with their men, in the same way as they are in today's army, many lavished more or the same affection on their horses. They cared for their men, but only up to a point. Officers were judged more on their ability to endure rather than inflict wounds. Soldiers expected bravery and technical skills from their officers, who were expected to stand firm under pressure. Lieutenant Thomas Lewis wrote to his father that their major had fled the 5th Dragoon Guards for fear of contracting cholera. 'If a man would run away, when the men were dying all round him, what would we do in action?' he condemned. 'We do not want to see his face again.' Officers were instead motivated by an abstract sense of 'honour', which was as tough a bond as 'mate-ship' was to the other ranks. They punctiliously obeyed orders, even if it should result in certain injury or death.

Commissions and advancement through promotion were by purchase and rarely by ability. An officer's commission was a financial investment, akin to owning a house by twenty-first-century standards, and it was a tradable commodity. His peers at home would comment upon conduct on the battlefield, therefore reputation was paramount. Officers expected total obedience from their men and the army's code of discipline exacted it, if all else failed. Peer pressure and the outward appearance of 'grit' also motivated soldiers. Death or mutilation would be risked before any doubts regarding courage might arise. Enlisted men existed in the smaller, harsher and every bit as demanding society of the regiment. Expectations from both groups underlaid the fighting power of the British army in 1854. No major war had been fought since 1815 and the 'Iron Duke' of Wellington had only passed away two years before. His complacent influence had had a stultifying effect upon the army. Very little had changed in nearly forty years and was reflected in the motivation and attitudes that were to influence some bizarre actions this day.[5]

War was seen as an aristocratic trade and bravery therefore as an essential military quality, exclusive to the wealthy. Commissions by purchase ensured that the wealthy with a stake in social order retained unchallenged social power. Incomes increased enormously during the Industrial Revolution in Britain and the untaxed aristocracy reigned supreme over tenants who did not possess a political vote. Soldiers, like the working classes, anticipated being told what to do by their 'betters'. 'I believe our steadiness under fire was mainly due to the splendid example of coolness set us by our officers,' Private Albert Mitchell explained, and they 'to a man were brave, both young and old':

It was very encouraging to the men in the ranks, when a shot or shell crashed through, thereby causing some confusion, to hear the voice of the Troop or Squadron leader saying 'steady men', 'close in' or some such words spoken quite coolly.

Mitchell did not, however, enjoy constantly striking and pitching his colonel's tent two or three times a week, when 'we the men at this time were without tents.'[6]

Shared harsh experience might soften the rigidity of the soldier/ officer interface, but only occasionally, while unconditional obedience was expected and exacted at all times. Officer behaviour could indeed be exasperating. Albert Mitchell and his companions coming off vedette duty on one occasion decided on a good breakfast of fried salt pork with biscuits soaked in fat. 'It was a breakfast that would have tempted anyone,' he remembered, 'who had lived (as we had) in the open air for three weeks, night and day.' Captain 'Jenks' Jenyns, his picket commander, rode by with Lieutenant Jervis sniffing the air and asking what 'smelt so nice'. They both indulged themselves with a taste, 'the Captain remarking that it was damn good' – so good, in fact, that 'we ourselves did not make so good a meal as we had anticipated'. Foreign commentators in the nineteenth century were intrigued by the extraordinary and eager deference the English appeared to show to their aristocracy. Novelist William Makepeace Thackeray labelled it 'lordidolitry'. After the breakfast incident Mitchell commented, 'It is remarkable how little pride there is in some officers at such times,' but there was stoic acceptance, and once 'in quarters such little incidents as this are soon forgotten.' Soldiers did what they were told, but they were not so obsequious that they did not recognise bad behaviour when it occurred. Nevertheless, they kept their thoughts to themselves until memoirs in later years.

Nineteen-year-old Private James Wightman, in his second year of service with the 17th Lancers, was bewildered by the succession of Commanding Officers they had experienced in the past few weeks. First to go had been Colonel Lawrenson, 'doubled up, as we thought, with cholera' at the Battle of Alma the month before. He was not generally liked, being 'a little too extra-dainty for the rough and ready business of warfare'. The no-nonsense Wightman had felled a Russian officer with his lance butt, after he fired a pistol at point-blank range, shooting off a ring from his horse's bit. Lawrenson told him off, calling the act cowardly, because he was taking the Russian prisoner; Wightman thought this petulant. His successor, Major Willet, 'was a good soldier, but a tyrant'. He had insisted his men should not wear cloaks during a night-long saddled alert when other regiments were comfortably cloaked, throughout an exceedingly cold night. 'This needless and wanton exposure' resulted in the sickly but obstinate Willet succumbing to hypothermia. 'He was a corpse before sundown the following day,' Wightman remembered. Now at daybreak this morning another CO had appeared, a total stranger dressed 'in blue frock coat and forage cap with a gold-edged peak'. This was 34-year-old Captain William Morris, or 'Slacks' as he was popularly called, the senior surviving 17th Lancer officer, fresh from the staff. The men did not know, but 'Slacks', or 'the pocket Hercules' as he was nicknamed by his officer peers, was the veteran of four cavalry charges and three campaigns in India. He was the consummate professional. Soldiers were generally trained by their NCOs, while officers supervised at a distance. On campaign the physical intimacy of the field brought them closer.[7]

The gulf between officers and men reflected the existing social divide and was more pronounced than it had been at Waterloo. Long years of Napoleonic campaigning had softened distinctions then, both sides being more familiar. Characterised by a slight stature, 'Little Hodge' or Colonel Edward Hodge commanding the 4th Dragoon Guards was, unlike many of his officer peers, a modest and humble man, but still could not easily identify with his men. His father had been killed at Genappe, the day before Waterloo, almost forty years before. 'We have had sad drunkenness amongst our men,' he confided in his diary en route to the Crimea in August. Hodge, being a devout Christian and generally humane, found his soldiers exasperating. 'The fools drink raw spirits, get horribly drunk and then wonder that they are ill. They do not give themselves a chance,' he wrote irritably. Hodge had no particular issue with Lord Cardigan, the unpopular Light Brigade commander, languishing every night aboard his luxury steam-driven three-mast yacht *Dryad* in Balaclava harbour. 'He seems very comfortable,' he wrote in his diary, the night Major Willet expired with exposure. 'This is the way to make war,' he commented, adding, 'I hope he will take compassion on me sometimes.'

Cardigan's yacht *Dryad* had arrived in the congested harbour two weeks before. Afflicted by diarrhoea, like most ranks sleeping rough on the Sapoune Heights, Raglan gave him permission to sleep aboard. He made constant use of his French chef; arriving late morning for duty, well after the normal dawn stand-to. At the opposite end of the spectrum were highly professional officers like Captain Louis Nolan, a 15th Hussars Aide-de-Camp (ADC) on Lord Raglan's staff. Nolan had served in Hungary with the Austrian cavalry for eight years and another eight in India, although had yet to see action. Sergeant Robert Henderson, a 15th Hussar depot instructor at Maidstone, remembered that like most officers who had served on the Continent or India, '[Nolan's] manner to those in the ranks, while it forbade the slightest approach by presumption, was so kind and winning that he was beloved by everyone.' Nolan was recognised for the intensely committed and professional soldier that he was. Sergeant Franks with the 5th Dragoon Guards recalled his easy and 'unpretending' attitude to the ranks. 'Familiarity breeds contempt' might often be the case, he recalled, but in Nolan's case 'it bred a very deep and lasting feeling of esteem.' Officers like Morris and Nolan were the forebeares of more compassionate and forward-thinking professional officers to come. In 1854 they were at the kinder spectrum of the essentially Napoleonic style of command: honour and courage for the officers and grit and obedience from the men.[8]

The British cavalry regarded itself as the army's senior service. Purchase of cavalry rank was the most expensive and the best investment. The seemingly unassailable aristocratic pinnacle of 'plungers' and 'tremendous swells', as they called themselves at home, was characterised by an air of elegant boredom. They drawled with affected jargon, pronouncing 'r's as 'w's, saying 'vewwy' (very), 'howwid' (horrid) and 'sowwy' (sorry), interspersed with pointless ass-like 'haw-haws'. Horses were their passion and dash the tactic of the day. The aim, not unlike foxhunting, was to ride like the devil at the enemy and run him over. Infantry were disdainfully regarded as a superfluous arm, better left at home, a drag on their arrogant belief that the cavalry could defeat any enemy single-handed. One pre-embarkation *Punch* cartoon summed up the horseman's sartorial attitude to war, with an affected cavalry officer complaining to a lady: 'Of course it's a bore just at the beginning of the season, and I shall miss the Derby! Wish they could have the Russians over here, because then we could have thrashed them in Hyde Park, and dined at Greenwich afterwards you know.'[9]

Generations of peace since 1815 had obscured the more visceral aspects of warfare. The large numbers of limbless ex-servicemen beggars that had roamed the streets during the Napoleonic era were largely gone.

The reality of warfare in the Crimea had already reduced the cavalry's stock among the infantry, artillery and engineers. Lord Raglan, the Commander-in-Chief, had sought to carefully husband his small mounted force of just two brigades, and the rest of the army had sensed it. When Russian cavalry was first encountered in strength at the Bulganek River before the Battle of the Alma, Raglan, fearing a trap, insisted the British cavalry retire. The infantry were much amused when the 'swells' were ordered back, amid much jeering and shouting, faced with an apparently small body of Russians. Lord Lucan, the cavalry commander, was labelled 'Lord Look-On' because of alleged timidity. British infantry then stormed the seemingly impregnable Russian position defended by 35,000 Russians on the Heights of Alma, in the face of fearsome casualties, and pushed them off. Raglan forbade the cavalry to pursue, despite raring to attack. Captain Louis Nolan on his staff echoed their frustration. 'When a routed army was in full retreat,' he indignantly wrote in his journal. 'What excuse can anyone find for those horse whose chief replied to an order to advance that the Russians were very numerous!' Captain Robert Portal with the 4th Light Dragoons complained they were commanded by 'old women' who 'would have been better in their drawing rooms'. 'Having no share in so glorious a victory was most galling,' Nolan concluded. The infantry, with its 2,000 casualties, typically joked that Raglan's dispatch likely had a cavalry section that only reported 'one horse wounded'.[10]

Cavalry were disdained as a 'showy' rather than 'a useful branch of the service'. Gentle fun poked at the absurdly gorgeous uniforms of the 11th Hussars by the *Times* newspaper before the war came home to roost: 'The brevity of their jackets, the irrationality of their headgear, the incredible tightness of their cherry coloured pants, altogether defy description; they must be seen to be appreciated.'

Lord Cardigan was rumoured to have spent £10,000 a year (multiplied by five for a modern estimate) for their uniforms in 1840. The only concession for the rigours of active service on going to war in 1854 was that the 11th were to sew leather patches on the seat of their cherry-coloured trousers. Prior to departure, the *Times* commented again that the constricted uniforms were 'as utterly unfit for war service as the garb of the female hussars in the ballet of Gustavus, which they so nearly resemble.'

Conditions around Sevastopol already resembled those that were to recur in Flanders in 1915. 'We have too much frippery – too much toggery – too much weight in things worse than useless,' Captain Nolan advised in his book on *Cavalry: Its History and Tactics*, shortly before the war. 'To a cavalry soldier every ounce is of consequence!' Nolan pointed out that cavalry duties involved riding and sleeping rough over all sorts of terrain. It required tough warm clothing on the lower half of the body, but needed to be loose on the upper half to enable unrestricted arm movement. Ornate and tightly fitting garb, designed with style in mind rather than wartime requirements, was prone to damage and offered little protection against the elements. Captain L.G. Heath, a naval officer assigned to shore duty in Balaclava, had already observed the deterioration of uniforms that had been little changed since Wellington. 'You have no idea of a campaign soldier,' he recalled, 'if you have only seen them in St James's Park or in a garrison ball room.' In the siege lines around Sevastopol 'they live in their full dress coats': 'The scarlet has turned to port wine colour and the gold lace and epaulettes to a dark coppery colour; the coat is generally full of holes and the individual wears no shirt.'

Ornate traditional uniforms were totally unsuited to trench warfare. 'The change of life to them must be very great,' Heath observed, noting their increasingly dilapidated state, 'and some of them feel it a good deal.' The weather and the rigours of campaigning were having a jaded effect; cavalry uniforms were coming apart. 'Our red coats are crimson and black stains all over them,' 23-year-old Lieutenant Robert Scott Hunter with the Scots Greys wrote home. 'Epaulettes no one wears, they are done away with, and we have to carry telescopes and haversacks, and pistols, so that with our brown faces and patched clothes, we look queer figures I assure you.'[11]

The physical condition of the British cavalry reflected its threadbare appearance, having bled men and horses since leaving England in March. Horses confined inside cramped stalls in ships' holds, roughly hoisted aboard by cranes, could not lie down and had to stand for six weeks. The Light Brigade alone lost fifty-seven mounts between England and Constantinople, twenty-six of these belonged to the 17th Lancers. They lost four more at Varna and then about 100 during Cardigan's so called 'sore-back recce' to Silistra. Cornet Fiennes Wykeham Martin remembers it being 'fearfully hot' aboard the steamship *Simla* with the 4th Light Dragoons ship 'going a great pace, 15 miles an hour' beyond Gibraltar. 'I cannot lay on the deck in a flannel suit without perspiring,' he recalled, whereas down below, 'there are about 20 horses on each side of the boiler, their noses about a foot from it; one is already dead from the heat, no air can get to them perfectly foaming with sweat.'

In late July they neared Malta beneath a searing Mediterranean sun, 'two horses gone mad from heat and being crammed up in the hold,' he wrote to his brother. Heavy Brigade transports tossed in a violent storm lost over 220 horses, the survivors being slung ashore in a wretched condition. 'On the 26th September the regiment lost more horses than at Waterloo,' remembered Lieutenant Colonel John Yorke, commanding the 1st Dragoons. Fearful transport conditions, heat, insufficient fodder and now a sudden dip in temperature with heavy dews and no shelter sapped the numbers and condition of the surviving cavalry horses.[12]

The health of the troopers was as jaded as their uniform and mounts. Three months before, cholera had surfaced at Varna in Bulgaria and 600 men died in two weeks; the French lost thousands. 'It is a thousand pities,' declared staff officer Lieutenant Henry Clifford with the Rifles, 'that our army did not go at Sevastopol on first leaving England when in rude health and full of spirits and enthusiasm.' 'All these have vanished,' he wrote in his diary. Cholera was frightening. Clifford recalled one young officer from the 77th fresh from England: 'he came up here on Tuesday, was taken ill on the Wednesday morning and buried that evening.' The intimidating aspect was complete helplessness in the face of an enemy one could not see or fight. It generally began with a day of painless diarrhoea with no vomiting. Victims often surmised it was a dose of dysentery, which would pass. Violent diarrhoea followed, with large purges of mucous membrane and vomiting with similar content, accompanied by intense thirst and pain with dehydration agues. After a day the skin became cold and took on a bluish-purple hue, familiar comrades' faces became pinched with sunken eyes, and an almost imperceptible pulse. Pain came from abdominal cramps with severe cramp in the legs and feet. There was nothing anyone could do. Horrified onlookers were surrounded by the stench of effluent coming from scores of friends or compatriots, struck down and rendered completely immobile by the disease.

'Men and officers are dying off like rotten sheep,' Lieutenant Robert Scott Hunter with the Scots Greys wrote home to his sister Molly. Cavalry camps were moved around at Varna to escape the insidious menace. 'Billy' Russell, the *Times* correspondent, reported the Guards and Light Division lost around 100 to 120 men each and the cavalry a similar amount, with 600 sick. The 5th Dragoon Guards lost three officers and forty other ranks at Varna, a loss rate appropriate to battle casualties. Squadrons had to be amalgamated before even meeting the enemy. Experienced NCOs and officers were replaced with whatever nominated replacements were available. Russell reported in early October that 'since we landed in the Crimea, as many have died of cholera as perished on the Alma,' where 380 of 2,000 casualties were killed. Only one in four, or 3,754 of 19,584 total soldiers who perished in the Crimea, were to fall in battle.

The cumulative impact was not just fewer experienced soldiers within a diminished chain of command; it also had an insidious impact upon morale. 'The depression of the army is increased by this event,' Russell observed at Varna prior to the Crimean invasion. 'It is doubtful' if they would exhibit 'the same pluck now that they were so full of a month ago'. Even before swords were crossed, men 'sup full of horrors and listen greedily to tales of death which serve but to weaken and terrify them.' Victorian soldiers were actually more phlegmatic than Russell and his readers gave credit. 'A private soldier does not care a bit about anything,' was Lieutenant Henry Clifford's more sanguine view, 'as long as he himself is not actually the victim,' a characteristic of soldiery throughout warfare. Danger needed to be visible before it became intimidating. Clifford observed: 'Tho' hundreds are falling about him he lives on, in the same thoughtless way and would not march 10 miles [to avoid cholera] to save himself from the fate of his companions.'[13]

Petty bickering between the Earl of Cardigan and Lord Lucan further undermined the parlous condition of the British cavalry. Cardigan, commanding the Light Brigade, had departed for Varna to take over the leading cavalry elements without the permission of his overall commander Lucan. Raglan, the Commander-in-Chief, compounded the issue by not consulting with his cavalry commander, encouraging Cardigan's erroneous belief that his brigade had some sort of pseudo-independent status. His insubordinate behaviour remained unchecked until Raglan, tiring of the stream of official complaints from Lucan and the Adjutant General, put the errant Cardigan in his place. The damage, however, had already been done; there was neither mutual regard nor trust between the two cavalry commanders. Mrs Fanny Duberly, accompanying the expedition, observed, they 'fight like cat and dog' and are the 'most pitiable old women you ever heard of'. Neither was their behaviour discreet: 'the very privates scoff at them and they drive the officers wild,' Mrs Duberly commented.

Lucan at Varna reverted to pre-war parade ground hype. Long field training days were conducted in the oppressive Bulgarian summer heat, weakening men and horses still further while he nagged at them with obsessive administrative trivia. His unsympathetic and unpredictable manner alienated officers and men alike. Meanwhile, Cardigan's 300-mile so-called 'sore back' reconnaissance from Varna to the Danube River at Silistra revealed just what an inept field soldier he was. Two squadrons of several hundred men were driven along at a 'cracking pace' for seventeen days on a mission, conducted in searing heat, which could have been likewise achieved by a few score men. Food and forage was not provided for in an area bereft of water. One aide dispatched by Raglan found the recce by following the dead horses that lined the route. Fanny Duberly witnessed the 'piteous sight' of the returning column, with 'men on foot driving and goading the wretched, wretched horses, three or four of which could hardly stir.' One hundred horses perished and cholera-prone cavalrymen weakened even further. 'Lord Lucan is a very sharp fellow,' acknowledged Major William Forrest with the 4th Dragoon Guards, 'but he has been so long on the shelf he does not even know the words of command.' Taken together, the bickering between the two commanders had negative implications for the future tactical efficiency of cavalry operations. Lord George Paget, commanding the 4th Dragoons, observed they were 'like a pair of scissors who go snip and snip and snip without doing each other any harm, but God help the poor devil who gets between them'.[14]

Captain Louis Nolan on Raglan's staff was disheartened by the contrast between British and French cavalry reconnaissance skills his practised eye detected:

Our French neighbours when called upon to reconnoitre to the front, to the right, to the left, dash off like a flight of swallows and spread far and wide, clustering around their leader again like bees bringing in the fruits of their expedition and that in a few minutes.

British light dragoons, he irritably observed, 'Trot off, keeping their dressing and looking to the rear instead of the front and if you move in another direction they stand there till they are sent for.'

These were parade ground tactics. Looking to their rear was perhaps advisable, because their rigid tactics were under the microscope of commanders focused more on unquestioning obedience than with the Russians. Lucan was constrained by Raglan's obsessive insistence on carefully husbanding his diminishing cavalry. He had ordered no forays across the River Chernya to the north-east, behind which it was known the Russians were gathering. When one of Captain Oldham's patrols from the 13th Light Dragoons lost a sergeant, taken prisoner across the river, Lucan had Oldham arrested for disobeying orders. Albert Mitchell witnessed Oldham's unsympathetic response to 'our mistake', the capture of the NCO by four Russian hussars. 'Serve him right too,' Oldham had said. 'Why did he not ride at them and bowl them over?' Now he was in trouble. Instructions were not to cross the river, but how else could they determine whether there were Russians in the village beyond? Lucan got the information but still insisted. Mitchell remembered, 'our captain was relieved and placed under arrest'.

The cavalry were the eyes and ears covering the open rear behind the Sevastopol siege lines as well as any approach to the vital British logistics hub at Balaclava. Lieutenant Colonel Anthony Sterling on Major General Sir Colin Campbell's staff, responsible for the inner defence of Balaclava, like much of the army, was singularly unimpressed with the cavalry. They had yet to be blooded. 'Cossacks are constantly roaming about,' he complained, 'and our cavalry are not very clever at outpost duty.'[15]

BRACKER FARMHOUSE, SAPOUNE HEIGHTS

MIDNIGHT TO 3.30 A.M.

Lord Raglan had taken over the Bracker farmhouse on the Sapoune Heights for his headquarters ten days before. The one-storey deep-roofed red-tiled house was north-west of the prominent col, where the road from Balaclava crested the Heights, 600ft above sea level. One of Raglan's staff described it as 'a sort of country villa, with large farm buildings'. It was close to the British siege lines and within a few minutes' ride to the Sapoune escarpment, offering a magnificent view of the approaches to Balaclava. Cottages and sheds joined by a low wall completed the square-shaped complex. All was quiet during the bleak, cold morning hours of 25 October. Raglan was asleep, as were most of the staff in tents located nearby. Staff watch in the warm flickering candlelight of the headquarters was far preferable to cavalry picket duty, enduring intermittent rain on the undulating plain below. Only the odd bang and iridescent trail of mortar shells occasionally disturbed the peace. Most officers and soldiers slept, if they were able, as soon as early darkness descended.

The 66-year-old Raglan modelled himself on the 'Iron Duke', having served him faithfully throughout his career up to Military Secretary. Raglan lost his right arm at Waterloo during the last hour of the battle and had been desk-bound for nearly forty years. He had never commanded even a company in battle. Like his master, who rested on his considerable laurels after 1815, Raglan was resistant to change in the British Army. He even affected Wellington's mannerisms: the habit of understatement, the dislike of military splendour or of being cheered by the men and cultivating favourites. Raglan was considerably out of his depth as army commander. He shared the Duke's impassive cool nobility, but not his drive or quick-thinking judgement. Four decades of paperwork and administration had sapped his initiative.

Unlike the Duke's practice, Raglan's key subordinates were bad choices, selected by virtue of their pleasant disposition rather than innate ability or drive. Lord de Ros, his quartermaster general noted for his good humour and eccentricities, was quickly taken ill. Although not without experience, he showed little inclination to acquire more. Raglan's primary subordinate commanders were all theoretically competent, but forty years of peace had given him little recent talent to choose from. All the infantry generals had Napoleonic war experience apart from the youthful Duke of Cambridge commanding the 1st Division, who was Queen Victoria's cousin. One of the youngest was his 54-year-old cavalry commander Lord Lucan, who had retired from service in 1838. This was in essence an army commanded by the spirit if not the substance of Wellington, out of touch with changing military technology and tactics. 'There is an old commander-in-chief, an old engineer, old brigadiers – in fact everything old at the top,' complained artillery Captain George Woronsov, which 'makes everything sluggish'.[16]

James Thomas Brudenell, the seventh Earl of Cardigan and Light Brigade commander, was, at 57, well past his prime and suffering from a chronic bronchial condition. He had purchased his way to lieutenant colonel and command of the 15th Hussars in 1830 after only six years. He was harsh and domineering towards his social inferiors and subjected his regiment, known to be a cheerful and efficient organisation before his arrival, to obsessive discipline and drills, antagonising every officer. Cardigan would flog for minor misdemeanours and insisted his regiment buy new expensive uniforms. After four years he was removed from command after a much-publicised petty altercation with a Waterloo veteran that diminished him. Despite public vitriol he managed to buy himself back into command of the 11th Hussars for an alleged £40,000, shamelessly exploiting family influence to persuade an ageing King William IV to reinstate him. Further regimental scandals and salacious court cases followed over the next sixteen years. Cardigan was catcalled at the theatre and booed in the street. The *Times* referred to him as 'the plague spot of the British Army', yet his wealth, good looks and louche charm exuded total indifference to criticism.

Raglan's overall cavalry commander George Charles Bingham, the third Earl of Lucan, detested him, hardly a positive auger for operations dependent upon mutual respect and trust. Lucan, like Cardigan, had judiciously purchased his way through five different regiments to gain a lieutenant colonelcy of the 17th Lancers by 1826. 'Bingham's Dandies' cost him £25,000, and like Cardigan he subjected his regiment to a heavy workload of drills, parades and inspections conducted with excessive zeal and discipline. Unlike Cardigan, who was lazy, Lucan was a martinet and workaholic, seemingly unable to distinguish what was important amid the minutia of administration. He was ambitious and brave and determined to experience campaign life, and served on the staff of Prince Vorontsov during the Russian invasion of the Balkans in 1828. Not only was he younger than Cardigan at 54, he was physically fitter and robust, and probably knew more about the Russian army than any other senior officer in Raglan's army. Bored with peacetime soldiering, Lucan had retired on half pay in 1837 to attend to his neglected family estates at Castlebar in County Mayo, Ireland. During the catastrophic Irish potato famine blight, his 'crowbar brigades' evicted thousands of peasant tenants from low yield smallholdings to create more productive farms. Detested and misunderstood for his ruthless actions, he exhibited the steel and energy that was sought to manage Raglan's cavalry. Lucan derided Cardigan as the 'feather-bed soldier', and when he divorced Lady Lucan, who was Cardigan's youngest sister, personal future enmity was assured. Given the degree of dislike between the two, most regarded the announcement by Horse Guards of their appointments as a ghastly practical joke. 'He and

Cardigan,' Major William Forrest with the 4th Dragoon Guards recalled, 'would be certain to have a row immediately'.[17]

The Bracker farmhouse headquarters was not populated with a wealth of talent. Raglan's aides included five nephews, pleasant young men, well known in society, but not necessarily competent. Nolan, who was the 'galloper' ADC to the more effective Quartermaster General Richard Airey, was professional enough, but background to the formation of this staff was the fact that there were only six students at the Sandhurst staff college in 1854. The later Field Marshal Lord Wolseley claimed he would not have trusted the staff with a subaltern's picket, because like the fountain in Trafalgar Square, they 'only played from eleven to five o'clock'. Only fifteen of Raglan's 221 staff officers were formally staff trained.[18]

Raglan, like the British government, had been largely bewildered by developments in this surprising war. The ostensible reason for its outbreak was the dispute over access to the holy sites in Turkish-controlled Jerusalem, pitting Russian Orthodoxy, French Catholicism and Moslem Turkish fundamental religious beliefs against each other. The complete destruction of a Turkish naval squadron at Sinope, by the Russian Black Sea fleet based at Sevastopol, alerted the British to its strategic situation in the eastern Mediterranean. The British press simplified the issue by describing 'poor little Turkey', the crumbling Ottoman Empire being menaced by the 'Russian Bear'. Likewise, France, after the recent coup by Napoleon III, saw the Mediterranean as key to the future restoration and expansion of influence abroad. Russia, seeking to profit from the power vacuum being created by Turkey's ailing 'sick man of Europe', miscalculated a series of arrogant moves that led to war first with Turkey and then Britain and France.

It was assumed the teetering Ottoman Empire would be no match for the Russians, so it came as a considerable surprise to all sides when Turkish forces stubbornly blocked Russian Danube offensives at Silistra, Varna and Schumla. Russian failure, coincidental with the arrival of an Anglo-French expeditionary force at Varna, and the possibility of Austrian involvement, transformed the strategic situation. Turkish military success negated the need for an Anglo-French presence at Varna in present-day Bulgaria and resulted in a proposed invasion of the Crimea to nullify the impact of the Russian Black Sea fleet and teach her a lesson.

British landings at aptly named Kalimita Bay, north of Sevastopol, had been a shambles. Fortunately unopposed, it took five days for the British army to disembark. The invasion decision was taken with no real intelligence. The British, delighted to move on from disease-riddled Varna, saw it as 'the Isle of Wight of Russia'. Raglan was still never really in control of events. Victory at the Alma had been a triumph of sheer bravery by exhausted and cholera-stricken troops, not generalship. Raglan, supposedly in overall command, isolated himself and rode about the battlefield as Wellington had done at Waterloo, but did not influence the outcome. 'There was a great want of generalship,' Captain Patullo with the 30th Regiment concluded after the victory. Raglan had a kindly disposition, and unlike Wellington, rarely admonished subordinates, being too courteous to make his own wishes clear and too diffident to force anyone against their will. All decisions were agonised on the basis of what the Duke might have done. Orders were expressed as his lordship's wishes rather than unambiguous direction. 'Never trouble Lord Raglan more than is absolutely necessary with details,' Captain John Adye was told on joining his staff. 'Listen carefully to his remarks, try to anticipate his wishes and at all times make as light as possible of difficulties!' Desk-bound for decades, Raglan at 66 was not going to fundamentally change now.[19]

Spying was not acknowledged as 'gentlemanly' conduct. Just before Raglan had departed for bed, a galloper had arrived at the Bracker farmstead with an urgent letter from Lord Lucan. A Turkish spy sent out to locate the position of the Russian army had identified enemy forces massed on the far side of the Chernya River, which would reportedly attack in the morning. 'Very well,' Raglan is alleged to have responded on reading the dispatch, but did nothing.

Charles Cattley was a civilian Russian interpreter attached to Raglan's staff. Few knew of the existence of the Secret Intelligence

Department (SID) that had been headed by Colonel Lloyd. When he died of cholera shortly after the Alma, Cattley took over. His encyclopedic knowledge of Russian regiments enabled him to interpret the sightings of uniforms and cap badges and offer Raglan likely deductions of what their strength and purpose might be. Cattley had worked in St Petersburg and was the British vice-consul at Kertch in the Crimea when war was declared, and expelled alongside the other British diplomats. Few of Cattley's intelligence summaries have actually survived, but those held in the National Army Museum in London suggest he was reporting directly to Lord Raglan. Raglan forbade intelligence-gathering patrols across the Chernya River, once it was appreciated the enemy was there in force, so Cattley had to rely on Turkish or locals of Greek descent to provide information.

The credibility of these foreign spies inevitably became an issue. Four days before, a spy reported 20,000 Russian infantry and 5,000 cavalry advancing on Balaclava from the direction of the Chernya River. Lucan ordered out the two cavalry brigades and Raglan directed that an infantry division march down from the siege lines to reinforce the Balaclava defences. They were out all night, the coldest yet of the campaign, and saw nothing. Another alert developed on the afternoon of 22 October, resulting in another exhausting and ultimately fruitless night. False alarms were exhausting the troops and Raglan was unimpressed. On the same day, Charles Cattley advised Raglan that according to an interrogation of two Polish deserters from Sevastopol, Prince Menshikov had received substantial numbers of fresh troops and planned 'with great force to attack us in the rear and deliver the town'. This too had not happened.[20]

Raglan went to bed early and was sound asleep during the early morning hours of 25 October. Analysis and thinking around the reports of the previous three days were giving separate but confirmatory indications that an attack on the 25th was increasingly likely. Royal Engineers to the right of the Sevastopol siege lines near the Chernya River had reported Russian bands playing at night in the outlying villages. 'I was told that "the Russkies" were very strong all over the place,' war correspondent William Russell heard in the cavalry camp, and 'that reports had been sent to headquarters that an attack was imminent, and that Sir Colin Campbell was uneasy about Balaclava'. He walked back to his tent area with Captain Louis Nolan, who loaned him his cavalry cloak because 'the evening was chilly'. Nolan 'let out' at the cavalry generals 'and did not spare those in high places'. Nolan had some credibility having written two books: The *Training of Cavalry Remount Horses* and *Cavalry: Its History and Tactics*. Russell respected his opinion and always had a nose for a good story. He listened as his companion vented his frustration. The British cavalry were the best in the world: properly led they could break infantry squares and ride over artillery. At the moment they were feeling vulnerable. There had been a succession of false alarms and all the indications were that the expanding Russian presence across the Chernya was becoming increasingly menacing.

An attack was considered likely to the rear of Sevastopol, but there appeared to be no plan apart from an infantry march down from the Sevastopol siege lines, and then only when the enemy was seen in force. The march to the plain from the Heights took an average of at least three hours. Successive Russian reconnaissance probes would likely have monitored this. So what was the plan if that happened?

'We are in a very bad way I can tell you,' was Nolan's parting remark.[21]

'LITTLE LONDON' BALACLAVA

MIDNIGHT TO 3 A.M.

The stench emanating from Balaclava harbour – 'little London' or the 'Liverpool suburb' as it was often called – permeated the deep narrow and seemingly landlocked narrow inlet. The harbour area was a tangle of masts, rigging and dark wooden hulls, dotted here and there by dim lamp lights. There were over fifty or sixty sailing ships and sail-rigged steamships moored, often two abreast, in the congested waterway. The muddy quayside, alive by day with curious Tatars, harassed commissaries, busy sailors and sick soldiers picking their way between piles of stores overflowing from requisitioned sheds, had died down. Some activity continued here and there, stores were kept on board ship, where they could not readily be got at or found. Troops often went on board to try and locate items carelessly secreted in the holds of vessels alongside the harbour. Merchant steamers haphazardly loaded with miscellaneous much-needed stores had trouble getting cargoes ashore. The shadowy forest of masts delineating the harbour area, encased in a spider's web of tangled rigging lines, seemed to encapsulate the ramshackle nature of the harbour's organisation.

The surrounding buildings looked Mediterranean rather than Russian, with pan-tiled roofs and whitewashed walls. Picturesque poplars and vines in well-kept gardens had once flourished amid the houses, but had been trashed by the occupation. Private Albert Mitchell remembered breakfasts were still on the table when the 13th Light Dragoons had arrived. Within hours sofas, pianos and elegant furniture were scattered everywhere. 'Many of these articles were ruthlessly destroyed, drawers and boxes ransacked, female attire held up and made the subject of ribald jest and laughter,' he recalled. Balaclava village had been a former favourite of Sevastopol day-trippers. Now gardens were trampled into mud, fences smashed, vines dragged down and doors and window frames broken up for firewood.

The harbour resembled a Scandinavian fjord, a narrow sea loch about half a mile long and not more than 300 yards wide. 'Balaclava is the queerest place in the world,' wrote the assistant surgeon with the 8th Hussars. 'Fancy a creek quite invisible from the sea, in which we found several line-of-battle ships, lying ten yards off the land, one of the great "Agamemnon".'

'He was a bold mariner who first ventured in here,' remembered war correspondent William Russell. He was 'astonished' to look down from one of the craggy hills surrounding the area to see 'under my feet a little pond, closely compressed by the side of high rocky mountains'. Nestled along the rocky sides were scores of ships, 'for which exit seemed quite hopeless'. The sealed aspect of the inlet intrigued Mrs Fanny Duberly, who first saw ships' masts through a fissure in the cliffs. 'How they got in, or will get out, appears a mystery,' she observed: 'They have the appearance of having been hoisted over the cliffs, and dropped into a lake on the other side.'

The still waters of the rocky inlet, not flushed by tides, had been transformed into a stinking midden. 'The town is in a revolting state,' Russell reported twenty days before. 'Lord Raglan has ordered it to be cleansed, but there is no one to obey the order, and no one attends it.' Offal from cattle slaughtered for the army was tipped into the harbour or left in fly-blown piles. Bales of unloaded rotting hay floated inside, unavailable to feed starving cavalry mounts. Unburied carcasses of worn-out pack ponies, bullocks and camels, worked and starved to death, lay around houses and streets. The human dead, harvested by cholera, had been buried in shallow graves and were smelling rank. One eyewitness described the harbour as a 'cesspool and the beach a bottomless pit full of liquid abominations − a putrid sea of black foetid mire, exhaling a poisonous stench even at this cold season.'[22]

Nobody was in overall control of this chaos. The army was in charge on shore, while shipping and the harbour were under two naval officers. Royal Navy Captain Heath maintained the harbour and allocated ships' berths; Captain John Christie oversaw men and supplies as the senior, but had no authority over merchant transports. They either ignored him or grudgingly accepted direction. On shore there were virtually no army supporting services. No preparations for living, hospital or supply accommodation had been made at Balaclava. The wagon trains of the Napoleonic era were disbanded after Waterloo and had not since been resurrected. Whereas the French army operating alongside had a properly organised supply corps, the *train des équipages*, operating from a bigger and more efficient harbour at Kamiesch Bay 9 miles away, the British did not. Individual British units were obliged to conduct their own piecemeal hand-to-mouth resupply by whatever means lay at hand, after finding their stores on whatever ship they be, amid the myriad of vessels in the confusingly managed harbour.

The 'little London' nickname was appropriate to the pseudo-commercial bustling activity that resulted. The harbour area was like a gigantic market place. Sergeant Timothy Gowing in the Sevastopol siege lines was waiting for first light on the morning of the 25th, when he would set off with a fatigue party on the 7- to 8-mile journey to the port, to bring up blankets for the sick and wounded. 'We got from the ship here some hams at two shillings a pound and some cheese, chocolate, paste etc., so we are doing well just now,' Lieutenant Richard Temple Godman with the 5th Dragoon Guards wrote to his father. 'Things are very dear, and the ships are stripped by crowds of hungry officers as soon as they come into harbour,' he recalled. Henry Clifford with the Rifles 'bought 12 candles for 6 shillings, a bottle of brandy for 8 shillings, 2 bottles of sherry for £1, a loaf of bread for 1 shilling' and tobacco and champagne for friends on board the *Sydney*. Troop Sergeant Major Richard Sturtevant with the Scots Greys remembered 'provision ships come to the harbour of Balaclava, but everything is too dear for the soldier.' 'Only fancy,' he complained, 'bottled porter 3s 6d per bottle; sugar 1 shilling a 1lb; salt and flour the same; a box of lucifers [matches] 3 pence; potatoes 21 shillings per hundredweight and other things equally dear.' His porter at today's prices would cost about £25, the potatoes £77 and the sugar £35.[23]

Part of the attraction of the bustling harbour area was the colourful and exotic activity around the evil-smelling venue, a contrast to the dour camps and siege lines. A motley throng of merchants and sutlers assailed visitors: Maltese, Greek, Armenian and every conceivable Levant race, lodging in every available nook and cranny of the dilapidated area. The authorities tolerated them because they were peddling food, clothing and drink – the latter especially sought after – but they charged the troops extortionate prices. Mrs Fanny Duberly relished the bustle and excitement of the place, which she passed through every day to visit her husband:

Either you are impaled on the horns of a couple of bullocks in an araba [cart], with which the streets are crammed, locked and blocked or bitten by a vicious camel – so that to save myself being crushed by a gun wheel I had yesterday to jump the pony over a bullock which was lying down in the shafts of an araba right across the road.

Surgeon George Lawson recalled the density of traffic serving the siege lines and port area:

The road is covered with conveyances of all sorts – Crimean bull-ocks or camel wagons, Turkish bullock wagons brought from Varna, Maltese mule carts … Then comes an occasional aide-de-camp at a gallop, or an infantry officer, dusty and weary looking, returning from Balaclava laden with whatever he has been able to buy – some preserved meats or a bottle of brandy, perhaps three or four ducks, or a pound of candles. He looks quite triumphant as he passes you with his prize.[24]

The lively and chaotic 'Liverpool suburb' was, however, vulnerable. The main siege and artillery park was located a mile to the north at the little village of Kadikoi. Two miles beyond to the north lay the Fedioukine Heights, on the south bank of the Chernya River. Two valleys stretched off to the north-east, bisected by the Causeway Heights, along which the Woronsov road ran, linking Sevastopol to Baider and Yalta beyond. Hills to the east, the foothills of the Yayla mountain chain, enclosed the open ground that approached Balaclava. Somewhere out there were the Russians. A swiftly moving enemy force could conceivably suddenly emerge from the Fedioukine Heights to the north or the wide valleys to the east and crest the Causeway Heights, 2 miles above Balaclava, without being seen from the port. These approaches to the rear of the Sevastopol siege lines had therefore to be defended.

As the entrance to the Balaclava gorge was beyond the range of Allied guns on the Sapoune Heights, it was decided to establish an outer defensive line. Six redoubts, little more than rough earthworks, were quickly thrown up, impelled by the recent disturbing recon-naissance and intelligence reports. The furthest outpost to the east – number 1 redoubt – was set up on Canrobert's Hill, 2 miles east of Kadikoi. The remaining five were built, each about half a mile apart, along the Causeway Heights, with the westernmost, redoubt 6, a mile and a quarter from the foot of the Sapoune Heights, the pla-teau where the siege lines were established. Turkish soldiers manned this outer line of redoubts. The biggest contingent, a battalion and three 12-pounder guns, was housed in redoubt number 1, furthest east. Half-battalion contingents with a couple of cannon supervised by English artillery NCOs garrisoned the remainder.

The inner defence line protecting Balaclava was manned by 1,200 sailors and Royal Marines, who had twenty-six guns emplaced on redoubts covering the eastern end of Balaclava gorge. The core contingent covering this final approach to the harbour area was a bat-talion of the 93rd Highlanders supported by a six-gun horse artillery battery. To their left was the cavalry encampment, with the Heavy Brigade under Brigadier General James Scarlett and the Light com-manded by Cardigan, tactically located to threaten the flank of any Russian incursion aimed at Balaclava.

Sixty-two-year-old Sir Colin Campbell was temporarily detached from the Highland Brigade to coordinate the rather ad hoc emergence of rearward inner and outer defence lines. He was probably Raglan's most capable and experienced formation commander, having served as a regimental commander under Wellington in the Peninsular War, a brigade command in the First China War and division command in the Sikh War. He took some 2,800 men under command, of which 1,000 were Turkish-Tunisian irregulars. Campbell was a canny and resource-ful commander, unimpressed with the defence scheme he inherited, which his staff officer Lieutenant Colonel Anthony Sterling claimed 'he never liked'. One of the redoubts was literally thrown up in a day, and its walls so shallow they could be ridden over with ease. Forty-eight hours before, Sterling had reported 'we of the Balaclava party are threatened continually with an attack from a very large force'. Like the cavalry, there had been many false alarms and 'the men lie down with their belts on at night ready to start up and fight at any moment'.

Lieutenant Colonel Sterling did not approve of war correspondents like 'Billy' Russell and was frustrated that he had to provide them with rations. 'No army can succeed,' he observed, 'with such spies in its camp.' Newspaper correspondents were an unwelcome emerging characteristic of warfare in the age of steam and telegraph communications. He had just drawn up a plan of their new defensive dispositions:

> And can quite imagine that if it got into the correspondent's hands, it would go straight to the *Illustrated London News* and from thence by Russian agents back direct to the enemy, who is watching every opportunity to force the position and burn our ships and stores in the harbour of Balaclava.

Campbell knew he would be dependent on Lucan's cavalry in the event of a crisis and made the effort to cultivate good relations. Lucan would normally have been slighted by Campbell's appointment, because he was his inferior, socially and by seniority. But Lucan's relationship with Raglan, the Commander-in-Chief, was noticeably cool, so he made no comment. Questions, however, did need to be asked, because there was no agreed contingency plan for the defence of the army's rear. It was based on the assumption that Campbell's force, only numbering 650 regular British infantry, would be enough to hold in place until British infantry divisions could descend the Sapoune Heights. Raglan, of course, was focusing on the front of Sevastopol, not its rear. 'I hear that Lord Raglan and his entourage are in high spirits about the progress [of the siege],' Sterling wrote three days before. This surprised him, so he assumed 'he knows more than I do.' Indications from false Russian alarms thus far had shown it would take an average of three hours for British infantry to emerge on the plain at the foot of the Sapoune Heights in front of Balaclava in the event of a crisis.

The Russian outposts had worked it out too.[25]

3

'THEM ROOSHANS'

3 A.M. TO 6 A.M.

SEVASTOPOL NIGHT

3 A.M. TO 4.30 A.M.

Inside Sevastopol, where 30,000 to 35,000 Russian soldiers and sailors were pinned, the streets came alive at night. 'During the day scarcely anybody could be seen,' Captain Robert Adolf Hodasevich observed, 'but now the whole town was alive.' His Taroutine Regiment company held the wall between the central and flagstaff bastions. Directly opposite were the main French batteries on Mount Rodolph, and below the deep ravine that separated the 3rd French Division from the 3rd British Division siege lines. While the town's citizens took the opportunity to forage for food and visit friends and hospitals, vital repair work on the battered defences feverishly went ahead. 'The people were as busy as ants,' Hodasevich recalled, working alongside the sailors and soldiers on the damaged fortifications. 'The streets of the town were crowded with guns, gun carriages, shot, timber etc.

that were being continually conveyed to the batteries.' There was very little time. 'No lights were allowed in the town, or in the batteries,' because that immediately attracted fire. 'All the works at the batteries were carried on with as little noise as possible.' Allied round shot was fired at the gun embrasures all day long, seeking to disable the artillery pieces inside, while shells were lobbed overhead to kill the crews. 'Much of the breastwork had suffered,' Hodasevich observed, 'while the embrasures looked liked great holes' where the shot had steadily chipped away the edges. During work groups of civilians, soldiers, sailors and officers 'formed motley groups about the streets in the darkness, where they discussed the events of the day past with anxious and gloomy anticipations of the one to follow.'

Following initial panic at the commencement of the Allied bombardment, 'our days began to be very monotonous'. Hodasevich remembered: 'We were obliged to remain in one place from daybreak till the evening, and the nights were spent in repairing the batteries, constructing new ones, or in improving cover for the men.'

This was the ninth day of the siege and the hard manual labour to shore up the siege lines was as exhausting as it was unremitting. 'During the time I was in the town,' Hodasevich recalled, 'I made with my company three batteries and four powder magazines.' The bugles and drum beats waking up the Allied lines were due to sound within two hours, the precursor to bombardments they would endure all day.

The cloud cover over Sevastopol thinned in the early morning hours and pinpricks of starlight shone through. Firing at this stage was intermittent. 'Our men on the lookout,' Hodasevich recalled, 'had become accustomed to the duty, so that we heard continually that the shells were going to the right, left or beyond us.' Eyes flickered skyward after the thud of a distant mortar to pick out the whispering incandescent trail of its burning fuse arcing through the night sky. It made a 'peculiar shou-shouing' sound, he remembered. Only after it reached the vertical plane and began to fall was there any chance of working out where it might strike. When the sentries shouted 'they were upon us, it was all helter-skelter to find some place of safety'.

Vertical shot was the most dangerous, especially the virtually invisible round shot. 'Those,' Hodasevich emphasised, 'we could not see or hear till they were too near to avoid them' and 'they did a great deal of damage during the night' because 'people ventured more out of their cover'.[1]

A young 25-year-old sub lieutenant, Leo Tolstoy, was to venture out to these parapets the following month. His vivid *Sebastopol Sketches* published the following year gave some indication of his emerging literary talent, encapsulating the Sevastopol siege experience. Sentries manning the parapet would shout 'Ca-a-nnon!' and then a cannon ball shrieks past you, slaps into the earth and showers everything around with mud and stones, forming a crater,' he recalled. A Russian gun would thunder out in response through the embrasure and then:

> Once again the sentry will shout 'Cannon!' and you will hear the same shrieking sound, followed by the same slap and showering of earth; or he will shout 'Mortar!' and you will hear the even whistle of a mortar shell, a sound that is quite pleasant and not at all easy to associate with anything dreadful.

After a 'ringing explosion', 'shell splinters will fly whistling and whining in all directions, stones will rustle through the air, and you will be splattered with mud.' 'We lost very few men at this time,' Captain Hodasevich remembered, 'not more than three men per company a day,' an uncertain lottery of death based on chance: 'Some days a company never lost a man.' Tolstoy remarked that the element of uncertainty stimulated 'a sensation that is a strange blend of fear and enjoyment': 'At the moment you know the shell is heading in your direction, you are bound to think it is going to kill you; but a feeling of self-respect will sustain you, and no one will observe the knife that is lacerating your heart.'

During the night preceding 25 October the Moscow Regiment lost two officers – Ensign Schwerin and Staff Captain Istenyev – with nine privates wounded. Casualties fell when it was realised the Allied infantry were not about to attack, so reserve troops could wait under cover until they were called forward. 'Officers were seldom killed,' Hodasevich remembered, 'as they were better able to take care of themselves'; soldiers manning gun embrasures and parapets, however, were forbidden to move.

Surviving a near miss was like an emotional born-again experience, 'if only for a moment' Tolstoy recalled, creating 'a sense of relief that is unutterably pleasant'. Tolstoy found himself actually willing shells and cannonballs to land closer; 'a peculiar fascination' that initiated a psychological high 'in this dangerous game of life and death'. Reality impinged when he saw a sailor 'covered in blood and dirt', blasted by a mortar to 'a strangely inhuman appearance', with a section of his chest blown away. 'During these first moments his face can register nothing but terror and the feigned, anticipatory look of suffering,' he remembered. The victim gasped out 'Sorry lads!' to the rest of the gun crew as he was stretchered away. They took it in their stride. A naval officer inside the embrasure lit up a cigarette and yawned. On noticing the look of horror on Tolstoy's face he casually remarked, 'we get seven or eight cases like that every day.'[2]

Hodasevich remembered that 'in a confined space, a shell is perhaps the most destructive thing that could be employed' and that 'frequently one would put from 10 to 25 men hors de combat'. Soldiers occasionally fell upon near misses pulling out spluttering fuses with a courage born of desperation, for which they might be awarded the Cross of St George. This was not simply lifesaving; the medal came with increased pay and exemption from corporal punishment. Sailor Grigori Pavliuk, serving with the 43rd Ekipazh, accepted the huge risk when a spluttering shell landed in his crowded casement inside the 5th Bastion. Pavliuk calmly approached it with a forage cap full of water to douse the fuse, but it exploded. Miraculously he was unscathed, 'a hero blessed by God' as his comrades proclaimed.[3]

Surgeons treating the wounded were grossly inexperienced, primarily university students who had 'not finished their term of studies

by about a year and a half', Hodasevich explained. Tsar Nicholas took
them on 'and there they were'. 'In our regiment,' Hodasevich remembered, 'we had one of these youngsters, who had no idea how he was
to set about an operation of any kind.' Tolstoy recalled that 'if you
have strong nerves' you might visit the wounded and watch the 'pale
and gloomy' surgeons with arms soaked to the elbows with blood,
examining chloroformed, delirious patients 'uttering meaningless
words which are occasionally simple and affecting'. He remembered
'fearsome sights that will shake you to the roots of your being':

> You will see the sharp, curved knife enter the white healthy
> body; you will see the wounded man suddenly regain conscious-
> ness with a terrible, harrowing shrieked cursing; you will see the
> apothecary assistant fling the severed arm into a corner; you will
> see another wounded man who is lying on a stretcher in the same
> room and watching the operation on his companion, writhing
> and groaning less with physical pain than with the psychological
> agony of apprehension.

Hodasevich suspected the students' knives were not even sharp
enough for vegetables, never mind amputation. Even the shovels
issued to soldiers to repair walls were inferior to British tools. Many
watching the British soldiers at work 'were astonished at the quantity thrown up at each shovelful, saying the enemy was digging his
trenches by means of machines'. Some would be captured from
Turkish redoubts before the end of this day. Russian shovels simply
received an annual coat of paint. Any repair money was pocketed by
unscrupulous officers so that 'when they came to be used, they are
good for nothing'. 'In my company the men broke *all* their tools after
three days' work,' Hodasevich complained, 'and we in consequence
were obliged to get new ones, which were little better.'[4]

Siege work was exhausting, monotonous yet tactically vital.
Repairs had to be finished before the bugles and drums on the other
side heralded another day. Russian batteries often found themselves

poorly sited after Allied siege lines shifted or were adjusted during the night, so gun embrasures had to be re-sited to bear on a new direction. Masses of sandbags and soil-filled wicker-basket gabions had to be firmly revetted to face such new threats. Colonel Franz Totleben, a gifted Russian military engineer, was responsible for developing a series of flexibly sited counter-gun emplacement measures, based upon what his lookouts, sited at strategic points overlooking the siege lines, had spotted. Casemates, which were bunkers dug into the earth and revetted with ships' timber, were constructed alongside as troop shelters. The psychological impact of these night-time measures had the effect of belittling the apparently successful damage inflicted by Allied guns by day.

Casualties and dysentery steadily thinned out the Taroutine Regiment. Soup used to be boiled for the soldiers in the streets beneath the parapet and house walls, but night-time bombardments had effectively precluded this, six days before. Food now had to be prepared in Fort Nicholas, on the Black Sea side of the city and transported to the other side in large tubs. What came forward was almost inedible and 'quite cold', Hodasevich described, 'with fat swimming in large cakes on top of the soup'. Diarrhoea was rampant. 'Many of the men calculated that they would soon be killed, so it was useless to eat, and lived almost entirely on their brandy.'

They received a double vodka ration morning and evening, which kept morale intact. Hodasevich had by this time survived two very near mortar bomb misses, which had not exploded. His men began to suspect he had supernatural powers: 'Burst not!' he allegedly commanded shells. 'They were convinced that I had the power of witchcraft,' he recalled, 'the way,' he rationalised, 'a Russian soldier always explains what he cannot understand.' Men placed their faith in the Tsar, God and Holy Russia.[5]

DAYBREAK NORTH VALLEY

5 A.M. TO 6 A.M.

Major General Nikolai Karlovich Gribbe's column was the first to leave the Chorgan village assembly area. They waded across the Chernya River ford in total darkness, moving through the Baider Valley towards the village of Kamara, known to be occupied by outlying British pickets. Lieutenant Koribut Kubitovich paused in columns of six men across, to let them pass by. Gribbe's column was the vanguard of General Pavel Liprandi's 'Detachment of Chorgun' spoiling attack on Balaclava. Seventeen battalions of infantry, thirty squadrons of cavalry supported by seventy-eight guns marched off in three columns snaking out of the Chorgun area. 'There was now not the slightest doubt,' Kubitovich reflected, that they 'were being concentrated for an attack on the enemy'. 'There would be a battle!'

Kubitovich watched four battalions of Dnieper Regiment infantry, preceded by a Cossack screen, pass by at the head of the column. Behind came squadrons of Uhlan cavalry, Cossacks and ten creaking horse artillery pieces. Yeropkin's lancers tagged onto the back. Grey-coated Russian infantry were barely visible in the early morning twilight. It was shortly after 5 a.m. and a blanket of mist hung around the peaks of high ground all around. 'The columns walked in deep silence,' Kubitovich remembered. 'Even the horses did not neigh as if they were afraid to attract the enemy's attention.' The sound of the approach was muffled by the dark mass of the surrounding valley walls. Nobody said a word. Gribbe's mission was to capture the village of Kamara at the head of the southern valley, unlimber his artillery and bring fire to bear on the easternmost Allied redoubt at Canrobert's Hill, opening the first phase of the Russian attack.

Major General Konstantin Semyakin's central column entered the valley north of the Causeway Heights. He was also to attack redoubt number 1, with four battalions of the Azov Regiment and another from the Dnieper, supported by ten guns. Before reaching the Woronsov road, Major General Levutsky would branch off to his right with three battalions from the Ukraine Regiment and eight guns to assault redoubt number 2, next in line to the west on the Heights. Colonel Aleksandr Skyuderi's column crossed the Tractir bridge over the River Chernya and began moving along a south-westerly track that traversed the Fedioukine Heights, where he would cross the North Valley and fall upon redoubts 3 and 4 with 300 Cossacks, four battalions of the Odessa Regiment and eight guns. Coming up behind were sixteen squadrons of Major General Ryhzov's Kiev, Ingermanland and Ural Cossack regiments to provide immediate support for this second phase. They would charge down upon the Allied siege and artillery parks outside Balaclava. On their right, Major General Zhabokritsky's eight battalions of 4,500 infantry were to establish themselves on the Fedioukine Heights as flank protection. He also had two squadrons of Hussars, another of Cossacks and fourteen guns. The screen would be in position once the redoubts were taken.

Within half an hour the heads of these menacing columns were approaching the Woronsov road, which snaked along the Causeway Heights. It was still dark. 'We understood,' recalled an optimistic Lieutenant Kubitovich, 'that the allied situation in the Crimea then, was far from good.' Sluggish developments after their victory at the Alma suggested 'they had changed from an offensive to a defensive attitude'. They knew the British faced two directions, Sevastopol under siege to their front while vulnerable to Russian attack from the flank and rear. 'We considered their situation to be not only difficult, but fatal,' he assessed.[6]

Ingermanland Hussar, Lieutenant Yevgenii Arbuzov, was at the rear of Semyakin's column. 'In front marched the infantry, in the middle the artillery and the cavalry came behind,' he recalled. At 5.30 a.m. the cavalry paused at the Chernya River while the infantry and artillery crossed over, wading the ford and using the narrow Tractir bridge. Off to the right the shadowy outline of Major General Zhabokritsky's division was already climbing the Fedioukine Heights. All this made heavy going for the horse artillery. Colonel Obolensky's Cossack Don Battery number 3 had joined Semyakin's central column the night before having to wend its way laboriously down from the MacKenzie Heights to the north. Heavy caissons and gun wheels had to be gripped by crews to brake the precipitous descent. One 'caisson drawn by excitable horses ran away downhill', one of the officers recalled, 'and flew full into the rocks where all fell down'. Miraculously, there was no damage and the driver and horses were 'all unhurt'.[7]

As they moved forward, Lieutenant Kubitovich's lancers were acutely aware of being observed by 'small enemy cavalry pickets on the elevated points'. Frustratingly, they could not get at them. 'The eyes see, but the teeth do not bite,' he recalled. 'Everyone has a special desire to fight the English cavalry, so famous for its furious attacks.' They would soon get the opportunity. As they approached, the squat outlines of four earth redoubts became distinguishable on the Heights, silhouetted against a lightening sky behind. 'These fortifications were out in front of the general line of enemy defences,' Kubitovich observed, and were more vulnerable. They did not cover each other and were only manned by Turks with some cannon crewed by the English. 'It was here that General Liprandi prepared to strike.'

Lieutenant Stefan Kozhukhov's 8th Artillery Battery, designated a reserve at the last moment, momentarily halted on the north side of the Causeway Heights. Shortly after 5 a.m. he noticed it was getting light and then 'we heard a distant shot'. 'Thick fog hanging in the air did not promise a clear day,' he recalled. It remained quiet until 'about ten minutes later another shot rang out, a third after that, and the business began.'[8]

With Major General Gribbe's force in place in front of Kamara village, Lieutenant Kubitovich watched as a squadron and a half of Cossacks and lancers 'threw themselves on an enemy picket located at the St John Monastery and forced it to hurriedly retreat'. Gribbe's artillery was now securely ensconced on the ridgeline at the head of the South Valley. Major General Semyakin's column was deployed just across the Woronsov road, ready to attack redoubt 1 on Canrobert's Hill. Colonel Obolensky's Don battery was unlimbering, and one of its officers remembered, 'the battery made a prayer to God and moved under the cover of a light mist towards the redoubt, which could clearly be seen against the heights.' Yeropkin's lancers, which included Kubitovich's squadron, were detached from Gribbe to screen Semyakin's right flank. All had gone like clockwork; at about 6 a.m. the attack was set to go.

Lord Lucan, the British cavalry commander, was trotting along the base of the Causeway Heights with his staff, conducting his normal early morning round of inspection. The British cavalry were already awake and standing by their horses, half asleep, hungry and tired. 'The brigade turned out as usual,' remembered Private Albert Mitchell with the 13th Light Dragoons. 'Anyone who may have been similarly situated can form some idea of the pleasure we felt.' The nights were cold: 'For several days nothing particular occurred, except for an occasional "Turn Out" after a few Cossacks who made their appearance for the purpose of harassing us.'

Early morning 'stand-to' alerts were resented, and Lucan, the instigator, was regarded as an irritant by many of his officers. 'He would send any officer home under arrest who left his post,' complained Lieutenant Colonel John Yorke with the 1st Dragoons, 'as well as the Commanding Officer who permitted it.' Despite this, Lord Cardigan, nicknamed the 'noble yachtsman', was allowed to languish aboard his luxurious steam yacht. 'When there is the least appearance of alarm,' Yorke commented, Lucan 'being excited to madness, abuses everybody and in the most uncourteous manner.' Such excitable behaviour promoted unease. 'We are constantly fearing his want of temper and judgement should anything serious occur,' Yorke had confided to his sister three days before. Just such a moment had arrived.

Captain Alexander Low was the 4th Light Dragoons Field Officer checking on the Kamara picket when he spotted a group of Cossacks stealthily approaching the village. His thirty-strong picket was likely dozing and had not detected them. Two squadrons of Cossacks and

Uhlans were coming up and they entered the village as the British hurriedly departed. The evacuation was so hasty that some of the Heavy Brigade officers 'lost their cloaks, a serious loss here' according to Lieutenant Richard Temple Godman with the 5th Dragoons, with winter approaching. Outlying pickets desperately tried to signal the approach of a substantial enemy force. Private Farquharson with the 4th Light Dragoons saw that 'Vedettes were circling to right and also to left, some of them being at a trot,' which indicated advancing infantry and cavalry. Sergeant Major George Smith with the 11th Hussars had also spotted his regiment's vedettes 'rapidly' circling, which meant a strong force. Meanwhile, Lucan's staff group continued its routine progress, completely oblivious to the mounting activity going on around it.[9]

As the staff group trotted up the Causeway Heights towards Canrobert's Hill, they saw what appeared to be signal flags flying over the redoubt. Lord George Paget, commanding the 4th Light Dragoons, was acting for Cardigan with Lucan's group, and drew rein within 300 yards of the Turkish-occupied redoubt: 'The first streaks of daylight showed us that from the flag-staff which had, I believe, only the day before been erected on the redoubt, flew two flags, only just discernible in the grey twilight.'

Nobody really knew what that meant. 'Holloa,' said the assistant Adjutant General, Lord William Paulet, 'there are two flags flying; what does that mean?' 'Why, that [surely] is the signal that the enemy is approaching,' Major McMahon on the staff ventured. 'Are you quite sure?' he was asked. 'We were not kept long in doubt!' Paget remembered. 'Hardly were the words out of McMahon's mouth, when bang went a cannon from the redoubt.'[10]

The crash reverberated around the valley sides and was quickly followed by more as Russian artillery, as was its practice, commenced firing in salvos. Staff officer Captain Charteris was immediately dispatched to British headquarters to tell Raglan the redoubts were under attack. Campbell, commanding the Balaclava defence force, was also alerted, but already knew, like everyone else, because the tempo of the cannon fire had perceptibly increased. All Lucan could do was order his two brigades of cavalry forward, there was nothing else available to support them. Charteris would not cover the 5 miles back to Raglan's headquarters much before 7.30 a.m. and the early morning relief of infantry divisions in the siege lines was going on, which would further complicate their response. Even in the event of a predetermined plan, the infantry could not arrive before 10 a.m., and there was no agreed plan. Cannon fire had at least disturbed the commander of the Light Brigade aboard his yacht *Dryad*, berthed in Balaclava harbour. It would take Cardigan more than two hours to arrive at the scene.

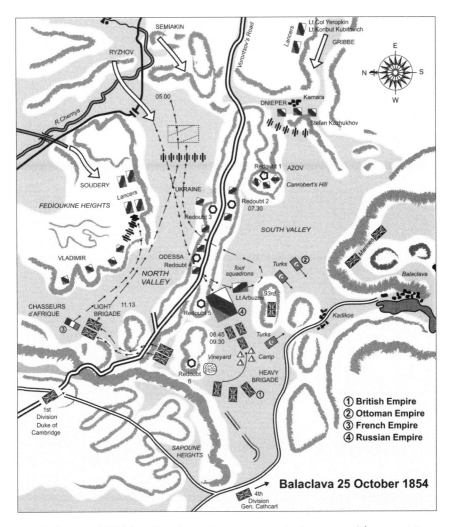

On 25 October 1854 four Russian columns unexpectedly emerged from a misty dawn to the north-east of the besieged city of Sevastopol. They swiftly occupied the key Allied redoubts along the spine of the ridgeline separating the North and South Valleys, capturing the outer defences of the port of Balaclava. By 9.30 a.m. the 93rd Highlanders' 'thin red line' and a remarkable cavalry action by the Heavy Brigade had checked the Russian advance and regained the Allied initiative. Before the belated arrival of two divisions of British infantry, Cardigan's Light Brigade recklessly charged a Russian battery at the end of North Valley, as a consequence of mistaken orders, and was badly mauled running a gauntlet of fire from three directions. The ensuing stalemate bedevilled British resupply to their siege lines for the whole of the following winter.

4

THE FIGHT FOR THE TURKISH REDOUBTS

5.30 A.M. TO 9.00 A.M.

THE ESNAN

5.30 A.M. TO 7.30 A.M.

The square-topped mounds coming into focus in the growing light of dawn atop the rolling Causeway Heights were manned by over 1,000 *Esnan* or Turkish militia. These North African irregulars were used to warm, sunny climes, not the bleak, cold and wet conditions they were enduring. It had rained the two preceding nights and at intervals by day and this night. Conditions underfoot inside the earth palisades were soft and muddy. Construction work had begun ten days before. The militia were in a miserable state and half-starved. Since the Battle of the Alma on 20 September to the beginning of the work on the redoubts, they had only received a daily allowance of two biscuits per man. Only recently had the British started to issue biscuits, rice and fresh meat, pork and rum was declined on religious grounds, so they received an additional ½lb of biscuit in lieu, which was barely sustenance. Pay was frequently in arrears, making them totally dependent upon the commissariat for the sort of comforts their British and French counterparts could readily buy. One of the Turkish soldiers had told John Elijah Blunt, Lucan's unofficial Turkish interpreter, 'that during the last two days they had nothing to eat but biscuit and very little water to drink'.[1]

Their small fortifications, which could be ridden over by a Cossack on horseback, were in a mile-long chain along the Causeway Heights. A battalion of Esnan defended the furthest eminence, which was redoubt number 1, roughly 600 men with three 12-pound cannons. Redoubts 2 and 3 further west had two guns each with half a battalion of militia, and number 4 redoubt had three guns. Redoubts 5 and 6 leading up to the Sapoune Heights were still being constructed. An English artillery NCO supervised each cannon. The Turks were not long enrolled, had never been in action, and could be forgiven for thinking they had been positioned there by the 'infidel' to be sacrificed. Their role as 'tripwire' was to ensnare any Russian approach materialising from the east, behind the Sevastopol siege lines. It was generally accepted that Turkish soldiers could do no more than defend fixed emplacements, because they were judged incapable of mounting operations in the open. The Ottomans were not entirely overawed by their allies, having already given a good account of themselves during defensive battles against the Russians along the Danube River. The Esnan in the redoubts were nervous, knowing there was a substantial Russian force somewhere out there to the east, across the Chernya River amid the foothills of the Yayla Mountains. Russian watchfires had been seen and military bands regularly heard playing in the outlying villages.

Only a week before, the redoubts had opened fire into dense white fog that had blanketed the advance of a large Russian force. Captain George Woronsov with I Battery Royal Horse Artillery screening Balaclava recalled just three days before at night, 'the Turks began to fire away in a great hurry at an imaginary enemy about 12 o'clock'. It was a false alarm. The cavalry were called out again but 'as the night was very dark it was some time before they found out their mistake'. Two hours later, nervous Marines outside Balaclava harbour were also blazing away with muskets and guns 'thinking the Russians were advancing, so we had a wretched night of it'.[2] Nerves were on edge. Turkish spies had detected an imminent attack, and yet the Esnan, glancing anxiously over their shoulders, could see no sign of any activity at all in the Allied camps to their rear. False alerts had demonstrated it took the British infantry hours to come up in the event of a crisis. If anything happened, they were clearly going to be on their own.

The first time the British met the Turks was at Constantinople, en route to Varna and the Crimea. 'Constantinople is a magnificent city to look at from the harbour,' Cornet Fiennes Wykeham Martin with the 4th Light Dragoons remembered, 'but when you get on shore it is the filthiest hole.' Lieutenant Henry Clifford with the Rifles commented that 'they look upon us I think with suspicion and wonder how it will all end'. The Ottoman Empire was clearly in decline, 'an old Pasha said the other day to me through an interpreter: "Oh! young man – we are not what we have been,"' Clifford recalled, '"we are fast going down hill."' They had been labelled the 'sick man of Europe'. 'We have allowed the Christians to build a church in Constantinople,' the Pasha explained, 'and the veils of our women fall lower and lower every day.' Not low enough for many young officers enraptured by the beauty of many of the 'one hundred wives' they sought to meet. 'I have no doubt the old Turks are delighted the troops are leaving Constantinople,' Clifford conjectured.[3]

The English lower ranks were as uncompromising as ever in their blatant disregard of any fighting qualities foreign soldiers might possess. Corporal Thomas Morley with the 17th Lancers glibly pronounced Turks are 'a dirty, lazy lot of people – they think about nothing but smoking'. 'When I was at Constantinople we were in the Turkish barracks,' he wrote to his father, 'and a very dirty barracks it was; we were eaten up with fleas, and they *were* fleas – the largest I ever saw.' He too was taken aback at the reports of successful Turkish resistance against the Russians besieging Silistra. 'They say the Turks have been fighting four and six to one,' but in his opinion 'one Englishman is worth six Turks'. He echoed the prevalent view in the ranks. Sergeant John Hill with the 1st Dragoons thought them 'an idle lazy race' and Corporal George Senior with the 13th Light Dragoons wrote them off as 'a degraded, dirty, idle lot, and they rob us whenever they can' and 'they are sure to give you the wrong change'. What made it worse was they were the wrong religion. Albert Mitchell with the 13th Light Dragoons remembered a small church desecrated by the Turks in the Crimea. 'The [altar] was broken down, and the pictures (of which there were many) torn to pieces and strewn about the floor, and to complete the work of desecration, all kinds of nuisances and abominations were strewn about the floor.'

The women had been chased off. Cornet Wykeham Martin summed up Turks as 'a most disgusting race of people and not worth fighting for'; in fact, 'I would almost sooner fight for a Russian if it was not a treason to say so.'

By contrast, and contrary to the British soldier's tendency to belittle foreign armies, the French were accepted, even though the Napoleonic Wars were a recent memory. 'You would be surprised to see the good feeling existing between the English and French soldiers,' Corporal George Senior wrote home. 'The latter you might see kissing our men and pulling them about, particularly our Guardsmen, whom they appear very partial to.' As was often the case, comradeship was alcohol-fuelled, with 'Yes', 'No' or 'Oui' exchanged with 'the greatest nicety, when at the same time neither party understood what the other was saying'. Whereas Raglan was leading an army very much in Wellington's image, it became quickly apparent to the British soldiers that the French were in a different league, practically schooled by recent warfare in their colonies. French infantry were seasoned veterans and tactically aware although British gunners and engineers were more technically proficient, well suited to the type of siege operations being conducted around Sevastopol. The British were led by 'gentlemen', the French had officers. French logistics were noticeably more competent than the hand-to-mouth subsistence conducted by English civilian sutlers and amateur merchants around Balaclava. The French shared the same jaundiced view of their Ottoman allies. 'The French detest the sight of them,' George Senior insisted, 'and say, "Turks no good, English good".'[4]

At 5.30 a.m. ten Russian guns supporting Gribbe's column opened up at redoubt number 1 from Kamara. They were soon joined by an eight-gun battery shooting in Semyakin's central column, deploying in the North Valley opposite the Woronsov road. After thirty minutes, Levutsky's ten-gun battery joined in, bombarding redoubt number 2. Lieutenant Koribut Kubitovich watched from the lancer screen. 'The redoubts loomed menacingly before us,' he recalled, and 'we did not doubt that we would take them and that they would fall on our first attempt.' He had a grandstand view of the battle, being left of Semyakin's Azov Regiment, forming up to assault Canrobert's Hill. For an hour Russian artillery lashed the redoubts on the crest of the Causeway Heights, with twenty-eight guns delivering fifty-six solid shot and shell each minute.

'The first rays of the rising sun' accompanied 'the opening shot from our cannons reverberating between the hills,' remembered Ingermanland Hussar officer Yevgenii Arbuzov. The sun was only on the high ground, whereas visibility in shadowy valley bottoms was patchy. Kubitovich observed General Liprandi ride by with the staff to encourage the infantry, dressing their lines for the assault. The men were 'electrified' and a 'tremendous "Ura!"' was bellowed out in response. Liprandi, unlike many Russian commanders, had charisma. 'This was not that response which is given so languidly and calmly on exercises,' Kubitovich recalled, 'it was a cry foretelling victory, unaffectedly rising from the mighty chests of our soldier heroes.' They watched and waited as salvo after salvo of heavy artillery fire crashed into the Turkish redoubts.[5]

No trace of the redoubts exists today. The largest, number 1, was pentagonal or square shaped, covering an area of 150 to 200 square yards, sufficient to house a battalion of infantry. Ramparts were shallow, negotiable by horsemen and being earthen and newly constructed, had settled in height with the rain. There was space for three 2-pound cannon, positioned to cover the main threat from the east. The soil depth on the hill was low, which meant walls had to be raised as distinct from digging down. Excavated soil was piled high to create a defensive ditch, but walls were relatively flimsy, depending upon thickness. Conditions inside were wet and unsanitary, disposal of human waste a problem, and the defenders had scant, if any, bomb-proof shelter, only rudimentary shelter from the elements. For an anonymous hour, while the Allies sought to react, Turkish militia had no recourse except to cower at the base of their earth walls and endure the storm of solid shot and shell. Round shot splattered and gouged chunks from the parapets or was aimed to bounce inside. There was no protection from shell bursts overhead. Russian artillery was the elite arm of the service and the competent gunners knew what they were doing. The Turks crouched at the far side of the ramparts, away from the direction of incoming shot, to avoid the worst of the velocity of incoming shot. Despite heavy losses, the Turks clung on. Tenacity was driven less by resolve, more by ingrained stoicism and acceptance they were more likely to survive inside the redoubt than outside, in the open. One soldier later complained, 'the guns in the redoubt were too small and ill supplied with ammunition'. They served the guns as best they could and continued to resist. [6]

The Russians did not have it all their own way. Colonel Obolensky's Cossack Don battery managed to unlimber at the foot of the Heights. 'At that moment a shot burst forth from the redoubt and hissed over the battery without causing any damage,' one of its officers remembered. 'As the fifth gun was moving into position, a cannon ball tore off the head of the driver on the first lead horse.' The rest of the battery were appalled by the crimson impact; Cossack Sazonov from the Veshenskaya Settlement was well known. 'He did not fall from his horse right away, but rode some distance without his head and then fell off,' a shocked eyewitness recalled. The decapitated torso riding a horse 'made a horrifying picture'. By now the leading elements of the

Russian infantry were entering the bushes that covered the slope in front of the redoubt summit.

Down in the shadowy low ground Captain George Maude's I Troop Royal Horse Artillery galloped up from base of the Heights and unlimbered between redoubts 2 and 3. They had been encamped in a vineyard by redoubt 6 and provided the Turks with the first tangible indication that support might at last be coming. He had four 6-pounders and two howitzers. 'It was so dark at first,' he recalled, 'that nothing could be seen but the flashes of the Russian guns on which accordingly our guns were laid.' The stand-off was unequal, thirteen to fifteen light British 6-pounders versus more than thirty Russian heavy guns, including many 18-pounders. Lord Lucan's cavalry, in the saddle at dawn, was beginning to move forward into the eastern part of the South Valley, behind the Woronsov road to the rear of the redoubts. Lieutenant Temple Godman with the 5th Dragoon Guards realised with the first firing 'something was going on', and on approaching they could clearly hear multiple battery fire. This was no false alarm; 'this time I knew we were in for it,' he recalled. They halted 300 yards from number 2 redoubt, with the Light Brigade on the left and the Heavy Brigade on the right. Lucan injudiciously halted close enough to receive stray solid shot off-shoots that glanced off the Heights, from Gribbe's battery firing in front of Kamara.[7]

After 6.30 a.m. Campbell's 93rd Highlanders, the only regular battalion of British infantry in Balaclava, hastily departed its encampment outside Kadikoi village, just north of the port. He marched toward the sound of the guns. Frequent false alarms had produced this well-rehearsed prompt response. Campbell was a seasoned campaigner, having fought with Moore and Wellington in the Peninsular War. Service in China and India had given him a practical understanding of the capabilities of irregular troops. He had an instinctive feel for what his Esnan Turkish militia might accomplish. 'Capital fellows,' he had confided to his aide Lieutenant Colonel Sterling, 'and dig better even than our own men.' 'But we cannot speak to them further than "Bueno Johnny" and "Bueno Ingles",' Sterling had observed. This was the fundamental problem. 'We will have race horses called "Bueno Johnny",' Sterling wrote home, and 'Johnny Turk's' nickname came into being.

Campbell had achieved his seniority through merit and was a no-nonsense robust-mannered soldier who did not suffer fools gladly. Lucan uncharacteristically deferred to his judgement because Campbell was non-confrontational with his superiors and mature enough to ignore Lucan's predictable idiosyncratic behaviour. He did not pose a social threat like Cardigan. Campbell had never been happy with the dispersed linear deployment of the redoubts he had inherited. His innate understanding of the Esnan, coupled with the ruthlessness that characterises most senior officers, led him to regard the Turkish redoubts as a virtual write-off. The absence of real support for the redoubts 'rendered a lengthened defence very problematical'. Sterling explained: 'The ditch and parapet, although as deep and thick as time allowed them to be made, were very poor defences; the Cossacks rode over both.'

A strong cavalry vedette posted behind, rather than on top of Canrobert's Hill, would have achieved the same purpose. Only infantry could hold ground and there was not enough of them to defend Balaclava, hence the Turkish 'tripwire' scheme. It worked so far as Campbell was concerned and was buying them the time they needed. The Esnan were correct in their estimation the infidel were indeed prepared to sacrifice them. When Campbell marched out of Kadikoi village he did not head for the redoubts, he made for a small hillock identified as a potential screen position blocking any passage of the gorge that led from the South Valley across Kadikoi village to Balaclava harbour. The artillery and siege park at Kadikoi village had to be protected.

The blunt-speaking Campbell could be pitilessly frank with 'foppish' young officers who did not understand the business of war. He had endeared himself to Lucan during the 'Look-on' affair, when Raglan had reined in the cavalry. Campbell was uncomplimentary about 'Those young officers of the cavalry who would fall out from their regiment and go to the front and give their opinion on matters they knew nothing about.'

In this he was in agreement with Lord George Paget, critical of the sniping from men like 'Captain Nolan, who writes books, and was a very great man in his own estimation'. 'These young gentlemen talk a great deal of nonsense,' Campbell pointed out; action was not all about honour and glory, 'he was there to defend Balaclava and he was not going to be tempted out of his strong position by jeers'. It was in this vein that the Turks would be sacrificed, for the greater good. They would not be relieved, the 93rd would occupy a secondary line in depth, blocking the approaches to Balaclava. The redoubts would be lost, but he might save some Turks.[8]

Lucan could do nothing with cavalry alone, except pose a threat from the flank, should the Russians try to rush Balaclava. He was in the correct place to menace the intent, but displayed inexperience by getting unnecessarily close to the redoubt fight. Perhaps he sought to reassure the Turks. Lord George Paget, in Cardigan's absence, took up the command position in front of the Light Brigade line. 'All sorts of gesticulations and cries of "Look out, Lord George!" met my ears,' Paget recalled as heavy fire came in. Bewildered by the shouting, he inadvertently moved his horse two or three paces directly into the line of the round shot his men had spotted coming through. One bounced between his horse's front and rear legs, throwing up a cloud of dust into his face. 'Ah, ha!' one of his orderlies laughed, 'it went right between your horse's legs.' Paget was not amused. 'I don't see anything to laugh at,' he said. Moments later another round shot shrieked through the ranks and spun a man round in the front line of the 4th Dragoons. 'I can well remember,' he later recalled, 'the slosh that sounded as it went through the centre of his belly.' It was to become a disturbingly familiar sound.

Campbell also sent Captain Barker's W Battery Royal Artillery to back up Maude's unequal firefight with the Russian gunners. Exchanges bouncing across the rocky ground produced frequent near misses amongst the cavalry. Many of the solid shot balls 'missing the hilltop fell among us,' Lieutenant Temple Godman with the 5th Dragoons recalled. 'One could see them drop, and in another moment the fragments flying far and wide.' The involuntary response was 'to bob one's head, though knowing it was no use, as the pieces whistled and hummed over'. Sergeant Maughan with the Inniskillings saw: 'Sergeant Bolton had his leg knocked off. The shot hit my horse first, came between us and doubled my sword up like a hoop and grazed my leg.'

Unnerved soldiers were obliged to sit, knee to knee in two ranks held together by discipline and the example of their officers out front. Officers sat motionless, conscious as much of their men's eyes on them as the incoming cannonballs.

Lieutenant Colonel John Yorke commanding the 1st Dragoons railed at Lucan's inept positioning in the line of fire. Shot arcing over the redoubts 'bowled like cricket balls into our ranks'. Corporal Joseph Gough nearby recalled 'the shot and shell were coming in pretty fast'. Unable to move, all they could do was shout 'look out boys!' 'They came with such force against the ground, that they would rise and go for half a mile before they would touch the ground again. Us and the Greys lost some horses there.'

Troop Sergeant George Cruse saw 'several round shot fall into the ranks' of the 1st Dragoons, 'breaking the legs of two horses'. 'One large ball struck a man named "M" right in the face,' he recalled, 'of course killing him instantly.' Cruse gave short shrift to the wobbling he detected in the ranks when 'the men began to bob their heads'. He and another NCO 'pitched into them for being so foolish, just as if they could avoid a 32-pound shot by moving their heads one side or another'. Yorke remembered the helpless predicament of soldiers having to remain in line. 'The officers could escape,' he recalled, 'we had only to move our horses a few yards to let the shot pass', but not the men. The shot 'generally took a front and rear rank horse, and sometimes a man, or a single horse'.[9]

Captain George Maude's I Battery began attracting considerable Russian artillery fire. Limbers were serving the guns while the horses remained in the traces. Five horses with the number 6 limber were struck down and spokes were punched out of the limber by shrapnel, but the crews seemed to have charmed lives. Shell bursts scoured gun carriages and round shot swooshed between the guns. After fifteen to twenty minutes of this a shell appeared to burst inside George Maude's horse. 'My God!' exclaimed Albert Mitchell's troop leader Lieutenant Smith with the 13th Light Dragoons, 'there is Captain Maude blown up'. Mitchell glanced across at 'what appeared at first to be a man blown to pieces'; the horse had been totally eviscerated. George Maude's left leg and arm were slashed to the bone by splinters carrying away much of the muscle, slicing the radial artery, and shattering his left hand. His left eye was blinded. Lieutenant Dashwood took over command but he too was abruptly bowled over by another round shot as he mounted his horse. He remounted and that horse too was struck down. Lucan rode up and seeing the shambles – a third of the battery's horses were dead in their traces and the limbers almost emptied of ammunition – ordered them to limber up and retire. As they moved off Gunner McBride with the 4th gun was knocked clean from his saddle, killing the centre two horses of the team. It was at this inopportune moment that Lord Cardigan suddenly appeared, having finally ridden up from Balaclava harbour.

Cardigan, a parade ground soldier, was late on parade. He was completely out of his depth in the midst of this crisis with the cavalry apparently committed and no infantry in sight. Lacking confidence in what to do, his only response was to raise his voice and project authority, as if he was on the drill square. 'Where are you going with your guns, Captain Shakespear?' Albert Mitchell heard him peremptorily ask. 'Who ordered you to retire?' 'We are going for more ammunition my lord,' was the response.

Thirty Russian guns firing at the rapid rate of two rounds a minute could conceivably fire over 3,000 rounds in an hour. This intensity of fire was directed against the redoubts and any identified British artillery. Like Maude's battery, running short of limber ammunition after an hour, the Russians were also limited by what they could carry on limbers and wagons. Some 1,800 to 2,000 rounds were likely poured into the Turkish redoubts. The Esnan had been at the centre of this crucible of fire for well over sixty minutes. They had retired to the back end of the redoubt, seeking cover from the worst of the shot and shell slapping remorselessly against the forward earthworks. Lord Lucan on the periphery of this storm had turned to his Turkish interpreter and shouted, 'Blunt, those Turks are doing well!'[10]

With the lessening of British artillery fire after 7.30 a.m. Russian infantry moved on redoubt number 1. Lieutenant Arbuzov saw 'the Turkish artillery began to slacken noticeably'. Lieutenant Kubitovich observed as 'under the leadership of Colonel Fabian Krüdener the Azov men went forward in company columns in a fine orderly fashion,' their long grey greatcoats hitched up by hooks to facilitate ease of movement. 'General Liprandi judged this moment to be the most suitable for the attack,' Arbuzov remembered. The Turks had clearly been battered into virtual submission. 'Accurate enemy artillery and rifle fire did not make them [the Russians] waiver,' Kubitovich observed, 'the soldiers went on with no regard to artillery and musket fire.'

Russian foot infantry tactics had progressed little since the Napoleonic Wars. Still armed with the M1845 smooth bore muzzle-loading musket, poorly factory made and maintained, their effective range was only 150 to 200 paces. The imperative, therefore, became to quickly close with the bayonet and rely upon shock action. Reloading the 12-pound musket was difficult and slow, and could only be done from a standing position. Only one round per minute was achievable and barrels became fouled by powder residue after a few cartridges, making it even more difficult to ram down the .700in spherical bullet. Effective firepower came from skirmishers sent ahead, armed with the more efficient semi-grooved Belgian Stutze rifle, and artillery fire. They attacked in dense columns, like the French revolutionary armies of the previous century.

The Azov Regiment advanced line after line at a regular measured pace in a compact square. A forest of bayonets approached as soldiers advanced with the musket carried at the vertical position close to the soldier's right side, only the front rank of the column marched in the 'on guard' position with the bayonet lowered towards the enemy. With drums beating and colours flying, the formation resembled a well-drilled ancient Macedonian phalanx. General Liprandi recalled the first 2,400 men marching forward in 'two lines in company column, not more than 100 paces between the lines' with two more battalions, some 1,600 men, coming on in attack formation in the third line. This appeared less an attack, more a well-drilled parade movement advancing in close formation. 'A Russian soldier forms part of a machine,' Captain Hodasevich with the Taroutine Regiment explained, 'which is composed of enormous masses of men that never have thought and never will think.' Colonel Krüdener leading the attack recalled, 'I didn't take my sabre from the scabbard. I only crossed myself and waved my hat on both sides.' He had set the machine in motion. 'Everybody rushed after me and I was protected by the stern Azovs,' he remembered. The Russian soldiers were philosophical about what lay ahead, they were told what to do and, as Hodasevich explained, 'it is the business of God and the Emperor, but none of his'.[11]

The Turks fought with the desperation of no options, knowing there would be no support. The Russian infantry assault spelt *finis* for them. Hussar officer Arbuzov watching from the North Valley saw his 'fine infantry fellows showered with a storm of bullets and canister, go bravely into the attack … With each casualty they closed up as if on training manoeuvres.' Kubitovich watched as 'now in a well-formed mass they reached the foot of the hill.' Bushes and undulating ground meant 'it is impossible to maintain the previous order'; they had 150 paces to go.

The British cavalry could only look on. Lieutenant Temple Godman saw 'the Turks outside the fort, on their extreme right commenced to fire musketry'. It was a confusing situation as the Turkish Esnan inside the redoubt attempted to reform in order to beat off the assault. 'As we were only about 300 yards off, with my glasses I saw everything,' he explained. 'Up the hill came the Russian infantry, meeting a warm fire from the Johnnys, who at that moment turned and rushed up again under their fort.'

It looked as though the Russians were enfilading the redoubt and trying to get in from the rear. 'On came the Russians, shouting and running up in a column in fine order, and giving a heavy fire. The Turks again showed a front, rushed at them, then waivered, and in went the enemy over their works.'

'The Turks made a brave resistance at this point,' recalled one Scots Greys sergeant, 'being nearly all killed before they gave in, and we could give them no assistance.' Albert Mitchell with the Light Brigade could see 'there was something up at the redoubt near Kamara [village], for the Turks were beginning to run down out of it down the hill into the plain.' The redoubt was being overrun:

> Soon we saw a compact body of Russian infantry, perhaps 300 strong, mount the hill in gallant style, cheering as they came. They soon entered the redoubt, not taking the slightest notice of the fire kept up by a few Turks who stood their ground for a time.

'A long drawn out shout of "Ura!"' accompanied this moment Kubitovich remembered, 'and the steep slope is covered with a dense crowd of soldiers making their way up.' The Russian infantry momentum was irresistible, 'success cannot be long in doubt,' he observed. 'Our soldiers climb up to the fortification itself and cover it like a swarm of buzzing bees!' They were soon inside. 'There are many already on the wall, many are going through the embrasures' and he saw 'a good many drop down into the fortification … Then the bayonet work of the Russian soldier began.'

About 170 Turks were killed inside the redoubt, a high proportion from a battalion of 600. The Azov Regiment lost two officers and 149 men storming the position and were unforgiving once inside. Few prisoners were taken because the enemy were the wrong religion. By 8 a.m. redoubt number 1 was lost, the anchor to the right of the line upon which the defence of Balaclava was based. The Azov Regiment colours now fluttered over the earth-walled bastion.[12]

THE MYTH OF JOHNNY TURK, THE SAPOUNE HEIGHTS

5.30 A.M. TO 9 A.M.

Lord Raglan probably took the first of his Balaclava decisions in his nightshirt. He was rudely awakened after 5.30 a.m. by the sound of a Russian cannonade reverberating around the valley floors at the foot of the Sapoune Heights. At the same time the strikingly tall Sergeant Timothy Gowing was making his way along the Heights to Balaclava, on fatigue duty. 'We could hear the firing at Balaclava,' he recalled, 'but thought it was the Turks and Russians playing at long bowls, which generally ended in smoke.' Raglan's headquarters began generating a flurry of anxious activity. 'We noticed too,' Gowing observed, 'mounted orderlies and staff officers riding as if they were going in for the Derby.'

William Russell was at the Bracker farmhouse by 7.30 a.m., just as Lucan's galloper from Balaclava arrived with the news that 'a strong corps of Russian horse, supported by guns and battalions of infantry, had marched into the valley.' Redoubt number 1 was under serious threat and redoubts 2 to 3 were teetering, 'unless the Turks offered a stouter resistance than they had done already'. The timings of reports are variable but it appears that Raglan did not set off to the edge of the Sapoune escarpment much before 7.30 to 8 a.m., which involved a twenty-minute ride. The rumble of artillery to the east was being picked up in the Sevastopol siege lines. Lieutenant John Hume, manning a 55 Regiment picket, learned he would not be relieved that morning, recalling, 'heavy firing was heard towards Balaclava'. Likewise, Lieutenant John Image near the French lines with Cathcart's 4th Division learned his 21st Royal Scots picket would also not be relieved as planned.[13]

As Raglan rode towards the edge of the Sapoune Heights he likely rued the decision not to respond to the Turkish spy's intelligence the night before, about this impending attack. 'What would the Iron Duke have done?' went through his mind. Russell remembered the ride toward the direction of firing 'over the thistles and large stones which cover the undulating plain'. He got there before the commander, whose arrival by inference was somewhat tardy. 'The booming of artillery, the spattering roll of musketry,' he recalled, 'were heard rising from the valley, drowning the roar of the siege guns in front before Sevastopol.' Battle was well under way.

Raglan, unlike Wellington, whom he subconsciously emulated, did not have a core of veteran subordinates around him able to take the initiative. Wellington had never been much of a delegator, because he was such an intellectual heavyweight himself, but he would quietly grip a situation with steely resolve. Raglan was neither; he cultivated a calm demeanour, maintained in a crisis, but was unable to grip reluctant subordinates to make things happen. He maintained his imperturbable facade, secure in his own mind that this was likely a feint. When he drew up at the edge of the escarpment, he was confronted with the same scene described by Russell: 'Looking to the left towards the gorge, we beheld six compact masses of Russian infantry, which had just debouched from the mountain passes near the Chernya [River], and were slowly advancing with solemn stateliness up the valley.' There had to be at least twenty artillery pieces deployed before them, while another two batteries 'were already a mile in advance of them, and were playing with energy on the redoubts, from which feeble puffs of smoke came at long intervals.'

Clearly, things were not going well. 'Enormous bodies of cavalry' were behind the guns and ahead of the infantry, 'in six compact squares, three on each flank, moving down in echelon towards us'. It was both a majestic and menacing sight. 'The valley was lit up with the blaze of their sabres, and lance points, and gay accoutrements,' while ahead of them 'were clouds of mounted skirmishers, wheeling and whirling in front of the march like autumn leaves tossed by the wind'. Hardly a feint, Raglan appreciated. Gallopers were dispatched to bring up the 4th and 1st British infantry divisions from the Sevastopol siege lines, many of whom were just emerging from a night in the trenches. This would be a thirty-minute ride; two more hours would be needed for the infantry to march down, therefore no appearance until much before 10 a.m. or later. All Raglan could do was anxiously scan the line of Turkish redoubts.[14]

His position at the easternmost edge of the Chersonese Plateau offered a striking view of the Balaclava plain, with its ridges and valleys arrayed before him like a three-dimensional map. The early morning light made the height differentials stand out in sharp relief. 'Fleecy vapours still hung around the mountain tops,' Russell remembered, 'and mingled with the ascending volumes of smoke; the patch of sea [by Balaclava harbour] sparkled freshly in the rays of the morning sun, but its light was eclipsed by the flashes which gleamed from the masses of armed men below.'

The Sapoune Heights, where Raglan and his staff stood, is a great bluff or escarpment rising 600ft above the plain. Directly ahead and to the east was the shallow South Valley, 2 miles long and half a mile broad. It was bounded to its left by the long spine of the Causeway Heights, running for 2 to 3 miles in the same direction. Russell, standing by Raglan, 'could see the Turkish gunners in the redoubts, all in a confusion as the shells burst over them'. He and his staff had arrived at the climax of the action, having missed the desperate stand fought from daybreak until now. 'Just as I came up, the Russians had carried number 1 redoubt, the furthest and most elevated of all,' Russell remembered, 'and their horsemen were chasing the Turks across the interval which lay between it and redoubt number 2.' Lucan's cavalry could be seen 'formed in glittering masses' on the south side of the Causeway Heights, concealed from the Russians by a 'slight wave' in the plain.

The view offered by Raglan's Olympian grandstand was virtual theatre. They overlooked the entire battlefield, but 600ft up was an entirely different perspective to that of his lesser mortal subordinates fighting down on the distant valley floors below. The 'slight wave' Russell distinguished was the key terrain feature, dominating both the North and South Valleys, the Causeway Heights. Line of sight at ground level below was, however, impeded by ridges and hills, which restricted the view of enemy positions. The 65-year-old Raglan did not appreciate that his 'bird's-eye' view from the Heights across the intervening terrain was not shared by his subordinates on the rolling plain below. Moreover, any commands he issued meant a ride of twenty minutes or more for his gallopers or dispatch riders to make their way down the scrub strewn rocky escarpment; and events were moving faster below.

'The successful seizure of redoubt number 1 decided the affair in our favour,' Lieutenant Kubitovich remembered. 'The Turks occupying redoubts number 2 and 3 hardly saw the right wing troops being directed towards them before they quickly turned to flight.'

The small Turkish garrisons, each of about 200 men and two cannon, were attacked by 3,800 men from the Ukrainian Regiment under Colonel Dudnitsky-Lishin. At the same time 3,500 men from the Odessa Regiment bore down on redoubt number 4 further right. Thousands of grim-faced grey-coated Russian infantry were cresting the Causeway Heights and Woronsov road at the point of the bayonet. The Turks were facing odds of nearly twenty to one. 'When the Russians advanced,' the newly arrived Russell saw that 'the Turks fired a few rounds at them, got frightened at the distance of their supports, and then "bolted".' This dispatch by Russell, perhaps more than any of the other later, often contradictory reports, was the genesis of the myth that 'cowardly' Johnny Turk simply ran at Balaclava.[15]

The impossible tactical situation in which the Turks found themselves, bereft of any support, was subsidiary to the racist view of the soldiery, that Johnny Turk was simply dirty and lazy. Constantinople, the exotic jewel of the East, had been an odious disappointment for many British soldiers. Turks did not drink, they hid their women and they had the wrong religion. The fact that the River Thames flowing through Queen Victoria's own capital was labelled the 'great stink' was irrelevant. The British soldier traditionally held a tawdry opinion of foreign martial skill, particularly non-European combatants. Few soldiers actually saw what happened at the redoubts, but prejudice – also voiced by officers – left them in no doubt. Private Charles Howell with the 1st Dragoons gave his opinion in later years 'as an old soldier and in the langue of an old soldier'. He was not 'grammatical' he explained, but described the manning of the redoubts by 'I was going to say Turkish soldiers, but they hardly deserved that name', who 'fled from the guns and left them before they [the Russians] got near them'. Howell's badly spelt opinion echoed that of the ordinary British soldier, who unquestionably accepted what others had seen: 'I have read that they stood theire ground until driven out by the Russian baynots, that may be so but it was the sight of it, and not the fell [feel] of it.'

Only about seven of ten defending Turks made it back to the British lines, the highest unit casualty rate that day. Corporal Thomas Morley with the 17th Lancers was similarly uncomplimentary. 'They have little bits of swords,' he wrote to his father, '… their firelocks all go off with flint and they alarm the Russians with them, and they can take an aim with them at half a mile's distance.'

What did people expect? Lieutenant Robert Scott Hunter wrote to his sister that 'the Turks absolutely ran away from the other batteries; before the enemy got there.' Albert Mitchell with the 13th Light Dragoons saw the Turks running down the hill 'Completely routed, everyone going his own way, with no one to direct or rally them. Many were shot down as they ran.'

Scott Hunter saw them pursued 'by a cloud of Cossacks, who speared the unfortunate Turks, who were running away and begging for mercy in all directions'. It was ending badly. Trumpet Major William Forster with the 1st Royal Dragoons watched as the Cossacks 'skewered the Turks as fast as they could handle their lances'.[16]

Contemplating all this from the Sapoune Heights, Lieutenant Colonel Somerset Calthorpe with Raglan remembered, 'many were the curses loud and deep heaped on their heads'. Raglan had ridden up just in time to witness the collapse. Russell nearby observed the Turks in redoubt 2 running in scattered groups towards redoubt 3 and Balaclava, 'but the horse-hoof of the Cossack was too quick for them, and sword and lance were busily plied among the retreating herd'. Not only could they see the debacle unfolding, the noises that came up gave the crisis an alarming immediacy. 'The yells of the pursuers and pursued were plainly audible.' 'Thus in a few moments,' Calthorpe complained, 'we lost, through the confounded cowardice of the Turks, the key of our advanced line of defence.' Mesmerised spectators around Raglan continued to watch as number 3 redoubt was subjected to intense cannon fire. Soon, 'the Turks swarm over the earthworks, and run in confusion towards the town, firing at the enemy as they run.' Russell from his ringside position authentically reported events with modern TV immediacy, enthralling readers back home with his descriptions of Cossacks falling upon running fugitives:

> Again the solid column of cavalry opens like a fan, and resolves itself into a 'long spray' of skirmishers. It laps the flying Turks, steel flashes in the air, and down go the poor Moslem quivering on the plain, split through fez and musket-guard to the chin and breast-belt.[17]

The Russians, like British soldiers, anticipated a rapid collapse of the redoubts. Liprandi's cavalry commander Major General Ivan Ryzhov recalled, 'Some kind of panic and fear overcame the Turks, so that they were unable to withstand the approach of our infantry and betook themselves away almost before they had to.'

The Cossack Don Battery positioned itself near redoubt 2 on the Causeway Heights supporting the Russian infantry attack. They approached to within 1,400 yards and opened fire, which silenced the guns. 'Our infantry attacks quickly took it and killed all its defenders.' They then moved to redoubt 3, requested once again to assist with their heavier guns 'setting off again into position at a walk'. They knocked out one of the Turkish cannon and managed to blow up an artillery caisson. 'The fire from the enemy guns slackened after a short but rapid bombardment from our side,' the officer remembered, 'and then the infantry stormed the redoubt.'

Some of the Russian low-level accounts suggest deliberate attacks were carried out in concert with artillery, which took time, not the rapid collapse described in Russell's accounts. General Liprandi's final after-action report to Prince Menshikov and the Tsar glosses over the detail. His account suggests steady progress from departure at 5 a.m. from his assembly area to the capture of the redoubts by 7.30 a.m. Nothing is said about Turkish resistance at all, apart from being irresolute. 'The Turks waivered' and 'did not stand firm' and ran, according to Major General Ryzhov's notes written after the battle. Lieutenant General Liprandi was hardly going to admit to the Tsar that 1,000 irregular Turkish militia had in any way thwarted the advance of his 27,000-strong force on Balaclava, with a superiority of twelve to one on the Causeway Heights. Neither was the two-hour delay imposed by the Turks recognised in any way by the British press.

For the moment the Russians were on a high. 'Russian flags were planted on the redoubts of the Balaclava Heights,' Hussar Lieutenant Arbuzov triumphantly remembered. 'The impression made by this magnificent attack was extraordinarily strong … Tears of joy and emotion were flowing freely,' he emotionally recalled. The cavalry brigade cheered the Don battery as its horse-drawn caissons rattled by and Arbuzov remembered 'the forage caps of the brave artillerymen flew high into the air, and with one voice a "Ura!" joyously spread through the ranks of our forces.' It was all going to plan.[18]

British cavalry, meanwhile, pulled back towards their original camp area. Russian artillery had made their position just short of the Causeway Heights untenable. Morale was intact and troopers were calmly phlegmatic about the retrograde movement. Trumpet Major Forster with the 1st Dragoons simply felt, 'let them [the Russians] come down from the hills and have a fair fight'; they were quietly confident.

Fleeing Turks streamed past Albert Mitchell's 13th Dragoon's troop, 'crying and calling upon "Allah",' he remembered, but 'however great their haste, they were very careful of their kettles and pans, for they rattled and clattered as they ran past us'. 'No bono Johnny,' the men called out, 'but that made no impression on them, for soon they were off as fast as they could go towards Balaclava.' A round shot shrieked past his head and splattered the ground in front of him; 'had it been a trifle lower, any troubles in this world would have been over,' he recalled. Looking up towards number 3 redoubt as they passed, 'we saw a man haul down the Turkish flag, which in their hasty flight the Turks had left flying,' which seemed to encapsulate the moment. 'At the same time someone, apparently an officer[,] mounted the breastwork and waved his sword at us triumphantly.' A disgruntled English artillery NCO passed them by and 'complained bitterly of the manner in which the Turks had left him'. Nevertheless, he assured them 'they won't fire the guns on you from this redoubt for I spiked them before I left.'

Lucan's interpreter, John Blunt, was sent off to try and rally the Turks to the 93rd Highlander's colours at Kadikoi, just north of Balaclava. He gathered a band of parched and exhausted Esnan around them and explained the order to their 'bimbashi'. 'One faint and bleeding from a wound in his breast asked why no support had been sent?' Another with a bandaged head and 'smoking a pipe half a yard long' confided to Blunt in Turkish, 'What can we do sir? It is God's will.' The British cavalry, as Troop Sergeant Major George Smith with the 11th Hussars recalled, could do little more than watch as Cossacks swooped around the foot of the Heights lancing and sabring fleeing Turks: 'Some of them being unarmed raised their hands imploringly, but it was only to have them severed from their bodies. Had a dozen or two of us been sent out, numbers of these poor fellows might have been saved.'

Lucan could have harassed these Cossack forays but, lacking tactical experience, he chose, as Raglan would have wished, to keep the British line together. It formed at an oblique, flanking the approach to Balaclava. Redoubt number 4 above them was carried at that moment and down came ragged files of running Turkish militia, preceded by an officer who Mitchell recalled rode by shouting 'all is lost!' Cossack cavalry was in hot pursuit, lancing fugitives in the back, one was impaled in front of them, 'who uttered a loud scream and fell'. Two Cossacks were seen bearing down on another Turk a short distance ahead. 'Before they could reach him,' Mitchell recalled, 'Johnny, who had his piece loaded and bayonet fixed, turned suddenly and fired at the foremost, knocking him off his horse.' The other had closed in and was about to lance the straggler and 'made a point, but whether it touched the Turk or not I cannot say; but in an instant he had bayonetted the Cossack in the body, and he also fell from his horse.' This sangfroid performance impressed the British, and 'Johnny resumed his journey at a walk', a fillip to everyone's morale. 'Now this exploit was witnessed by many of our men,' Mitchell remembered, 'who cheered Johnny lustily.' The Turks still had teeth. The implications of the fall of redoubt 4 were not lost on the simplest trooper in the British line. Private Charles Howell explained that the Russians:

> Knew all the supplies were taken from Balaclava to the army in front of Sevastopol. So if they could drive us from that position we should have been in rather an unpleasant fix. If our supplies had been cut off we could not fight long without food.[19]

Raglan had ordered up two divisions of infantry but they were unlikely to appear for at least two hours. At 8 a.m. he sent a galloper off to Lucan with an order for the 'cavalry to take ground to the left of the second line of redoubts occupied by the Turks'. Its imprecise wording caused confusion amid the welter of activity on the valley floor below. Which redoubts occupied by Turks? They had all been abandoned. There was no second line of redoubts, only the one seized along the Causeway Heights. Left or right depended on which way Raglan was facing when the order was written. Lucan correctly deduced his commander meant west, where he would be in dead ground and therefore unseen by the Russians covered by the Causeway Heights and able to potentially menace their flank.

Fortunately, the aide and Lucan sorted out the detail on the ground, but clearly Raglan's three-dimensional view did not equate to the two-dimensional realities on the valley floor below. The order took the cavalry nearly 2,000 yards from Campbell's position, occupying the small knoll at the entrance to the main approach to Kadikoi and Balaclava. Visibility for the cavalry was virtually nil and they were barely on the extremity of being able to support Campbell's infantry.

Fanny Duberly had been summoned by a note from her husband Henry that said a 'hot' battle was about to take place. She was soon clattering through the 'narrow and crowded streets' of Balaclava as fast as she could. A commissariat officer advised 'that the Turks had abandoned all their batteries, and were running towards the town'. She should therefore veer left to avoid them and 'lose no time in getting amongst our own men'. 'For God's sake,' the officer appealed, 'ride fast, or you may not reach the camp alive.' The road ahead was almost blocked by Turks fleeing towards the town, some 'running hard' and shouting 'Ship Johnny! Ship Johnny!' She saw that, bizarrely, they were 'laden with pots, kettles, arms and plunder of every description'. Caught up in the popular myths and rumours of the collapse, she later recalled, 'had I known more of their *brutal* cowardice, I would have ridden over them all.' 'Every Turk turned tail and *ran*,' she complained, 'like rabbits.' She could not understand why so many insisted on carrying 'old bottles, for which the Turks appear to have a great appreciation'. Henry met her at the camp, 'where I stood, superintending the striking of our tent and the packing of our valuables'; 2,000 yards away Cossacks were running down Turkish stragglers to the accompaniment of scattered musket fire. 'Henry flung me on the old horse; and seizing a pair of laden saddlebags, a greatcoat, and a few other packages', they made their way up to the high ground that Raglan's staff was occupying.[20]

One of the ship's officers aboard HMS *Himalaya*, a steam troopship off Balaclava harbour, was attracted by the sound of heavy firing on shore, 'increasingly towards 9 o'clock and from that time incessant'. It looked serious. The harbour appeared under threat because he 'could see occasionally shells bursting over the high hills by which the bay is surrounded'. Frantic efforts were being made by ships' crews to raise steam and unfurl sails to get out of the crowded harbour. With Turks running into the harbour area crying 'Ship Johnny!' it looked as though anything might happen. 'There was literally nothing' beyond the 93rd Regiment, Lieutenant Colonel Sterling with Campbell admitted, 'to hinder the cavalry which came down on the 93rd from galloping through the flying Turks, and destroying all the stores in Balaclava.' The confined shelter offered by the precipitous harbour walls might instead prove to be its nemesis. Craft could not swiftly exit the harbour without the certainty of chaotic entanglements. 'There was indeed, a frigate in the harbour,' Sterling remembered, but should Russian cavalry appear in the streets, 'the frigate must have fired through our own shipping, if she could have got a spring on her cable in time to fire at all.' There was no plan to evacuate the harbour in the event of a crisis; there was not even an agreed procedure to disembark stores.[21]

Fleeing Turks poured through the Highland camp, liberating anything of usefulness, especially food in their starving state. As they ran through, Mrs Smith, married to Private Smith, a soldier servant with Quartermaster Sinclair of the 93rd, was still attending her washing, despite the sound of round shot whooshing overhead. Described as a 'large powerful bony woman' she assumed the first Turk entering her tent was intent on stealing or taking liberties. She was to become the stuff of legend, further embellishing stories of Turkish cowardice. Surgeon George Munro with the 93rd remembered, when the Turks 'trampled on things, which being washed, she had spread out to dry, she broke out into a towering rage, and seizing a large stick … laid about her right and left in protection of her property.'

Realising they had bolted from the battle and deserted her regiment, 'she abused the "Johnnys" roundly in braid Scotch'. Captain Edward Fisher-Rowe with the 4th Dragoon Guards summed up popular army feeling when he commented: 'the Turks are found out at last; they are a black-guardedly, cowardly race, without honour amongst the officers or honesty amongst the men.' Whereas before he received 'a nod and "Bono Johnny" from everyone', now he more likely 'stands a good chance of a blow across the mouth'. The 93rd, Fisher-Rowe pointed out, 'who like all Highlanders can bear malice, swear, if they get a chance, to drive bayonets through the whole lot' of them, adding indignantly, 'they stole all the highlanders kits while they were actually defending them from the enemy'. Mrs Smith became known as 'Kokana Smith', meaning 'woman' in Turkish and attained celebrity status, myth was transformed by word of mouth to fact.[22]

Private John Vahey and Paddy Heffernan had come to their intoxicated senses in the 17th Lancers' guard tent. 'We must have had a long snooze,' Vahey recalled, 'for it was broad daylight before we were wakened by the loud thundering of a tremendous cannonade close by, making the very tent poles quiver.' Both had monumental hangovers. 'I still felt decidedly muzzy, for commissary rum, as you would know if you ever got tight on it, is hard stuff to get sober off.' Reverberating booms gave 'a shrewd guess what all the row was', but there was no sentry at the tent flap to tell them what was going on. They languidly stretched in the cool air outside and realised the camp was 'utterly deserted'. Nonplussed but cheerfully unconcerned, they went back inside to confer 'over a refresher out of the inexhaustible rum bottle', and try 'in a boozy sort of way, to argue out the position'.

Private Christopher Fox with the 4th Dragoons, another incorrigible hard-case, had also been left behind in the Light Brigade camp on extra fatigues. The 26-year-old Fox had a jaundiced view of authority, having appeared forty-three times in the regimental defaulters' book, court-martialled four times and imprisoned twice during seven years' service. Fox had watched the brigade saddle up and ride off towards the sound of firing early that morning. He had no intention of missing what appeared to be the first likelihood of action that campaign and took a troop horse and set off after them, to find his unit. His action leaving his post against orders constituted a flogging offence.

Vahey and Heffernan, left in camp, could hear but not see what was going on. The sound of continuous gunfire was kept up on the other side of a low ridge, projecting from the Causeway Heights, which blocked their view. 'We could tell it must be pretty warm work,' Vahey remembered. 'Why the devil should we be out of the fun?' they agreed, and went to the horse lines 'half drunk as we were' to look for sick horses. Vahey picked up his butcher's axe while Heffernan still had a sword. Two lame horses had been left behind, one with 'a leg like a pillar box' and the other 'down on his side and did not look much like rising again'. Increasingly frustrated, they strode off toward the Heavy Brigade, which they could see forming up in the distance behind the escarpment to their front.[23]

By now Raglan's gallopers had reached the Sevastopol siege lines to summon the 1st and 4th Infantry Divisions. The irrepressible and cheery Captain Jem Macdonald, the Duke of Cambridge's ADC, had no problem getting the 1st Division moving. 'There's a row going on down in the Balaclava plain,' he told the staff, 'and you fellows are wanted.' Captain Ewart, Cathcart's 4th Division ADC, met with reticence. 'Lord Raglan requests you, Sir George,' he appealed, 'to move your division immediately to the assistance of the Turks.' They were still in the midst of a relief operation. 'It is impossible for my division to move,' the irritable Cathcart responded, 'the greater portion of my men have just come from the trenches'; they were tired and reorganising and had yet to eat. There was bad blood between Cathcart and Raglan. The former held a dormant commission to be Raglan's successor if anything should happen to him. It produced tensions, not helped when Raglan ignored Cathcart's advice to storm Sevastopol after the flank march, when its defences had been at their most vulnerable. Just two days before he had marched his division down to the plain, responding to yet another false alarm. 'The best thing you can do is to sit down and have some breakfast with me,' Cathcart advised Ewart. The ADC pluckily stood his ground, saying he was not going anywhere until he saw Raglan's clear instruction being carried out.

The stand-off caused another forty-minute delay. The 4th Division was the nearest to the Col entry point descending to the plain. Raglan forbade the use of the Woronsov road, which was a more direct route because the French feared an unexpected engagement with the Russians, who had already occupied its east end. 'I will see if anything can be done,' Cathcart acquiesced and bugles were blown and drums rolled until the division set off at a leisurely pace towards Balaclava.

On the Russian side, Liprandi's opening moves had gone completely to plan, aside from the tripwire delay imposed by the Turkish redoubts. The first four redoubts had been captured at the eastern end, giving the Russians control of the Woronsov road leading to Sevastopol. By driving back the British cavalry and artillery, they had swung open a door enabling clear access to Balaclava. Lieutenant Kubitovich with Yeropkin's lancers had spotted English cavalry off to their right flank. 'The appearance of the English cavalry made us glad,' he remembered; 'we hoped that our wish to fight them would come true.' The route to Balaclava looked open and 'after a short period of inactivity following the occupation of the redoubts, Major General Ryzhov, the cavalry commander in our force, received the order to make an attack.' Ryzhov's cavalry formed the 'enormous bodies of cavalry' that Russell had seen advancing in 'six compact squares' behind Semyakin's central column, on the north side of the Causeway Heights.

All Kubitovich could see in the way was a 'Scottish regiment', which had appeared 'almost at the very beginning of the battle,' he remembered, and 'alarmed by our attack, deployed in the front of the village of Kadikoi, in the main path of our force's advance'. Fleeing Turks had congregated around the ends of this 'thin red streak', identified by correspondent William Russell, from the Sapoune Heights. This small red line appeared dwarfed in the immense space it was trying to block ahead of the wide gorge leading down to Kadikoi and Balaclava.

Lord Raglan pensively regarded this space. Thirty minutes before he had caused confusion, diverting Lucan's cavalry away from the same gap, isolating Campbell's 93rd regiment 2,000 yards from its nearest support. Raglan now dispatched a second galloper to Lucan at 8.30 a.m., directing 'eight squadrons of heavy horse to be detached towards Balaclava to support the Turks who are wavering'. Lucan had barely reached this position twenty minutes before when he received an exasperating order to go back. Thirty minutes in a cavalry action can be an eternity. The Turks were not wavering around Campbell, they had been overrun and were seeking support. Lucan was being asked to move four regiments of the 'Heavies' back onto the open plain, separating them from the five Light regiments and isolating the last Heavy Brigade regiment from its parent command. Transmission of orders from Raglan's Olympian heights to the reality of the fast-moving action below took twenty to thirty minutes. It was unwise to divide the cavalry force by as much as a mile in the face of the enemy. Frustrated and nonplussed, Lucan told Brigadier General James Scarlett commanding the Heavy Brigade to execute the move and go back to where he had come from.

Back up on the Sapoune Heights, William Russell remembered watching every move 'as though they were looking on the stage from the boxes of a theatre'. The time was approaching 9 a.m. – thirty minutes after Raglan had dispatched his last order – already invalidated by the disturbing developments they saw shaping up below. The huge masses of Russian cavalry that Russell had spotted coming across the North Valley were emerging on the 'crown of the hill across the valley'. Starting from the left they began to trickle over the spine of the Causeway Heights. Riding beneath, and oblivious to the storm about to break over them from above, was Scarlett's painfully thin lines of four regiments of horse marching in open column. Both sides were clearly unable to see each other. Tension on the Heights became physically palpable.

The enormous Russian mass below came to a halt, 'and squadron after squadron,' Russell recalled 'flies up from the rear, till they have a body of some 1,500 men along the ridge – lancers, and dragoons, and Hussars'. They regrouped into two huge squares, with another in reserve, and began to trickle forward onto the lower slope. Brigadier General Scarlett could be seen at the head of his column below, unaware of this dark, menacing cloud forming and about to burst over them. On the Heights, Russell remembered 'nearly every one dismounted and sat down, and not a word was said'. It had taken Lord Raglan barely twenty minutes to set up Scarlett's command for likely execution. Every man on the escarpment knew the storm would break in a lot less time than this. They were helpless inanimate observers, resigned to accepting the calamity that must ensue.[24]

5

EIGHT MINUTES OF CUT AND SLASH

8.55 A.M. TO 9.15 A.M.

A THIN RED STREAK TIPPED WITH STEEL

8.55 A.M. TO 9.05 A.M.

Fifty-five-year-old Brigadier General Sir James Scarlett, commanding the Heavy Brigade, was a large, florid, ruddy man and short-sighted. Popular with all ranks, he had recently commanded the 5th Dragoon Guards but had never seen active service. He was, nevertheless, open to advice from his official staff ADC Lieutenant Alexander Elliot and Colonel Beatson, both of whom had campaigned in India. Glancing left, Elliot spotted the tips of Russian lances fretting the high ground, followed by the heads and horses of Russian cavalry coming over the edge of the Causeway Heights. Scarlett had not noticed but the sky-line was pointed at as Lucan and his staff came galloping up, shouting, 'Scarlett! Scarlett! Look to your left!' About 400 yards away and 100ft above a huge grey Russian wave was gathering, about to break over and engulf his column. 'Left wheel into line,' Scarlett immediately

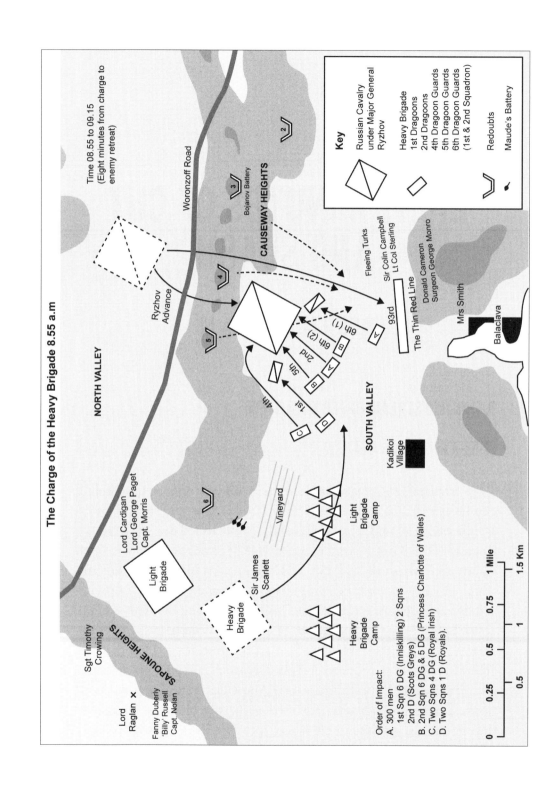

The Charge of the Heavy Brigade 8.55 a.m

Time 08.55 to 09.15
(Eight minutes from charge to enemy retreat)

SAPOUNE HEIGHTS

Lord Raglan ×

Sgt Timothy Crowing

Fanny Duberly
'Billy' Russell
Capt. Nolan

NORTH VALLEY

Woronzoff Road

Lord Cardigan
Lord George Paget
Capt. Morris

Light Brigade

Ryzhov Advance

CAUSEWAY HEIGHTS

Bojanov Battery

2

3

4

5

6

Light Brigade Camp

Vineyard

Heavy Brigade Camp

Sir James Scarlett

Heavy Brigade

4th
1st
5th
2nd
6th (2)
6th (1)

A
B
C
D
A
B

93rd

The Thin Red Line

Fleeing Turks

Sir Colin Campbell
Lt Col Sterling

Donald Cameron
Surgeon George Monro

Mrs Smith

Balaclava

SOUTH VALLEY

Kadikoi Village

Order of Impact:
A. 300 men
 1st Sqn 6 DG (Inniskilling) 2 Sqns
 2nd D (Scots Greys)
B. 2nd Sqn 6 DG & 5 DG (Princess Charlotte of Wales)
C. Two Sqns 4 DG (Royal Irish)
D. Two Sqns 1 D (Royals).

Key

Russian Cavalry under Major General Ryzhov

Heavy Brigade
1st Dragoons
2nd Dragoons
4th Dragoon Guards
5th Dragoon Guards
6th Dragoon Guards
(1st & 2nd Squadron)

Redoubts

Maude's Battery

0   0.25   0.5   0.75   1 Mile

0.5   1   1.5 Km

ordered, which brought his squadrons into one line, two troopers deep. Because the rough ground of the cavalry encampment and an old vineyard lay to his left, Scarlett moved his first three squadrons further right to enable the 5th Dragoon Guards to come up in between to the left. Coolly oblivious to Lucan's shouted demands to charge immediately, Scarlett set about fixing his brigade's alignment. Officers sat motionless on horses, with their backs to the enemy as NCOs darted about dressing the ranks. Their only hope of survival was to present the Russians with a compact front.

The Russians on the ridgeline pulled up so abruptly that the rattle of accoutrements was clearly audible to spectators on the Sapoune Heights. The appearance of British cavalry below had been completely unexpected. They gaped, fascinated, at the scene below. The absence of hurry and the imperturbable dressing of ranks going on below appeared menacing. Scots Greys with busbies and red tunics seemed terribly like the bearskins of the awful Guards they had faced at the Alma. Had they taken to horseback? The immediate halt led to a spillage of Russian horsemen beyond the flanks, so that the tight phalanx of mass cavalry took on a crescent-shaped appearance. A trumpet sounded and the advance resumed, this time hesitant and slow.

Major General Ryzhov commanded Liprandi's cavalry and he had been ordered: 'On the occupation of the last enemy redoubt by our infantry, to immediately – even starting from the spot at full speed – to throw ourselves at the English cavalry occupying a fortified position near the village of Kadikoi and the town of Balaclava.'

He decided to move forward at a quick trot, 'not at full speed as ordered', because charging an enemy thought to be a mile distant would blow the horses. But suddenly there they were, right in front

---

Four squadrons of Russian cavalry were repulsed by Sir Colin Campbell's 93rd Highlanders barring the way to the British logistic base at Kadikoi village and Balaclava. Meanwhile, the British Heavy Brigade charged uphill against a mass of Russian cavalry more than six times their number. They struck the compacted Russian cavalry with four successive attacks from different directions, which unhinged the mass and caused it to break and flee. It was a remarkable success.

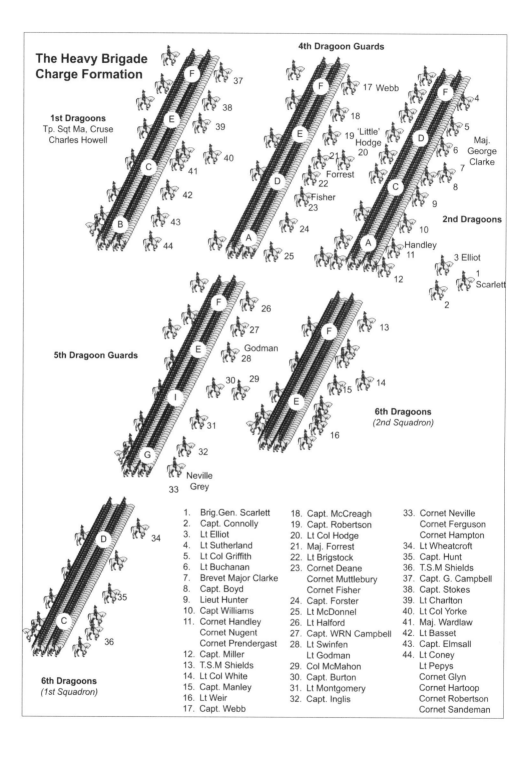

The Heavy Brigade Charge Formation

4th Dragoon Guards

1st Dragoons
Tp. Sqt Ma, Cruse
Charles Howell

F
E
C
B

37
38
39
40
41
42
43
44

F
E
D
A

17 Webb
18
19 'Little' Hodge
20
21
Forrest
22
Fisher
23
24
25

F
D
C
A

4
5
Maj. George Clarke
6
7
8
9
10
Handley
11
12

3 Elliot
1
Scarlett
2

2nd Dragoons

5th Dragoon Guards

F
E
I
G

26
27
Godman
28
29
30
31
32
Neville
33 Grey

F
E

13
14
15
16

6th Dragoons
(2nd Squadron)

D
C

34
35
36

6th Dragoons
(1st Squadron)

1. Brig.Gen. Scarlett
2. Capt. Connolly
3. Lt Elliot
4. Lt Sutherland
5. Lt Col Griffith
6. Lt Buchanan
7. Brevet Major Clarke
8. Capt. Boyd
9. Lieut Hunter
10. Capt Williams
11. Cornet Handley
    Cornet Nugent
    Cornet Prendergast
12. Capt. Miller
13. T.S.M Shields
14. Lt Col White
15. Capt. Manley
16. Lt Weir
17. Capt. Webb

18. Capt. McCreagh
19. Capt. Robertson
20. Lt Col Hodge
21. Maj. Forrest
22. Lt Brigstock
23. Cornet Deane
    Cornet Muttlebury
    Cornet Fisher
24. Capt. Forster
25. Lt McDonnel
26. Lt Halford
27. Capt. WRN Campbell
28. Lt Swinfen
    Lt Godman
29. Col McMahon
30. Capt. Burton
31. Lt Montgomery
32. Capt. Inglis

33. Cornet Neville
    Cornet Ferguson
    Cornet Hampton
34. Lt Wheatcroft
35. Capt. Hunt
36. T.S.M Shields
37. Capt. G. Campbell
38. Capt. Stokes
39. Lt Charlton
40. Lt Col Yorke
41. Maj. Wardlaw
42. Lt Basset
43. Capt. Elmsall
44. Lt Coney
    Lt Pepys
    Cornet Glyn
    Cornet Hartoop
    Cornet Robertson
    Cornet Sandeman

of him. Ryzhov, like many of his contemporaries in the Tsar's army, followed battle tactics as a form of parade evolutions. Instead of immediately attacking, utilising height and surprise, he paused to execute a drilled approach. With the British equally acting as if on parade, Ryzhov decided 'as the rest of the divisions each came up the slope, I directed them to parts of the enemy formation'. This resulted in the Russians stretching and extending their line along the Causeway Heights. This ponderous allocation of deliberate tasks was distracted by the Ural Cossack regiment on the right, whose 'commander tore off at high speed without any thought or any of the necessary arrangements'. The predatory Cossacks wanted instinctively to attack the vulnerable British. Ryzhov saw the English cavalry had anchored its left flank on the rough vineyard terrain to his right, and were protected 'by a rather strong battery emplaced in Kadikoi village'. His Cossacks were already moving on this side, which further complicated the spillage over the ridge on both flanks, created by the sudden halt in the centre. 'An officer sent with my orders was no longer able to stop them,' he remembered with exasperation.[1]

Cossacks occupied a unique position in the Russian forces, recruited for just three years before entering the reserve. They originated from the Russian and Ukrainian settlers that used to secure the frontiers of Old Russia. Military service, long compulsory for Cossacks, was regarded as an honourably martial way of life, affecting a man's stature in society. A Cossack father would provide the horse, sabre and accoutrements his son would need at his own expense; the government only issued the carbine. Cossacks were better educated than the dull Russian soldiery, and less amenable to its unthinking rigid discipline. They had a robust frontier attitude that led to a looser

---

The positions of the various squadrons and regiments of Scarlett's Heavy Brigade are shown in this schematic, as well as the location of some major witnesses of the action. The 6th and 2nd Dragoons hit the Russian assembly first, followed by the 6th's second squadron and the 5th Dragoons. The 1st Dragoons and lastly the 4th Dragoons were the *coup de grâce* that finally split the Russian mass apart.

and more informal relationship between officers, junior leaders and men. Unthinking Russian infantry were resolute in defence, whereas Cossacks were observant and cautiously independent, with a highly developed instinct for self-preservation. Dying in place was hardly a virtue if one could fight advantageously elsewhere. They were born raiders, merciless in pursuit and particularly adept at sniffing out defence gaps. Their proclivity for precipitate retreat, and placing loot above duty did not endear irregular Cossacks to the more traditional regular Russian cavalry. Captain Robert Hodasevich with the Taroutine Regiment remembered their scruffy, unruly appearance, with clothes often 'in tatters':

> They have few words of command, but all their movements are directed by signals. These signals are imitations of the cries of different animals found in the Caucasus: they howl like jackals and wolves and bark like dogs, and mew like cats.[2]

The men understood these signals, but their training did not suit them for conventional cavalry operations.

As Ryzhov's Hussar columns began to descend the slope, the Cossacks, he recalled with irritation, 'moved with a frightful "Ura!"' and quickly shifted back and forth in a long row like some kind of flock or flight of birds, but not however, closing with the enemy'.

Instead of swiftly plunging down the slope, having caught out the British in a chance meeting engagement, Ryzhov busied himself sorting out Hussar squadrons as they reached the crest. Meanwhile, 'the enemy stood calmly,' he recalled, 'and waited as if by agreement.' An ominous silence reigned on both sides; 'only the Cossacks were shouting,' he remembered, 'and that was far off and nobody paid them any attention.'

A tense William Russell on the Sapoune Heights saw a sudden movement to the left of the assembled mass, when an element 'drew breath for a moment, and then in one grand line dashed at the Highlanders' covering the Balaclava gorge. Partially obscured by a small hillock were 550 93rd Highlanders occupying a 150-yard frontage blocking it. They were reinforced at each end by 100 sick and convalescents from Balaclava, and Turkish survivors from the stormed redoubts.

The Highlanders watched attentively as the Causeway Heights suddenly came to life. Hundreds of Russian cavalry were starkly silhouetted against the skyline, amid the protrusions of the captured redoubts. A great slice detached itself from the mass, and four squadrons of 400 Hussars came hurtling towards them. Charging cavalry often looked forbiddingly more numerous than they actually were. Russell found them frightening. 'The ground flies beneath their horses feet,' he observed from 2 miles away. 'Gathering speed at every stride, they dash on towards that thin red streak tipped with a line of steel.' Campbell, confident in the capabilities of the Minié rifle, chose not to form square, but engage from a line two deep. With the front rank kneeling and the rear standing, the whole firepower of the regiment could be brought to bear, rather than the quarter side of a square.

Surgeon George Munro with the 93rd remembered Campbell riding along their front 'telling the regiment to be "steady"', for if necessary every man should have 'to die where he stood'. His aide, Lieutenant Colonel Sterling, recalled, 'he looked as if he meant it'. 'Ay, Ay sir Colin,' the cheery soldiers responded, 'we'll do that.' Campbell was an experienced soldier, sure of his ground, and his infantry outnumbered the approaching cavalry three to one. Munro recalled, 'I do not think there was a single soldier standing in the line who had an anxious thought as to our isolated and critical position or who for a moment felt the least inclination to flinch before the charge of the advancing cavalry.' They knew what to expect and anticipated 'a regular hand to hand struggle'.

Onlookers predicted a grim outcome. 'Ah what a moment!' remembered Mrs Fanny Duberly, standing by Russell. 'Charging and surging onward, what could that little wall of men do against such numbers and such speed?' The Russian cavalry 'passed in front of us a few hundred yards', remembered Private Charles Howell with the 1st Dragoons, and 'the thought was in my mind, oh the poor 93rd, they will be all cut up, their's more than fifty to one against them.' The Russians were galloping so boldly and fast that one trooper remarked to Major William Forrest with the 4th Dragoon Guards, 'Bedad, they must take them for Turks.' 'They never expected to meet English there I am sure,' agreed Lieutenant Temple Godman with the 5th.[3]

'The sudden appearance of a steady line of redcoats, as if sprung from the earth, caused the enemy to falter,' Munro remembered. Campbell had learned his trade in the Peninsular War. 'As we sat our horses,' Howell remembered, 'we heard quite plain the sharp words, *Kneeling ranks Ready – Present* and in an instant many a Russian soldier's saddle empty.' The first volley, a flash and billowing cloud of smoke, accompanied by rapid crackling one second later, was likely premature, probably at 600 yards. Few Russians fell and they came on. 'The distance is too great,' Russell tersely reported:

> The Russians are not checked, but still sweep onwards through the smoke, with the whole force of horse and man, here and there knocked over by the shot of our batteries above. With breathless suspense every one awaits the bursting of the wave upon the line of Gaelic rock.

'*Present!*' the command rang out again. By now, with just 100 yards to go, the scarlet line would have felt the reverberation of hundreds of thundering hooves through the ground. '*Fire!*' Campbell bellowed as the rear rank of rifles with fixed bayonets erupted with crackling fire and spluttering smoke. There was a notable recoil within the Russian mass, horses plunged and reared amid a chorus of shrieks from riders. As the smoke rolled back on the Highland ranks they brought their bayonets up to charge, 'manifesting an inclination to advance and meet the cavalry half way,' Munro recalled. Campbell sharply checked them: '*Ninety-Third! Ninety-Third! Damn all that eagerness!*'

Private Donald Cameron in the ranks remembered that after the second volley 'they seemed to be going away. We ceased firing and cheered.' But it was not over yet. The Russians changed direction and 'wheeled about and made a dash at us again'. Colour Sergeant J. Joiner with the 93rd saw that 'they found it too hot to come any further' and swung round to take them in their right flank. 'The Grenadiers, under my old friend [Captain] Ross, were ordered to change front,' Munro remembered, 'and fire a volley,' which caused visible damage: 'This third volley was at much nearer range than the previous ones and caught the cavalry in flank as they were approaching, apparently with the intention of passing our right.'

Joiner claims, 'volley after volley was fired into them so fast' that 'their own dead and dying choked their way'. Campbell, with a keen veteran eye, had anticipated the Russians would seek to envelop a weak flank, and shared the insight with his ADC. 'Shadwell!' he said, nodding towards the Russians, 'that man understands his business.'

Russell's subsequent vivid dispatch composed from 2 miles away created an iconic account of what was in effect simply a brief cavalry-infantry skirmish. The 'thin red streak' became the 'thin red line', immortalised by British military history as an example of inspirational courage: rock-hard Highland infantry seeing off masses of Russian cavalry seeking to trample them. Mrs Fanny Duberly standing alongside was hardly likely to contradict the respected correspondent of the prestigious *Times* newspaper. 'One terrific volley,' she recalled, 'a sudden wheel – a piece of ground strewed with men and horses.' Russell's exciting dispatch climaxed with 'another deadly volley flashes' that 'carries death and terror into the Russians', who 'wheel about' and 'fly back faster than they came'. 'Bravo, Highlanders! Well done!' was the predictable patriotic applause from spectators on the Sapoune Heights. The gripping yarn was embellished in similar newspaper accounts that published eyewitness letters. The '93rd opened such a fire upon them that you could see them falling out of their saddles like old boots,' claimed one private with the 1st Dragoons. 'Dozens of saddles were soon empty,' another 1st Royals eyewitness claimed. Other depictions point to a paucity rather than multiplicity of corpses sprawled in front of the Highland line. Surgeon Munro, coming forward to treat them, found 'not more than 12', while Captain George Higginson on the high ground with Russell 'could not observe any casualties'. Lieutenant Stotherd with the 93rd wrote to his parents, convinced the stand had been a resounding success: 'We gave them three British cheers and peppered them so much that they turned and swerved away and finally beat a retreat at a hard gallop, leaving many a corpse behind.' Whatever the body count, the 93rd had mastered a crisis.[4]

Two years later Surgeon Munro received an insight into the true extent of the Russian casualties. He met a Russian Hussar officer in the Crimean capital Simferopol with a severe limp, who had participated in the charge. 'In the first place, we did not know that you were lying down behind the hill close to the guns,' he explained, 'which were keeping up a galling fire on our columns.' They were heading to capturing them and were in mid-stride, when:

> You started from the ground and fired a volley at us. In the next place, we were unable to rein up or slacken speed, or swerve to our left before we received your second volley, by which almost every man and horse in our ranks was wounded.

When they tried to wheel left, 'a wing of your regiment changed front' and delivered another punishing volley, 'one of your bullets breaking my thigh and making me the cripple that you see'. Russian cavalry were generally strapped to the saddle in action, which explains the relatively low casualty count. 'A mounted man,' the Russian pointed out, 'though severely, or even mortally wounded, can retain his seat in the saddle long enough to ride out of danger.' Much of the cavalry fleeing back to the Causeway Heights was reeling, semi-conscious but fastened to their saddles.[5]

The first crisis in front of Kadikoi village and Balaclava was settled in minutes. The attention of the onlookers on the Sapoune Heights now shifted to the unfolding catastrophe about to overwhelm the British cavalry.

SUCH A CHARGE! EIGHT MINUTES OF CUT AND SLASH

9.05 A.M. TO 9.13 A.M.

An axiom of cavalry warfare was that no mounted unit should ever receive an attack standing stationary. Forward momentum was vital, to stave off defeat. Strangely enough, Brigadier General Scarlett's insistence on standing still and calmly dressing the ranks in front of the Russian menace proved sound. Every British trooper knew they were in a bad place. Corporal Joseph Gough with the 5th Dragoon Guards looked up, thinking, 'at first we thought they were our Light Brigade, till they got about twenty yards from us, then we saw the difference'. Corporal John Selkrig grimly realised, 'we were taken completely at a disadvantage'.[6] Officers sitting motionless on their chargers and ignoring the enemy while waiting for NCOs to dress the ranks was enormously reassuring to men acutely aware of their vulnerability. It represented order in the face of pending chaos. Lord Lucan, the British cavalry commander, was so impatient to get Scarlett moving he ordered his own duty bugler, Trumpet Major Joy of the 17th Lancers, to sound the charge. Scarlett studiously ignored the call, intent on aligning his squadrons to present a cohesive front. No officer would move without his order.

There was much to reflect upon during this interval between life and death. Squadron commander Major George Clarke in the lead Scots Greys line was apprehensive that his charger 'Sultan', habitually unnerved by galloping squadrons during training, would revert to form and swerve across the line of advance. Troopers uneasily fidgeted and fingered sabre pommels. Newly sharpened sabres had been issued in England six months before. Troop Sergeant Major George Smith with the 11th Hussars remembered 'an order was given that they were not to be drawn till required, when in the presence of the enemy'. Sword practice was banned for good reason. Every time the blade was withdrawn from its steel scabbard and replaced, it lost some of its keen edge. Experienced cavalrymen stuffed straw down the full length of the scabbard to protect newly sharpened blades. Not everyone had done so. Lack of training, tedious picket duty and constant false alarms had resulted in a dropping away of standards by the less experienced. The sudden early morning alarm gave no time to remedy blunt blades.

Cornet Henry Handley with the Greys fingered his prize purchased acquisition, one of the new Colt and Adams revolvers, vastly superior to the conventional one-shot pistols. A number of officers and NCOs had chosen to purchase these five or six percussion cap models. Some of the unease in the ranks was mellowed by the euphoria of the moment. They were living the heavy cavalryman's dream of battle, for which many had joined. Nothing on this epic scale had occurred since Waterloo nearly fifty years before. Then, as now, the Inniskillings and Scots Greys were drawn up together, and were going to replicate the glorious charge of the Union Brigade. This produced an upsurge of tribal regimental fighting spirit. 'There is something grand and exciting in a charge,' recalled one Inniskilling private. 'You brace up with all your nerves and prepare yourself for mortal combat.' 'But,' he added, 'it is not very pleasant to have showers of musket balls whistling over your ears.' Cornet Grey Neville waiting with the 5th Dragoons in the centre of the second line remained nervous. Since the outbreak of war, he was convinced he was going to die; he had a brother in the infantry siege lines in front of Sevastopol. Grey Neville was a promising and popular young officer but not a good swordsman or horseman and up ahead were Cossacks, reputed experts.

Further to the left and rear Major William Forrest waited motionless in the second line with the 4th Dragoon Guards. On the verge of battle, he remembered, his thoughts were of his wife Annie. Cardigan had hounded him from the 11th Light Dragoons in 1843, when as Commanding Officer he refused Forrest's reasonable request for leave to attend her when she was ill with her first pregnancy. Even the Duke of Wellington had to intercede in the scandalous society quarrel that resulted. His new Commanding Officer, Edward Hodge, was more reasonable and likeable, but disapproved of wives on campaign.

He would later have to share a hut with her, because Forrest was his second in command. 'In my mind a very disgusting exposé to put any lady to,' he insisted. Hodge was loved by his soldiers, but he was exasperated by their tendency to drink themselves to death, but paternal enough to care. Hodge's father had been killed in the cavalry skirmish at Genappe the night before Waterloo, adding to the poignancy of the moment. This was the first major cavalry action since.[7]

Trickling slowly down the slope towards them came the Russians. Those ascending the ridgeline, coming up from the North Valley, were getting their first view of the South Valley. On the left, they were being hit and occasionally unhorsed by Captain Barker's W Battery. They did not expect to see British cavalry arrayed – as if on parade – before them. They also had brief time for reflection. Captain Khitrivo, commanding the 8th Weimar Hussar Squadron, was comforted by the thought that if he should fall, his old father would not be saddled with his regimental debt, cleared the night before. Cornet Veselovski in his regiment had just been reinstated months before, having been demoted to private following a scandalous fracas with another cornet in a guard house three years ago. He was determined to distinguish himself in the coming battle, but had barely minutes to live. The pressure of more and more squadrons coming up the slope behind them was precipitately pushing the lead units into a totally unexpected situation. Lieutenant Yevgenii Arbuzov on the left with the Saxe-Weimar Hussars remembered: 'While still on the move we saw that we would not have to deal with an artillery park, as supposed in our battle orders, but with English cavalry fully ready for battle.'

The advance was going to be tricky, because 'between us and the English, we could see their horse lines and serving tables'. An abandoned English cavalry encampment was in the way with partially struck tents. Lieutenant Stefan Kozhukhov was watching the cavalry advance from his artillery placement on the high ground at the head of the South Valley, near Kamara village. His impression was that the Russian cavalry, having overrun the Turkish redoubts, were complacent, believing the battle to be virtually over. There was neither command dexterity nor time to react to this unexpected development. 'Either General Ryzhov ordered the attack too late,' he subsequently surmised, 'or it was commanded when the Hussars had not yet managed to form up.' He watched as the hesitant Russian cavalry moved down from the Causeway Heights like 'an unorganised mob'.[8]

When Scarlett was satisfied his men were ready, he ordered his own trumpeter, Monks, to sound the charge and the Heavy Brigade started to spur their mounts uphill. From the Sapoune Heights, the action looked lost, as Russell recalled:

> The Russians advanced down the hill at a slow canter, which they changed to a trot, and at last nearly halted. Their first line was at least double the length of ours – it was three times as deep. Behind them was a similar line, equally strong and compact. They evidently despised their insignificant looking enemy.

Lord George Paget, watching to the north with the Light Brigade, had identified the difficult ground the 'Heavies' would have to cross, because they had been encamped on it: 'Anyone who has ridden, or attempted to ride, over an old vineyard will appreciate the difficulties of moving along its tangled roots and briars and its swampy holes.'

It was no conventional charge, *Trot* through *Gallop* at 200 yards and then *Charge* for the final fifty. There was neither time nor space. 'The pace of the Heavy Brigade never could have exceeded 8 mph,' Paget remembered, 'during their short advance across the vineyard', and they were going uphill. 'Suddenly within 20 yards of the dry ditch,' when it appeared the Russians 'must annihilate and swallow up all before them' with a 'handful of redcoats, *floundering* in the vineyard,' Paget saw 'the Russians halt, look about, and appear bewildered, as if they were at a loss to know what next to do!' The bizarre scene 'is forcibly engraved in my mind', he remembered. 'They stop! The Heavies struggle-flounder over the ditch and trot into them!'[9] Scarlett's first three squadrons of the Heavy Brigade, one of Inniskillings and two of the Scots Greys, barged into the centre of the Russian mass. The Greys keened a low tribal-like moan while the Inniskillings gave a high-pitched cheer. Three hundred men were attacking about 1,600 Russians. The swift change of direction from open column into line and further reorganisations to enable units to close up, meant by accident rather than design that the Heavies would hit the Russians in multiple waves of regimental attacks from different angles.

Another axiom of mounted tactics, creating the elan characteristic of cavalry troops, was that once the charge was sounded, it was 'do or die'. There could be no recall or turning back, commitment was total. As the first scarlet wedge plunged into the Russians, it disappeared from view. Onlookers on the Sapoune Heights were horrified. They appeared to be swallowed in the maw of the grey Russian mass, whose flanking arms unfolded to pull the British inside. Sergeant Timothy Gowing, viewing to the right of the Heights, remembered 'a number of the spectators, as our men dashed into that column, exclaimed, "They are lost! They are lost!"' Private Albert Mitchell with the Light Brigade was thrilled. 'I have often heard of cavalry charging cavalry,' he recalled thinking, 'now will be a chance of seeing it.' Although cavalry charge in lines, head-on collisions with opposing lines, the stuff of feature films and novels, only rarely occur. Horses instinctively swerve or pull up when confronted with obstructions, always stronger than the pain of the spur or pull of the bit. One side generally loses its nerve and turns about even before horses begin to baulk at self-destruction. Sergeant Timothy Gowing, viewing at distance, described the essence of this initial collision: 'heavy men mounted on heavy horses, and it told a fearful tale'. British horses were larger in girth and height than their more wiry adversaries. Fear of possible Austrian intervention had resulted in a dearth of Russian cavalry available for the Crimea, with poor quality ponies and insufficient fodder.[10]

Mitchell remembered 'we could see little else but smoke and dust' on impact, 'for the Russians fire their pistols when they charge and then use the sword'. Firing from the saddle is futile unless the muzzle is almost touching the target, because pistols and carbines were notoriously inaccurate. One of the earliest casualties was Lieutenant Colonel Darby Griffiths, the Greys Commanding Officer, struck in the head by a carbine shot. It took off his bearskin and had him reeling in the saddle, blood pouring down his face. Aiming was haphazard, with barrels jerked about by horses producing little control where shots went. It was dangerous to let the enemy get too close before resorting to swords. Sergeant Charles McGrigor with the Scots Greys recalled: 'When within two yards of our enemy, they fired upon us with pistols, but 'ere they could get them out of their hands, we were into them with our swords like the very devils, laying them low at every blow.'

'All I saw was swords in the air in every direction,' remembered Lieutenant Temple Godman with the 5th Dragoons, 'the pistols going off, and everyone hacking away right and left.' 'On the smoke clearing away,' Mitchell 'could plainly see our red jackets had gone clean through their leading squadrons and were engaged with the next.' Russians turning about at the approach of Scarlett's wave were sabred as the Inniskillings and Greys 'threaded' their ranks, spurring their horses between the gaps. Scarlett and his staff were the first inside the line. The general with his helmet looked less conspicuous than his ADC, Lieutenant Elliot, whom he insisted wear the cocked hat appropriate to his staff appointment, thereby attracting much of the Russian ire. They broke the line and the Greys, resplendent in their prominent bearskins, drove a wedge through the opening.[11]

'Oh such a charge!' a captain in the Inniskillings wrote home: 'Never think of the gallop and trot which you have often witnessed in Phoenix Park when you desire to form a notion of blood-hot, all mad charge, such as that I have come out of.'

Troopers sat well back in their saddles at the instant of shock. Horses were totally unrestrained by the bit and spurred forward to give it its head. Swords were pointed forward as men rose in their stirrups. 'Such splendid cutting and thrusting never was seen,' claimed Sergeant Thomas Kneath in the Scots Greys. 'Their horses, little cats of things, could not stand the jumping forwards of our powerful animals, with a pair of spurs driven into their sides.' The greater height of the British horses meant every cut and thrust had the advantage of gravity. Kneath was confident of the superiority of:

> Our heavy dragoons swords, longer and straighter than the Russians' which is a complete curve, and is not the slightest use in giving point, so that all they could do was to cut at our fellow's helmets, which they did heavily, but only dented them. [12]

The perennial cavalry debate about cut versus thrust was still not settled after the French wars. Stab wounds penetrated deeply, pierced vital organs and caused internal bleeding, a killing rather than disabling stroke. Penetration was invariably mortal, whereas a man with several cuts might fight on. French Colonel Antoine de Brack, called 'Mademoiselle' on account of his elegant good looks, wrote after the Napoleonic Wars: 'It is the point alone that kills; the others serve to wound. Thrust! Thrust! as often as you can: you will overthrow all whom you touch, and demoralise those who escape your attack.'

Attacking with the point as the Inniskillings and Greys closed in extended line was the only practical offensive option when riding knee to knee. Lieutenant Elliot saved Scarlett's life on breaking the line when the short-sighted general failed to notice a tall Russian officer bearing down on him. Elliot barged him with his horse and ran him through the body with such force that the thrust went home to the hilt. The complication of the thrust, as evidenced by training notes, was that the blade needed to be parallel to the ground to slide between the ribs without being entangled in the cage. 'The Russian was turned quite round in the saddle before the sabre could be disengaged,' described a witness, 'and then he fell dead to the ground.' Elliot barely managed to retain his sword with the momentum, as he passed him. Instinctive slashing took over in most melees, because it took a cool head to target, thrust and withdraw the sword. [13]

The Heavies' 'do or die' effort was pressed home with maniacal courage. 'I never in my life experienced such a sublime sensation as in the moment of the charge,' confessed an Inniskilling officer. 'Some fellows talk of it being "demoniac" like the Beserkers of ancient Irish history, because it "made me a match for any two ordinary men" and "gave me an amount of glorious indifference to life".' 'From the moment we dashed at the enemy,' he later wrote, 'I can tell you I knew nothing but that I was impelled by some irresistible force onward.' Only with maniacal cutting, thrusting and energy-sapping slashing would they get through this Russian mass. They had to keep moving forward to survive, otherwise they would be blocked, surrounded and cut down.

> Forward-Dash-Bang-Clank … It was glorious! Down, one by one, aye, two by two fell the thick skulled over numerous Cossacks … I could not pause. It was all push, wheel, frenzy, strike and down, down, down, they went. Twice I was unhorsed, and more than once I had to grip my sword tighter, the blood of foes streaming down over the hilt, and running up my very sleeve.

Major George Clarke's horse Sultan was predictably spooked at the outset and in the process his imposing bearskin was knocked off. Superstitious Russians gave him a wide berth, convinced that a bare-headed man taking on acres of flashing swords had to be imbued with satanic powers. Clarke looked the part when he emerged on the other side, blood streaming over his face and neck from a deep cut across the skull. 'They say you could not see a redcoat, we were so surrounded,' recalled one Scots Grey officer, 'and for *ten minutes* it was dreadful suspense.'

The charge was soon a 'scrimmage', 'more like a row at a fair', recalled Lieutenant Robert Scott Hunter. 'The scene was awful, we were so outnumbered and there was nothing but to fight our way through them, cut and slash.' The bluntness of swords against thick padded Russian greatcoats caused problems. 'I made a hack at one,'

Scott Hunter remembered, 'and my sword bounced off his thick coat, so I gave him the point' and he reeled from the saddle. 'Such a *mill* you could not imagine,' Cornet Daniel Moodie claimed, describing the metal-on-metal noise as being akin to an industrial workshop. The Russian mass became so tightly compacted, they could barely swing a sword. 'The slaughter was awful,' claimed Sergeant Charles McGrigor, with many Russians 'lying dead on their horses' necks or cruppers, for being strapped into the saddle, they could not fall from their horses', snagging and entangling those fighting around them. Cornet Henry Handley blessed the day he purchased his Colt and Adams revolver. Lanced and severely wounded he was surrounded by four Cossacks, three of which he managed to shoot from the saddle. This intensity of hand-to-hand fighting could not be physically maintained for more than eight to ten minutes, without succumbing to exhaustion. Scott Hunter described the energy-sapping fight through a succession of whirling and fleeting images:

> I made a hack at one, and my sword bounced off his thick coat, so I gave him the point and knocked him off his horse. Another fellow just after made a slash at me, and just touched my bearskin, so I made a rush at him, and took him just on the back of his helmet, and I didn't wait to see what became of him, as a lot of fellows were riding at me, but I only know that he fell forward on his horse, and if his head tumbled like *my* wish, he must had have it *hard*, and as I was riding out, another fellow came past me, whom I caught slap in the face, I was bound his own mother wouldn't have known him.[14]

If Scarlett's intrepid 300 from the Innskillings and Greys failed to punch through, they would lose momentum and be overwhelmed. They were being surrounded, as Scots Grey Sergeant David Gibson realised:

> I was in the centre, cutting right and left, when a Russian came in rear and gave me such a clip on the bearskin that it came off my

head, and I got two cuts on the cranium before I was aware of it. I thought it was all up with me.

Faint with loss of blood and blinded by the flow gushing down his face, 'one gave my sword a crack and sent it spinning out of my hand.'

Both Russian flanks had changed direction and imploded at Scarlett's penetration, seeking to take the English in flank and rear. As they exposed their own sides and backs in doing so, the second Inniskilling squadron crashed into the Russian left flank. At the same time the 5th Dragoon Guards, following up the Greys, hit the Russian centre for the second time. Gibson was rescued, but badly cut up. He had been lanced, received two sword cuts on his left hand, one on the right hand and left arm, and two cuts to the head with another across the brow. As he was led off to hospital, he was regarded a very lucky man.

Paget, viewing from the Light Brigade lines, watched these successive blows against the Russian mass. 'One body must give way,' he appreciated. The noise was completely deafening, 'the clatter of the swords against the helmets, the trampling of the horses, the shouts!' The unearthly din became an enduring memory and 'still rings in one's ears!' Successive blows from arriving British waves were visibly destabilising 'the heaving mass' of Russians that 'must be borne one way or other'. It was not certain which way it would go.[15]

CRACKING OPEN THE MASS

9.10 A.M. TO 9.15 A.M.

'I held my breath, waiting to see how this would end,' recalled Major General Ryzhov, 'as I did not have any reserve.' Ryzhov's later account of the battle was somewhat disingenuous in avoiding unpleasant truths. Dismayed at the sheer ferocity of the British assaults, he began to assume the worse. 'If the hussars turned back,' he recalled, 'I would not have anything with which to stop the enemy.' Successive squadrons of Russian cavalry coming up the rear slope were jam-packed together, unable to fend off barging British cavalry on big horses thrusting and cutting their way through from all directions. Ryzhov claimed: 'Never had I seen a cavalry attack in which both sides, with equal ferocity, steadfastness, and it may be said – stubbornness, cut and slashed in place for such a long time.'

He estimated the contest 'slashed away at a standstill for about seven minutes', before they were pushed, teetering over the top of the Causeway Heights. Witnesses claim the Russians fought in silence except for a deep moan-like noise, punctuated by a constant hissing between determinedly clenched teeth. Ryzhov worried that any 'descent from the heights,' if he were pushed over, 'with its unavoidable disorder, would help the enemy cavalry deal us a great defeat.'

Major General Khaletskii's Ingermanland Hussars were in serious trouble. The general discharged his pistol at close range in the melee and was set upon and slashed about the ear and neck, which sent his sabre spinning. His orderly, 55-year-old Corporal Karp Pivenko, gave him his own and slipped from his horse to recover the general's sabre and fended off another attack on him, for which he was to be subsequently decorated. Within a year, though, he would be dead from typhus. The Ingermanland Hussars on the left were unhinged by the two successive blows to the Russian centre punched in by Scarlett's group followed by the 5th Dragoons and the second Inniskilling squadron that emerged from the left oblique. Lieutenant Yevgenni Arbuzov's command was caught off balance and disorientated: 'Our regiment's 2nd Squadron, being pressed from the left side, veered to the right at full gallop, pushed on the 1st Squadron and forced it unwittingly to do the same.'

This meant his own platoon 'did not have any enemy facing it at the moment we collided with the English'. They chased the English left and rear and 'hewed into it'. He had only dim memories of the crazed melee that resulted: 'I only remember that I struck one dragoon in the shoulder, and my sabre bit so deep into him, that I only drew it out with difficulty.'

The cut Englishman pitched from the saddle, his spurs snagging on Arbuzov's reins as he went down, tearing at the bit in the horse's mouth. 'My horse reared up' in the closely packed fighting 'and nearly fell over,' he recalled.[16]

Russian officer casualties, many at the front when the English tore through, were considerable, perhaps four out of ten. Captain Petr Marin, ahead of the 3rd Squadron, which he commanded, was knocked from his horse. By the time he managed to remount, he was slashed about the head, one cut down to the bone. He presented a ghoulish appearance, his moustache clotted with blood as he managed to rally his men. Captain Khitrivo's 8th Squadron was hit as he attempted to form line from column. His debt was settled, having been paid the night before to protect his old father. He went down with his horse, struck by a bullet and multiple sabre cuts; when he got to his feet the squadron saw him cut down again. He was subsequently recovered to Scutari Hospital, Constantinople on an English steamer but died before he got there. Cornet Veselovski, seeking to redeem the regimental disgrace that had reduced him to the ranks, disappeared underfoot, never to be seen again. Wounds were horrific, medieval in character. Staff Captain Prince Mutsal Khamzaev received a slash to the left rear of his skull and lost two incisors on the return stroke to his left chin. Shell fragments pitted his right elbow. Pitching from the saddle decreased survival chances even further. Horses had the equivalent of a heavy mace at the end of each leg, and these were kicking out in the tight press.

The size and weight of the English chargers was a combat multiplier, as dangerous as the men riding them. Weight conferred momentum, every slash from greater height was aided by gravity, while Russian counterstrokes required more effort. Padded Russian greatcoats offered some protection to the torso; the most injuries were to the face, neck and upper extremities. Captain Matveeski in Arbuzov's regiment was slashed across the face to the right, the blade snagging the corner of his eye socket, penetrating the cheekbone to the skull and inflicting massive trauma to his brain. As he momentarily reeled, unbalanced by the stroke, his assailant plunged his blade into Matveeski's chest, entering the ribcage above the eighth rib. Amazingly he lingered on in regimental service until succumbing to his devastating injuries in 1857. Russian casualties were rising. Arbuzov briefly broke off the action, 'I wanted to see my squadron better,' he recalled, 'and bring it to good order.' But half his men were already down.[17]

'Then we went in and gave them what they will not forget,' remembered a 5th Dragoon Guards officer, chasing after the Greys through the centre. 'Some of the Russians seemed to be rather astonished at the way our men used their swords' – it was light curved versus heavy straight, Troop Sergeant Major Henry Franks recalled. 'It was rather hot work for a few minutes; there was no time to look about you.' Disturbing images of bloody viscera was Private James Prince's enduring memory as the 5th Dragoons plunged in after Scarlett's 300 Inniskillings and Greys. It was a gory passage. 'There was some being with their heads half off, and some with their bowels out, and some with their legs shot off with cannon balls.' 'We soon became a struggling mass of half frenzied and desperate men, doing our level best to kill each other,' Franks remembered. 'Swords were flying about our ears as if by magic,' one Inniskilling trooper recalled, 'but we drove them back in queer style.' 'We're heavier than the enemy,' Franks realised, 'and we were able to cut our way through them, in fact a good many of them soon began to give us room for our arms.'

Up on the Sapoune Heights, Raglan and the staff watched mesmerised as scarlet threads irresistibly stitched a passage through the grey Russian colossus. 'Grey horses and red coats had appeared right at the rear of the second mass,' William Russell observed. Sergeant Timothy Gowing, watching further to the right, was equally excited. 'At times our men became entirely lost in the midst of the forest of lances,' he remembered, 'but they cut their way right through as if they had been riding over a lot of donkeys.' Elements suddenly broke out of the rear of the Russian mass. 'A shout of joy burst from us and the French, who were spectators,' he recalled, 'as our men came out of the column.' Incredibly, Scarlett's first 300 had got through.[18]

Anyone knocked from a horse was in serious trouble. Corporal Joseph Gough's horse 'was shot; he fell, and got up again' but Gough 'was entangled in the saddle, my head and one leg were on the ground'. The horse galloped forward again, snagging him even further in a hopeless predicament, until it fell again. At the point of being impaled by a Russian lancer 'and I could not help myself', his friend 'Macnamara came up and nearly severed his head from his body; so thank God I did not get a scratch!' Gough caught a loose Inniskilling horse, snatched a pistol from its holster, and managed to shoot a Russian bearing down on him through the arm: 'He dropped his sword, then I immediately rode up to him and ran him through the body, and the poor fellow dropped to the ground.'

Corporal James Taylor was less fortunate; he was surrounded and set upon by Russians and 'a good many of them' suggested one eye-witness, 'as he was very strong and a good swordsman'. Taylor's left arm was nearly chopped through in four places, 'all the Russians seemed to cut at the left wrist,' the witness claimed, because 'so many men lost fingers, and got their hands cut.' Taylor's body was later found, but it 'was nearly cut to pieces'.

Cornet Grey Neville with the 5th Dragoons, a poor rider and swordsman, also ended up on the ground. He had had a premoni-tion of death. He rode at a group of Russians and in trying to bowl them over went down with them. Totally winded, he was lanced four times on the ground, feigning death. When Grey looked up he saw a Russian dragoon had dismounted to finish him off. The sword came down cutting at his head and sliced his ear, but Grey's helmet saved him. He lay with both sides trampling over him until his plain-tive cries for help attracted Private John Abbot from the Dragoons. Once he recognised him, he stood defiantly astride his prostrate body. Abbot held onto his horse's bridle and killed three Russians who tried their luck, until he slung Grey across his back and sought medical assistance. Grey's sad premonition of death came to fruition; a broken rib that had pierced his chest was to finish him off, though he lingered for nineteen more days. As he lay dying his final wish was that his father, Lord Braybrook, should provide for his gallant rescuer. Abbot was decorated and awarded £20 each year for life.[19]

Just as Scarlett's 300, chased by the 5th Dragoon Guards, was starting to overwhelm the first Russian echelon, the Russian crescent-shaped formation was hit on the right flank by the 4th Dragoon Guards. At virtually the same time, as if orchestrated, the 1st Dragoon 'Royals' crashed in from a right oblique direction. Its Commanding Officer had charged up from redoubt number 6 on his own initiative. The Russian mass had now been struck five times in a succession of staggered frontal and flank attacks. Lord George Paget, watching from the Light Brigade lines, observed the discernible cumulative effect the successive blows had:

> Their huge flanks lap round that handful, and almost hide them from our view. They are surrounded and must be annihilated! One can hardly breathe! Our second line, half a handful, makes a dash at them! One pants for breath! One general shout bursts from us all! It is over!

The *coup de grâce* was administered to the right flank by 'Little Hodge' and the 4th Dragoon Guards, while the Royals plunged in from the oblique. Major William Forrest riding with them recalled 'we had very bad ground to advance over, first thro' a vineyard, and over two fences, brush, and ditch then thro' the camp of the 17th'. General Richard Dacres 'saw it all from the hill', the Sapoune Heights, and remembered the cool and deliberate way the flank was turned: 'The 4th came up at a very slow trot, till close to [the enemy], when they charged them right in flank at a gallop and sent them right about.'

Colonel Edward Hodge's account was conspicuous by its simple brevity. 'The Greys were in a little confusion and retiring,' he explained, 'when our charge settled the business.' Hodge's men burrowed swiftly from flank to flank across the entire Russian mass.

The fight now became a scrap; it was not about swordsmanship, more about 'laying about' with one's blade, which was often blunt. Forrest cut at a Russian:

> But do not believe that I hurt him more than he hurt me. I received a blow on the shoulder at the same time, which was given by some other man, but the edge must have been very badly delivered for it has only cut my coat and slightly bruised my shoulder.[20]

Darby Griffiths, the Greys Commanding Officer, later admitted the Greys' swords were indeed defective. 'Whenever our men made a thrust with the sword, they all bent and would not go into a man's body.' Private Isaac Stephenson got 'one slight cut on the arm from a "cut 6" by a Russian Dragoon'. But before he could get at him, 'there were no less than three sabres of our fellows going on him thicker and faster' and he was down. Private James 'Jack' Auchinloss 'bowed to the pommel of his saddle' to dodge a pistol shot fired by a 'huge' Russian lancer, which ricocheted off the hilt of his sword. 'Fair play, mate,' he shouted and spurred after him incensed through the crowd until he clasped his assailant around the neck 'and battered his face to a jelly with his sword hilt, then throwing him down'. Blunt blades led many a soldier to aimlessly flail about in the compressed mass, lost in the fury and terror of the moment, when cool heads might have dispatched opponents with a simple thrust. Private Thomas Ryan in the 4th Dragoons had his helmet battered off in the fight and his reddish fair hair clearly showed 'he had about 15 cuts on his head, not one of which,' according to a witness, 'had more than parted the skin'. Death came from 'a thrust below the armpit, which had bled profusely'. He was the only man in Hodge's regiment to die.[21]

'My friends it is a thing impossible for a person that is in battle to give anything like a true account of it,' declared Private Charles Howell, with the 1st Dragoon Royals. 'He knows scarcely anything, only what he happens to do himself, not always then,' he recalled. 'All that I know is that I used my sword the best way I could.' These last two attacks on the right flank completely unhinged the Russians. 'It was the first time I ever crossed swords with the enemy,' admitted one trooper with the 1st Dragoons, 'and it was very sharp work.' In the exuberance of the charge they sensed they were turning the battle. 'I never enjoyed such a sport in my life,' the trooper admitted; 'it was far beyond my expectations; I actually felt overjoyed meeting them at a gallop.' 'The Russians,' he recalled, 'went over the hill again like a drove of scattered sheep.'[22]

Trumpet Major William Forster recalled: 'when the Royals saw that they could not be restrained, they gave one loud shout and let us at them … Without waiting for the command of an officer or any one else we rushed as hard as they could gallop at the enemy' catching them in the flank and rear. 'It became a frightful scene of slaughter' and 'the Russians had to turn tail and run for it.' As they linked up with the Greys, who had preceded them, there was 'a real British hurrah'. 'They give way!' Paget observed from the Light Brigade lines on the flank. 'The heaving mass rolls to the left! They fly! Never shall I forget that moment!'

The time had arrived for the Light Brigade to administer the *coup de grâce* and hit the teetering Russian mass in the flank. But they remained stock-still. 'They bolted,' remembered Sergeant Timothy Gowing watching the Russians from the Sapoune Heights, 'that is, all that could – like a flock of sheep with a dog at their tails.'[23]

The remarkable fight was over in barely eight to ten minutes. Eight hundred British cavalry had put twice their number to flight, despite being tactically wrong-footed and obliged to charge uphill over difficult ground. Casualties among Ryzhov's cavalry were some forty to fifty killed and over 200 wounded. Virtually every squadron commander in the Ingermanland Hussars was dead or wounded, with one man in six a casualty, despite outnumbering their opponents two to one. The British Heavy Brigade lost ten killed and ninety-eight wounded. In ten minutes, despite catching the British unawares at the beginning of the day and overrunning the Turkish redoubts on the Causeway Heights, the main Russian objective of the day was already lost. The British logistics park at Kadikoi remained intact and the ostensibly open route to Balaclava harbour was blocked. General Liprandi's primary objective for this probing attack was compromised by two of the most iconic actions ever celebrated in British military history. A third was to come later that same morning.

6

DECISIONS

9.30 A.M. TO 11.10 A.M.

MISSED OPPORTUNITIES

9.30 A.M. TO 11 A.M.

The Heavy Brigade regiments were too intermingled to immediately pursue the Russians as the psychological reaction to the stress of the moment set in. 'The realities of war were very apparent,' a Scots Grey officer recalled. 'Excited cheering and congratulations from men covered with blood and cut about dreadfully.' Eight minutes of psyched-up adrenalin, terror and unremitting laying about left and right with their swords had physically and emotionally drained them. They realised with surprise and gratification that they lived, and had unexpectedly carried all before them, against the odds. Only minutes before every onlooker had given them up for lost. 'A cheer burst from every lip' on the Sapoune Heights, Russell remembered, puncturing eight minutes of gut-wrenching silence. 'In the enthusiasm, officers and men took off their caps and shouted with delight' and, like spectators in an opera box, 'clapped their hands again and again'.[1]

Sitting or standing by their horses 500 yards away and watching it all was the Light Brigade, with Cardigan already grumbling, 'those heavies have the laugh of us this day'. 'All this time we sat expecting an order to pursue,' remembered Private Albert Mitchell with the 13th Light Dragoons, 'but no order came.' An opportunity was slipping away. Private James Wightman watched as his Commanding Officer Captain Morris 'moved out and spoke very earnestly to Lord Cardigan' in front of the brigade. 'My Lord, are you not going to charge the flying enemy?' he pleaded. 'No,' Cardigan peremptorily replied, 'we have orders to remain here'. Morris, a veteran of the Sikh Wars, was aghast; he had charged with the 16th Lancers at Aliwal. 'But my Lord it is our positive duty to follow up this advantage,' he insisted, yet Cardigan rebuffed him three times. He had no instinctive feel for the course of this battle, he was a parade ground soldier. Completely inexperienced, he lacked sense, but not courage. He was both bewildered by the unexpected outcome of the Heavies' audacious charge and supremely self-satisfied that he might deny Lucan some success by refusing to budge. There was a distinct murmuring from the ranks behind that he should get going, and Cardigan was not going to be influenced by that. Momentous decisions were the business of officers, not the other ranks. All the men heard, according to Wightman, were 'hoarse sharp closing words' terminating the exchange of views. 'No, no, sir!'

Morris wheeled his horse about and rejoined his right squadron, muttering, 'My God, my god, what a chance we are losing!' He sharply slapped the blade of his sword against his leg in frustration or in anger. 'I among others distinctly heard the words and marked the gesture,' Wightman observed. Clearly 'Cardigan had rebuffed him'.[2]

Lord George Paget with the 4th Light Dragoons was also surprised at the stunning result of the Heavy Brigade charge. 'Could it then have been foreseen that the affair would terminate as it did,' he admitted, 'the Light Brigade might have been made available.'

But he indicated the difficulties. They were not best placed he felt, on elevated ground slightly to the rear, to intervene. They would have to cover a quarter mile 'down a somewhat steep and broken descent'. Intelligent reading of the battle would have suggested the need to react in some capacity, aggressive or defensive, but psychologically they were unprepared for the moment. 'The probabilities were against the actual result,' Paget concluded, lamely adding the Russians were of course looking out for 'an attack from another direction'. A convincing rout of Ryzhov's cavalry would likely have deterred Liprandi from continuing the action, but the opportunity was allowed to quietly slip away. 'I was never so vexed in my life,' recalled an NCO with the 1st Royals: 'To think that 3,000 Russian cavalry were within the grasp of our small force, and our commander allowing them to retire unmolested!'

'We felt certain that if we had been sent in pursuit,' an exasperated Mitchell remembered, 'we should have cut up many of them, besides capturing many prisoners.' But it was not to be. They moved off by threes to the right and went back through their old camp, before crossing over the ridgeline of the Causeway Heights further down to enter the other side of the North Valley.[3]

Ryzhov's cavalry regiments quit the Heights and galloped back in some disorder through the North Valley back to the Chorgun Gorge. He was badly shaken, his adjutant and orderly were wounded and his horse had been killed beneath him. His performance, he knew, would be perceived as underwhelming. General Liprandi judiciously made scant mention of the debacle in his report at the end of the day and Prince Menshikov in overall command chose to omit any mention of the cavalry advance and rout in front of Kadikoi. The Russian cavalry reformed in depth at the eastern end of the valley, behind a screen of eight 6-pounders belonging to the 3rd Don Cossack Battery. This screen was linked to ten guns on the Fedioukine Heights to their right, where Major General Jobokritsky's column had established itself to cover the Russian northern flank. On the left side of the North Valley were four battalions of the Odessa Regiment's infantry, sited between captured redoubts 3 and 4 with a battery of six guns. The valley was now enclosed from three directions.

'The enemy being gone, and we all right, had time to look around,' remembered Lieutenant Temple Godman with the 5th Dragoon Guards. 'The ground was covered with dead and dying men and horses.' All around were 'swords, broken and whole, trumpets, helmets and carbines etc.'. Fanny Duberly came to look and was struck by the transition of 'a few minutes – moments as it seemed to me – and all that occupied that lately crowded spot were men and horses, lying strewn on the ground'. Cornet Daniel Moodie with the Scots Greys observed 'an awful spectacle'; dead and dying horses lay in all directions among the bodies of many Russians. 'The place was stinking so much that I was glad to get out of it,' he remembered. The exuberant Inniskilling officer who had revelled in the moment – 'oh such a charge' – had now to confront the carnage they had caused. 'I cannot depict my feelings when we returned,' he admitted. 'I sat down completely exhausted and unable to eat, although deadly hungry, and wept. All my uniform, my hands, my very face were bespattered with blood.'

The blood was Russian. Lieutenant Alexander Elliot's brother officers came to his tent after the battle to find him gazing in a looking glass. His cocked hat had attracted much of the violence that would otherwise have been directed at his general, Scarlett. 'Haloa, Elliot, beautifying are you?' they asked. 'Yes,' came the response, 'I am sticking on my nose.' It had been nearly slashed off his face during the brutal melee.[4]

Infantryman Lieutenant Colonel George Bell walking the ground saw one Russian dragoon had nearly reached the British tents. 'He lies quiet on his back, with a sabre cut almost through his head, and his long beard is matted in crimson gore.' Nearly all the dead he noticed had been pierced rather than slashed with the sword:

That man is more hideous to look upon, a sabre point let out his life blood under the bridle arm and he is smashed too about the face with the broad sword of England. Here's another lying on his back in a bath of his own blood, both hands clenched tight in the agony of his departing spirit.

Another, where 'a home thrust through the abdomen finished his career', a fair-haired young man in blue hussar uniform had been 'first gashed about the head and then let out his life below the left arm'. Fanny Duberly, with characteristic Victorian sentimentality, focused on the horses. 'One horse galloped up to where we stood,' she remembered, 'a round shot had taken him in the haunch, and a gaping wound it made.' She was particularly distressed by another hit in the nostrils by shell splinters, 'which staggered feebly up to Bob [her own horse], suffocating from inability to breathe' before it toppled over. George Bell decided 'not go any further' checking out the fallen; 'only one redcoat lay here.'[5]

At about 10 a.m. the Duke of Cambridge's 1st Infantry division began to descend the Sapoune Heights and entered the North Valley. Their prompt departure put them forty minutes ahead of Sir George Cathcart's 4th Division, which had yet to reach the entry point at the Col to the right of Raglan's viewing point. The battlefield looked inactive, a lull that was to last some ninety minutes. The North Valley appeared mostly empty, except for the main Russian force massed at the far end, obscured faintly by haze. At the near end to Raglan's observation platform, the Heights on either side could be seen occupied with grey-clad infantry mixed between batteries of cannon.

Captain Arthur Hardinge, delivering messages from Raglan's staff to Lucan, had taken the opportunity to join the Greys during their mad dash with the Heavy Brigade. He now galloped up to Raglan's group to describe in breathless and animated language what Brigadier General Scarlett had done. With his tunic clearly ruffled, and the straps of his overalls slashed apart, he was the envy of the rest of the staff. Flushed and triumphant he saw war correspondent William Russell, 'Did you see it all?' he asked as he passed by on the slope. 'Was it not glorious!' Raglan had already dispatched an aide to Scarlett to say 'well done!' and he sincerely meant it. The short fifteen-minute action had changed everything. The British had regained the initiative, demonstrated by increasing numbers of British infantry coming down onto the plain and North Valley. Raglan intuitively perceived the Russian Army had been rattled by the audacious charge by the Heavy Brigade and probably only needed to be threatened again by British cavalry in order to withdraw. Indignation and impatience was surfacing on the British side in the valley below as Lucan and the cavalry appeared to sit motionless in their saddles.[6]

'Butcher' Jack Vahey from the 17th Lancers, hungover and still semi-intoxicated, arrived at the scene of the Heavy Brigade charge alongside his equally boozy partner Paddy Heffernan with the Royals. They had absconded from the Light Brigade detention tent determined to be part of the ongoing 'fun'. 'The heavies had already charged the Russian cavalry,' Vahey recalled, 'and emptied a good many saddles.' Riderless horses were galloping around in all directions and they separated to apprehend a mount. He captured 'a tidy little iron-grey nag' which he assessed from the quality of its gear was an officer's charger. 'It was easy to see from the state of the saddle,' he recalled, 'that the former rider had been desperately wounded, and the reins too were bloodier than a dainty man would have liked; but I was noways squeamish.' He mounted and attached himself to the left flank of the Royals, where his pantomime appearance elicited a lot of laughter. 'There's no mistake,' he admitted, 'I was not much of a credit to them.' He was bare-headed with hair 'like a birch-broom in a fit', no jacket, shirt sleeves rolled up to the shoulder with 'my shirt, face and bare arms all splashed and darkened with blood', offal smeared from butchering the day before. He wore thigh-long 'greasy' jackboots with an axe instead of sword at the shoulder looking 'as regimental as you please'. The horse's previous Russian rider was likely very short, 'for my knees were up to my nose in his stirrups'. An eruption of mirth spread through the ranks, attracting the ire of Regimental Sergeant Major John Lees. 'Taking me all in all, I was a hot looking member,' Vahey admitted, as well as being 'fully half-seas over'. Lees was not amused and came up at the gallop roaring, 'Go to Hell out of that!'

Vahey, meanwhile, had caught sight of the 'light bobs' up ahead and swung out of the line and spurred off in pursuit. 'Behind me,' he remembered, were a couple of officers from the Greys, 'who tried to stop me for decency's sake'. All around the Heavy Brigade troopers laughed and cheered in astonishment. Vahey intended joining his unit.[7]

Raglan felt he could relax. For the first time since the battle had opened early that morning, he was able to take decisions free of crisis. Nevertheless, he was becoming impatient. At 9.30 a.m. he dispatched an order to Lucan: 'Cavalry to advance,' he directed, 'and take advantage of any opportunity to recover the heights. They will be supported by infantry, which have been ordered to advance on two fronts.' Raglan could see British infantry on the Woronzov road, but Cathcart's 4th Infantry Division was taking too long.

When Cathcart's infantry had left the plateau amid all the excitement, he was instructed by Raglan's Chief of Staff Airey to recapture the lost redoubts. But neither of the two infantry division commanders had been told they were to advance in conjunction with the cavalry. Cathcart was entering the South Valley, completely out of sight of the cavalry on the other side of the Causeway Heights in between. When the redoubts were pointed out to him by Captain Ewart, Airey's staff officer, his immediate response was 'you must be mistaken', muttering, 'it is impossible that there can be one [on Canrobert's Hill] as far away as that.' Not only was Raglan's coordination of the cavalry and infantry advance a failure; the orders regarding objectives appeared equally unrealistic. 'Well, it is the most extraordinary thing I ever saw,' Cathcart complained. 'The position is more extensive than that occupied by the Duke of Wellington at Waterloo.' He had been there, and Wellington's army then had been four to five times larger.[8]

Raglan's Olympian view from the Heights enabled him to see everything, but at valley level the ground was broken and undulating. The angle of the sun at this time of the day and year makes the outline of the valley lines indistinct. From the Heights, the hills and curves of the valley floor appeared flatter than they were. Raglan overlooked the fact that what was *below* him, was *above* the cavalry. Men on the Causeway Heights could not see into the valleys, and those on the valley floor could not see what was happening on the Heights above. Lucan, seeking clarification of his orders, could see no infantry. Convinced his commander would not wish him to attack alone, he determined to wait for their arrival. He had seen Russians to the left and right of the valley where his brigades were lined up. He would need infantry to clear them. Raglan, looking down, perceived Lucan for some inexplicable and exasperating reason was not following his orders.

The ante was raised on the Sapoune Heights when a sharp-eyed staff officer pointed out that Russian artillery horses had come forward to tow away the captured British guns. Cathcart's infantry were taking too long, the enemy remained still, and Lucan's cavalry remained motionless. Clearly irritated, Raglan urgently dictated another order to Airey, the fourth of the day. 'Lord Raglan wishes the cavalry to advance rapidly to the front,' he wrote, 'follow the enemy and try to prevent the enemy carrying away the guns.' Wellington had never lost a gun in the Peninsular Campaign, and Raglan consciously aped his benefactor. It was a point of honour not to lose guns in battle, they were for artillery, the equivalent of colours to the infantry. 'Troop Horse Artillery may accompany,' Raglan added, 'French cavalry is on your left. Immediate.' Raglan wanted the removal of these guns threatened by a cavalry advance, he was not ordering an uphill charge. But the men who were to receive the order in the valley below could not even see these guns.

Captain Louis Nolan was recognised as one of the army's most accomplished equestrians, and he was chosen instead of the next ADC – Lieutenant Somerset Calthorpe – in line for duty. The most direct route was a precipitous track 650ft down to the plain below. Nolan would make the best time. Staff 'gallopers' always asked if there were any supplementary verbal observations to add. Raglan called out as he set off, 'Tell Lord Lucan the cavalry is to attack immediately.' This was music to the ears of the highly opinionated and professional equestrian commentator Nolan, who sped off, galloping past Mrs Fanny Duberly. As Nolan descended, the whole perspective of the valley sides and floor changed. Intent on guiding his horse and maintaining a precarious foothold on the track, the staff officer would not have noticed the fundamentally changed terrain perspective until he arrived at the valley floor.

A myth has since grown around an apparently impetuous Nolan, fuelled by Hollywood characterisations played by screen icons such as Errol Flynn in the 1930s and Terence Stamp's portrayal in the 1970s, in epic film recreations of *The Charge of the Light Brigade.* That Nolan held strong opinions is evidenced by his journal, which is critical of both Raglan and Lucan. However, an ambitious young cavalry officer seeking advancement would hardly have aired these publicly. His published treatise on cavalry appears obsessed with the tactical virtues of light cavalry, even able, he suggested, to charge directly at artillery. He was as surprised as everyone else at the remarkable accomplishment of the Heavy Brigade that day, at variance to his own embedded theories. Contrary to colourful personality myths since, serious research around Nolan's career suggests he got on well with his superiors, as one would expect from a selected Aide-de-Camp. Future advancement would be dependent upon senior sponsors. His treatises on cavalry give no intimation of a reckless, hotheaded or impatient individual, they rather espouse scholarly and analytical study. Utter conviction might be mistaken for arrogance, but modesty was not a common trait among his Victorian cavalry officer peers. Nolan sought and garnered positive reactions to his ideas from the popular press. He was clearly someone who shrewdly watched and listened. Despite his enthusiasm to transmit Raglan's immediate and aggressive intent to his Commanding General, Nolan was unlikely, like any deferential junior officer, to pick a verbal fight with his superior officer.

Nolan's ride took fifteen minutes, arriving at the assembled Light Brigade and cavalry staff shortly after 11 a.m. 'Where is Lord Lucan?'

he shouted to his friend Captain William Morris, waiting ahead of the 17th Lancers. 'What's it to be, Nolan?' he was asked, as he directed him on, 'are we to charge?' It was an exciting moment. 'You'll see! You'll see!' he responded. Private Albert Mitchell watched Nolan 'come galloping down' from the 13th Light Dragoon lines, 'and handed a paper to Lord Lucan'. There was a palpable air of expectation; 'we now felt certain,' he recalled, 'there was something cut out for us.'⁹

Lucan read and re-read the order but was totally nonplussed. There was no mention of Heights, simply to 'the front'. No word of the infantry he had been waiting for since the previous order forty-five minutes before. He was to 'follow the enemy' but he could not see any Russians on the move, 'and try to prevent the enemy carrying away the guns'. Both he and Nolan appeared to be exasperated according to the many eyewitness accounts during the verbal exchanges that followed. Nolan insisted 'Lord Raglan's orders are that the cavalry should attack immediately.' Lucan could not see this was a continuation of the order he had received just before. 'Attack Sir! Attack what?' he asked irritably. 'What guns sir? Where and what to do?' Nolan had seen the guns from the Heights, but they were lost from sight on entering the valley. He was still re-orientating himself having ridden the precarious descent. It is conceivable he was not entirely sure, when he pointed, apparently with some exasperation, 'There my Lord! There is your enemy! There are your guns.' 'I saw Lucan's evident astonishment at the message,' remembered Captain Arthur Tremayne with the 13th Light Dragoons nearby, 'because Nolan pointed right down the valley.' This was a sobering moment. 'Surprised and irritated at the impetuous and disrespectful attitude and tone of Captain Nolan,' according to Sir John Blunt, Lucan's Turkish interpreter, which could conceivably also have been interpreted as urgency, Lucan 'looked at him sternly, but made no answer'. It seemed they had been directed to commit virtual suicide.¹⁰

Raglan's viewing point on the Sapoune Heights was several hundred yards south-west of the present Russian Great Patriotic War Museum, where most tourist guides claim he stood. Standing at the same point at almost the same time, day and time of year when the order was given reveals how difficult it is to discern the line of the North Valley and Causeway Heights. This is because of the hazy view presented by the angle of the sun, shining directly face-on. The ground below looks disarmingly flat and gentle from this height. Nolan's difficult mounted descent into the North Valley looks all the more remarkable. He would have had eyes only for the route he was hurriedly following, not for the Russian positions, now coming into three-dimensional view. Driving by car to the point where Nolan met Lucan's staff, near the present-day petrol station, one is struck by the total change of scenery and perspective. The gentle downward slope of the North Valley floor is ominously overlooked by the medium rise of flanking valley sides, which were occupied by Russian artillery and infantry. Lucan could see little from his position at the head of the valley, but would have seen a lot more if he had ridden his horse up the small rise upon which the petrol station sits today. It is a dramatic and disorientating contrast from the Sapoune Heights behind, which appear massively high, with the white speck of the present-day museum readily discernible, just below the horizon, offering ready identification of Raglan's viewing point to its left. Nolan would have faced this same confusing, disorientating perspective when asked by Lucan to precisely point out the guns he was to attack. They were not visible from Lucan's staff group. Nolan was perhaps understandably vague, pointing in what was roughly the approximate direction, because he had clearly seen the guns from above, but not now. All this left Lucan at his wits' end. Raglan's vague formulation of orders all that day had made little sense, the last direction often contradicting the previous. There appeared no connection between the third instruction received forty-five minutes before this one. Surely Raglan did not expect him to advance uphill with cavalry unsupported by infantry? By now the 1st Division infantry had arrived, but the 4th were out of sight on the other side of the Causeway Heights in dead ground to the North Valley.

It has been attractive for historians to explain the muddled transmission of orders in terms of a dramatic personality clash. Lucan was
predictably on a short fuse following a series of conflicting directions, and now this young 'bookish' aide was arrogantly, to his mind,
demanding he follow Raglan's latest incomprehensible demand.
Nolan's urgency was less conceit stemming from his own experience
and strongly held tactical views on cavalry, but likely more about
his keen desire to participate in the pending action. Like the lucky
Hardinge, the aide who had attached himself to the Heavy Brigade
charge, here was Nolan's chance to bathe in some reflected glory. If
Lucan demurred, he would have to ride back to Raglan to clarify, or
the moment might slip away, as in the case of Cardigan's failure to
strike the retreating Russian cavalry ninety minutes before. William
Russell recalled: 'the Russians had succeeded in carrying off our guns
out of the Turkish redoubts before Captain Nolan had well left the
plateau'. The situation on the valley floor was constantly shifting. The
guns were already disappearing into the rear of the Russian lines.

Much of the evidence about Nolan's earlier career suggests he was
not only a paternal officer, who cared for his men, but he was non-
confrontational. He was a messenger, and also common to many of
the Light Brigade cavalry troopers that morning, increasingly indig-
nant he might miss out on the action. It was clearly incumbent on
Lucan, as the senior cavalry commander, to respond in some way to
Raglan's confusing directive himself.[11]

After the crushingly successful charge of the Heavy Brigade, the
inaction that followed suggested to many troopers in the Light
Brigade that the battle was actually over. 'Considering all immediate
action was over,' recalled Captain J.D. Shakespear, with the accompanying horse artillery, 'if not indeed, the whole thing for the day, I rode
over to the [Causeway] Heights to reconnoitre.' Russian troops were
consolidating their positions on both sides of the valley. The Light
Brigade waited, amid the familiar smell of horses and manure, bits
jingling as they shook their heads, free momentarily from the stench
of battle. Troopers patted horse necks and comfortingly muttered to

steady them amid the occasional bang of an artillery piece. Officers shared flasks of rum in the cold morning. Some of the men had dismounted, utilising the pause to peel and munch hard-boiled eggs. Jemmy, the rough-haired terrier belonging to an 8th Hussars officer, was gently teased; the dog was a favourite, like 'Boxer', the adopted mascot with the 11th Hussars. The arrival of French cavalry with the Chasseurs d'Afrique, who formed to the left of the brigade, elicited predictable ribald comments and jesting, common between units.[12]

'SOMEONE HAD BLUNDER'D'

11 A.M. TO 11.10 A.M.

Eighth Hussar Private John Doyle was 'warming our noses each with a short black pipe' he recalled, 'and thinking no harm of the matter'. His view was not shared by his Commanding Officer, Lieutenant Colonel Frederick Shewell, who was a strict disciplinarian and pious Christian. Shewell had risen from his sick bed to lead his men during the early morning sudden flap and was not in the best mood. Doyle was disturbed to see as 'all at once his face expressed the greatest astonishment, and even anger'. He peremptorily asked: 'What's this? What's this? One, two, three, four, six, seven men smoking! Sergeant! Sergeant Pickworth!'

The NCO appeared and was ordered to 'advance and take these men's names'. This caused a momentary stir in the ranks, and Doyle acknowledged 'it might not be quite according to regulation to be smoking sword in hand, when the charge might be sounded at any moment'. The inquisition gathered momentum when Shewell rode through the 8th Hussars' ranks. A hapless Sergeant Williams was confronted by 'did you not hear what I said about smoking just now?' 'I have not lit my pipe yet, sir,' the Sergeant answered respectfully, but others had: 'Fall back to the rear, and take off your belts.

Why here's another! To the rear, fall back. I'll have this breach of discipline punished.'

Without realising it, Shewell had condemned Sergeant Williams to conduct the coming charge unarmed. He was not a popular commander. Lord Paget in front of the 4th Light Dragoons, cigar in mouth, heard all the commotion in the ranks to the right. 'Am I to set this bad example,' he considered, 'or should I throw away a good cigar?' Life, as he had already witnessed that morning, could be nasty, brutish and short. 'Well, the cigar carried the day' he decided and it was still clamped between his teeth when they subsequently charged.[13]

Artillery Captain Shakespear had already discerned Russian positions on both sides of the North Valley on his reconnaissance ahead of the forming Light Brigade. Scanning the Heights, he picked out ten cannon 1,500 yards opposite and 'there were other guns further on to the left of these'. There were also cavalry, infantry and artillery up ahead, strung out across the plain, and he saw the Russians occupied the former Turkish redoubts: 1, 2 and 3 to his right. Sharp-eyed cavalry troopers had also identified the impending trap. Albert Mitchell with the 13th Light Dragoons had dismounted and was peering down the valley:

> Soon we could see the enemy had placed a number of guns across the lower part of the valley nearly a mile and a half from us. At the same time a field battery ascended a hill on our left front, where it was placed in position facing us. They also placed a field battery on the slope between the redoubts and the valley on our right.

Russian infantry was very much in evidence around these guns. The North Valley was shaping up to be a deathtrap.[14]

It was at this moment that Captain Nolan arrived. Realising something was going to happen, all eyes were on Lord Lucan as he trotted across to Cardigan to share the contents of Raglan's imprecise order. Shared mutual loathing cloaked in the formality of rank was to contribute to the events that followed. 'Lord Cardigan, you will attack the Russians in the valley,' Lucan directed. Cardigan was quick to object, stating he would be subjected to flanking as well as frontal fire. 'I know it,' Lucan cut him short, but 'Lord Raglan would have it,' having decided to accept the command without formally challenging it, beyond the brief exchange with Nolan. 'Certainly my Lord,' Cardigan responded, saluting with his sword, 'but allow me to point out to you that there is a battery in front, a battery on each flank, and the ground is covered with Russian riflemen.'

Formal Victorian deference and mutual personal hostility precluded any form of rational discussion of the order's contents. Both men assumed Raglan's intent was to attack the guns 1¼ miles to their front, almost indiscernible at the end of the valley. Later recriminations over whether it was 'attack' or 'advance' were irrelevant. No horse could sustain a galloping charge over that distance. Raglan's imprecise direction thus far in this campaign made it impractical for Lucan to refuse or demur, while seeking further information. Honour was at stake as was the remorseless passage of time. It would take an hour to question and respond to further clarity and the situation might well have changed by then.[15]

Action for the Light Brigade was now pending, but not what anyone could have envisaged. Every officer down to private soldier appreciated the likely outcome. 'Then we got the order to advance,' remembered Private Thomas Williams with the 11th Hussars. 'I could see what would be the result of it, and so could all of us,' he later wrote to his father. 'But of course, as we had got the order, it was our duty to obey.'

Lord George Paget commanding the 4th Light Dragoons had never really got on with his second in command Major John Halkett; they hardly spoke to each other. Paget, thinking through the consequences of what lay ahead, suddenly offered him his flask, a gesture of reconciliation. They were not to know that Halkett had barely twenty minutes to live. The brief flurry of activity in the 13th Dragoon lines, as they readied themselves for an advance, increased Lieutenant Percy Smith's feelings of vulnerability. His right hand had been maimed in a past shooting accident, but he was accepted for active service. An iron guard, especially made for him by his brother officers, normally held it up but he had mislaid it during the sudden alarm that morning. Smith would ride the charge unarmed, all he could do was cheer his men on.

Private James Wightman with the 17th Lancers was suddenly startled by the bizarre spectacle of 'Butcher Jack' Vahey galloping up, with belt and arms festooned over his white canvas butcher's smock, 'face, arms and hands smeared in blood'. He obviously 'had some drink in him' because he shouted 'that he'd be damned if he was going to be left behind his regiment and so lose the fun'. His comical arrival was something of a morale boost, 'a gruesome yet laughable figure' Wightman agreed. The Adjutant Cornet John Chadwick and an NCO directed him to rein back and join his own troop in the second squadron. He still had an axe at the slope on his shoulder.

'I suppose you would like to know what I had about me through all this danger,' Lieutenant Edward Seager later wrote home to his wife Jane. He had a picture of her in his sabretache, the flat decorative leather satchel suspended by long straps at the thigh; inside he also carried the 'darling children's picture', with his mother's prayer book. 'In the pocket of my jacket was your letter,' he recalled, 'containing little Emily's hair' and 'around my neck was the dear locket you gave me in Exeter'. Seager was festooned with talismans, which numerous eyewitness commentaries appreciated they would need, because it appeared that they were about to charge the whole of the Russian army. Troop Sergeant Major George Smith with the 11th Hussars knew they were 'to attack the battery of guns which was placed across the valley immediately in our front about a mile off'. Private John Richardson saw 'the thirty guns which we had to take were stretched right across the valley'. Smith also knew there was 'a battery of guns on the Fedioukine Heights on our left and the enemy had possession of the redoubts on our right,' where another battery and riflemen were posted. It did not look good. He judged they were attacking an 'army in position numbering about 24,000 and we, the Light Brigade, not quite 700'.[16]

In the ranks there was realisation that some officers were uneasy about this order. It made so little sense. But as Poet Laureate Alfred Lord Tennyson suggested in his later epic poem, Victorian soldiers were expected to do what they were told: 'Theirs not to reason why, theirs but to do and die'. Private Edward Woodham chatted with Private Wootten, 'an unsophisticated west countryman' in the second line with the 11th Hussars. 'Ted, old fellow,' he confided, 'I know we shall charge,' at which Woodham scoffed, 'Oh nonsense! Look at the strength in front of us. We're never going to charge there.' Wootten would be proven correct, but would not live to make the point.[17]

At the end of the North Valley, Russian Lieutenant Koribut Kubitovich, lined up with Colonel Yeropkin's composite lancer regiment, watched as Russian units consolidated either side of the valley during the lull. General Liprandi, he believed, anticipated an advance after the debacle of the Heavy Brigade attack, and 'saw it was necessary to make some changes in his troop deployments and reinforce his right flank'. The North Valley was gradually boxed in, and 'the right flank was deployed in stepped back echelons,' which included eight guns from Bojanov's battery and the Odessa Jäger Regiment. Kubitovich's lancer regiment was redeployed from the left to the right side of the North Valley, where it waited between redoubts 2 and 3.

'I cannot say with certainty,' recalled Major General Ryzhov, 'but I believe that about an hour and a half went by in which there was absolutely no activity on the enemy side.' The Russians put this to good use, consolidating their grip on the far end of the Causeway Heights, despite the cavalry setback. Ryzhov surmised 'it appeared that the battle could be considered at an end'. He was at the far eastern side of the North Valley, discussing the day's events with Colonel Prince Obolensky, whose Don Battery Number 3 was positioned across to block any Allied approach. To his right were ten guns under battery commander Colonel Brombeuss, dispersed in twos and threes among Major General Zhabokritsky's infantry. These pointed out from the lower re-entrants of the Fedioukine Heights and completely covered the North Valley opposite Bojanov's battery on the other side. The left, centre and right of North Valley was boxed in by twenty-six or so cannon. The Russian artillery was the most technically proficient arm of the Tsar's army. White willow wands were already set out in the North Valley to measure and indicate the key ranges. Massed behind the Don Battery were two Hussar regiments lined up in echelon. Swarms of Russian infantry dominated the high ground, enabling the supporting artillery batteries to sweep the North Valley below. Liprandi now felt able to draw breath and await Raglan's next move. Lieutenant Kubitovich felt they were in an unassailable position because any advance would 'have to pass through a crossfire from our artillery and riflemen, and afterwards – when in disorder due to enemy fire – he would have to meet an attack by Russian cavalry'.

There seemed little likelihood of further action that day. Both sides were in strong face-off positions, except the British had regained a psychological ascendency.[18]

Sharp-eyed troopers waiting with the Light Brigade had picked out much of this movement. Private Robert Farquharson overheard a man muttering what they all suspected, that 'many of us will not get back to the lines again'. Twenty-one-year-old William Pennington had only been with the 11th Hussars for six months and had reconciled himself to acceptance that 'he had no hope of life'. 'A child might have seen the trap that was laid for us,' Captain Thomas Hutton, waiting with the 4th Light Dragoons rear ranks, observed. 'Every private dragoon did.' Private William Nicholson with the 13th Light Dragoons thought the same: 'we knew that the order was a blunder, and when we started we never expected to come back alive.'

'All we had to do was obey orders,' Nicholson remembered. 'I can safely say,' Private Thomas Williams with the 11th Hussars insisted, 'that there was not a man in the Light Brigade that day but what did his duty to his Queen and Country.'[19]

Unlike the Heavy Brigade, the distinguishing colour of Cardigan's Light Brigade was blue, albeit faded and showing signs of campaign wear and tear. They formed the first echelon with the 13th Light

Dragoons to the right in front with the 17th Lancers to the left. Lances were held at the vertical carry, pennants fluttering in a light breeze. The 9ft lance coupled with the momentum and weight of the horse could be a formidable weapon. They were placed in the front line to intimidate the Russians and inflict maximum damage on first contact. The small pennant just short of the spearhead was designed to confuse the horses of opposing cavalry, only later being retained for parades and ceremonial heraldry.

Regiments in the brigade were identifiable by strikingly different headdress. The 17th on the left had leather chapskas, which were square-topped caps resembling academic mortar boards, but with a peak. To their right the 13th Light Dragoons were distinguishable by beaver-skin shakos, shaped like a top hat with a peak. Behind them in the second echelon line were the 11th Hussars, who wore fur busbys like a shako, without a peak, with a decorative bag arrangement hanging on one side. Bringing up the third echelon to the rear were the 4th Light Dragoons on the left and the 8th Hussars right, likewise distinguishable by their headgear.

Wellington's cavalry advice had always been to attack in three such lines and European cavalry tactics had hardly evolved since the Napoleonic Wars. The idea was that the first and second lines, with 400 to 500 yards between them, should strike two successive blows across a consolidated front. The second line aimed to avoid the initial melee and hit the enemy line at a steady pace. The third line, a similar distance behind, constituted the ready reserve to fight off enemy cavalry counter-attacks. Bringing the greatest number of sabres to bear over as wide a front as practical aimed at immediately enveloping and overflowing the enemy's flanks. The problem, in the emotional pell-mell of a charge, was for officers and NCOs to prevent their two lines merging into one. Moreover, the pace of the clash with the enemy had to be at a speed that maximised the controlled use of sabre cut and thrust and lance. Cardigan's force numbered 664 officers and men, advancing on a two-squadron front of some 140 yards, with about 125 men in the front rank.

Behind the Light Brigade came Scarlett's distinctive red-tunic Heavy Brigade, riding in close support. They were led by Lucan, the senior cavalry commander, well out in front, so as to maintain contact with the advance Light Brigade. Despite the desperate action just ninety minutes before, the 'Heavies' were still in good shape. Behind them came long trains of horse artillery, jogging along, ready to peel off and provide close-in artillery support.

'I remember as if it were but yesterday,' recalled Private James Wightman, the smell of the horses and dust raised by the squadrons forming line. Up ahead he saw: 'Cardigan's figure and attitude as he faced the brigade and in his strong hoarse voice gave the momentous word of command: "The Brigade will advance! First squadron 17th Lancers direct!"'[20]

Conditions in the Russian siege lines at Sevastopol. Captain Robert Adolf Hodasevich fought for 'Holy Russia'. (Central Armed Forces Museum Moscow)

Sevastopol under attack. (Sevastopol Cyclorama)

Conditions in the Russian siege lines. (Sevastopol Cyclorama)

The Russians blockaded Sevastopol harbour with sunken ships. (Moscow Museum)

Sevastopol harbour today, near the former sunken line of ships. (Author's collection)

Infantrymen like Sergeant Timothy Gowing had tight-fitting uniforms that were totally unsuited to static siege warfare and reduced to patched rags. (Author's collection)

The Bracker farmhouse, Lord Raglan's HQ. (Author's collection)

Ismail Pacha and Turkish soldiers. Corporal Thomas Morley with the 17th Lancers declared 'one Englishman is worth six Turks', they are 'filthy and lazy'. (Library of Congress)

Opposite: A noxious stench from rubbish mixed with stinking offal from slaughtered animals emanated from Balaclava harbour, packed with ships. (Library of Congress)

This contemporary photograph of a Turkish irregular in the Crimea, with his 'camp follower', encapsulated the disdain felt by many common British soldiers to their erstwhile ally. (Author's collection)

The 55-year-old Brigadier General Sir James Scarlett, the commander of the Heavy Brigade, coolly dealt with the overwhelming Russian force that emerged on his flank. (Library of Congress)

Four squadrons of Russian cavalry detached themselves from the mass and charged down the slope toward the 'thin red line' covering Balaclava harbour. (Sevastopol Fort Museum)

They were heading for the British logistics park at Kadikoi village outside Balaclava. (Library of Congress)

The Turks retreated through the camp lines shown here to the left toward the ships in Balaclava harbour. (Library of Congress)

The site of the Heavy Brigade charge today, conducted uphill and marked by the white obelisk. (Author's collection)

Lieutenant Halford rode with the 5th Dragoon Guards in the charge of the Heavy Brigade; his tight-fitting uniform and brass helmet were hardly suited for hard cavalry campaigning. (Library of Congress)

The area around the cavalry camps where much of the initial action took place. (Author's collection)

A diminutive hillock, the site of the 93rd Regiment's stand, on the battlefield today.
(Author's collection)

The resourceful veteran commander Sir Colin Campbell directed the fire of the 93rd Highlander's 'thin red line'. (Author's collection)

Paymaster Henry Duberly, 8th Hussars, and Mrs Fanny Duberly who joined Raglan's staff on top of the Sapoune Heights. (Author's collection)

Fanny Duberly remembers riding through 'the narrow and crowded streets' of Balaclava as fast as she could. (Library of Congress)

The tangle of unloaded stores at Balaclava harbour. (Library of Congress)

Lord Raglan's viewpoint, overlooking the Valley of Death and the site of the Heavy Brigade charge today. This photograph was taken at the same time of year, and the battlefield is indistinct. (Author's collection)

Lord Raglan, the British Commander-in-Chief, dictated the order for the charge of the Light Brigade. (Library of Congress)

Lord Lucan, the Commander of the British Cavalry, received the order and ordered Cardigan to carry it out. (Public domain)

Lord Cardigan, the Commander of the Light Brigade, received and executed the order.
(Public domain)

Captain Louis Nolan was Raglan's 'Galloper' who delivered the order. (*Illustrated London News*)

The start point of the Light Brigade charge today ,looking east toward the Russian guns. (Author's collection)

The mid-point of the charge; the guns were beyond the modern poplars. (Author's collection)

Lord George Paget was the 4th Light Dragoons Colonel and Cardigan's deputy commander, riding to the left of the line in the third and final wave of the Light Brigade's charge. (Library of Congress)

The scene encapsulated in Tony Richardson's 1968 film, *The Charge of the Light Brigade*. (Author's collection)

The mid-point today, showing the height of the redoubts beyond, to the right of the riders charging right to left. (Author's collection)

The view ahead towards the guns today from the same point as previous. (Author's collection)

William Simpson's painting captures this view from the Russian-held Heights. (Library of Congress)

French General Bosquet captured by Roger Fenton in a similar pose in the Crimea, when he declared of the charge, '*C'est magnifique, mais ce n'est pas la guerre*'. (Library of Congress)

By this time much of the charge formation had been shot to pieces. A still from Tony Richardson's film. (Author's collection)

The savage melee at the guns. (Public domain)

Cornet John Wilkin rode the charge of the Light Brigade as assistant surgeon with the 11th Hussars in the second wave. He wears the distinctive tight blue cloth jacket with crimson 'cherry bum' trousers, more suited to ceremonial parades than battle. (Library of Congress)

The uniforms of the Chasseurs D'Afrique, veterans of French colonial Morocco, were far more loose-fitting and suited to campaigning in the conditions of the Crimea. (Author's collection)

The site of the Russian guns at the end of the Valley of Death today. (Author's collection)

A cookhouse scene, with survivors from the 8th Hussars who rode to the left of the third wave of the charge of the Light Brigade. (Library of Congress)

A group of survivors from the charge of the Light Brigade attend one of the many commemorations in England, which began twenty-one years afterwards, in 1875. (National Army Museum, London / Bridgeman Images)

7

THE RIDE OF THE SIX HUNDRED

11.13 A.M. TO 11.20 A.M.

FOUR MINUTES

11.13 A.M. TO 11.17 A.M.

The first newspaper reports describing the charge of the Light Brigade were to arrive in England at Victorian breakfast tables a fortnight later. They were all based on observations made from the clinical standpoint of the Sapoune Heights and it was this detached view that inspired Poet Laureate Alfred Lord Tennyson to pen his famous poem six weeks later. Clinically observed at a distance, it was indeed epic and glorious. From the perspective of the Russian artillery and infantry firing into the valley from the flanking Heights, it was insane. On the valley floor below it was viciously brutal.

War correspondent William Russell glanced at his pocket watch shortly after 11.10 a.m., as the brigade set off, and started jotting notes. 'They swept proudly past, glittering in the morning sun,' he later wrote, 'in all the pride and splendour of war.' 'There was a lot of

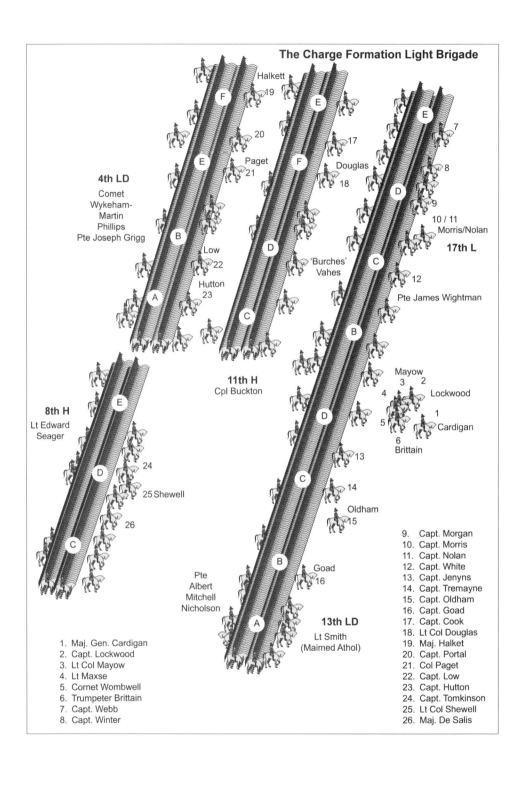

The Charge Formation Light Brigade

Halkett
19

20

4th LD
Comet
Wykeham-
Martin
Phillips
Pte Joseph Grigg

Paget
21

Low
22

Hutton
23

E

F

D

B

A

C

Douglas
18

'Burches'
Vahes

E

F

D

C

E

D

C

B

7

8

9

10 / 11
Morris/Nolan

17th L

12

Pte James Wightman

Mayow
3   2

4   Lockwood

5   1

          Cardigan
6
Brittain

8th H
Lt Edward
Seager

E

D

C

24

25 Shewell

26

11th H
Cpl Buckton

D

C

B

A

13

14

Oldham
15

Goad
16

Pte
Albert
Mitchell
Nicholson

13th LD

Lt Smith
(Maimed Athol)

1. Maj. Gen. Cardigan
2. Capt. Lockwood
3. Lt Col Mayow
4. Lt Maxse
5. Cornet Wombwell
6. Trumpeter Brittain
7. Capt. Webb
8. Capt. Winter

9. Capt. Morgan
10. Capt. Morris
11. Capt. Nolan
12. Capt. White
13. Capt. Jenyns
14. Capt. Tremayne
15. Capt. Oldham
16. Capt. Goad
17. Capt. Cook
18. Lt Col Douglas
19. Maj. Halket
20. Capt. Portal
21. Col Paget
22. Capt. Low
23. Capt. Hutton
24. Capt. Tomkinson
25. Lt Col Shewell
26. Maj. De Salis

excitement on the hill-side when we found the Light Brigade was advancing,' remembered Sergeant Timothy Gowing, watching further along the Sapoune Heights to the right. Mrs Fanny Duberly simply recalled, 'I only know that I saw Captain Nolan galloping' and 'that presently the Light Brigade, leaving their position, advanced by themselves, although in the face of the whole Russian force'.[1]

Unlike Russell's grandiose description, down on the valley floor, the Light Brigade were not looking their best. Bedraggled plumes had long since been discarded and busbies, jackets and overalls were patched and discoloured by hard campaign wear. Sleeves were coming apart, jackets showed rents and with much of their gold lace was tarnished. Many no longer wore shirts beneath, long since rotted away. The 17th Lancers had their death's head badges hidden beneath oilskin covers that cased their square-tipped caps. Hussar pelisses were worn as extra garments in the 11th, while the 8th only had jackets because their pelisses had been lost during the voyage out. Occasional flashes of red stood out from busbies that were still intact, on the overalls of 'cherry bum' 11th Hussars and the odd cuff in the 4th Light Dragoon ranks. White facings were universally stained grey and shoulder scales and epaulettes had long since disappeared.

The horses they rode were gaunt, half-starved and hangdog-looking, having been denied decent forage since their awful sea passage east. They suffered for want of grooming, encapsulating the shrunken appearance of squadrons, which had lost men to cholera, hyperthermia and illness. But these men were erect in the saddle, rode with studied precision and were itching to get at the Russians. Private Dennis Connor with the 4th Light Dragoons remembered the normal chafing in the ranks as they waited for the lead squadrons to distance themselves from the second and third lines. 'One would tell another that he would lose the number of his mess that day,'

Cardigan's Light Brigade formed into three lines as it moved off, as shown in this schematic, which also charts the location of many of the primary witnesses who gave accounts of the charge.

The Charge of the Light Brigade

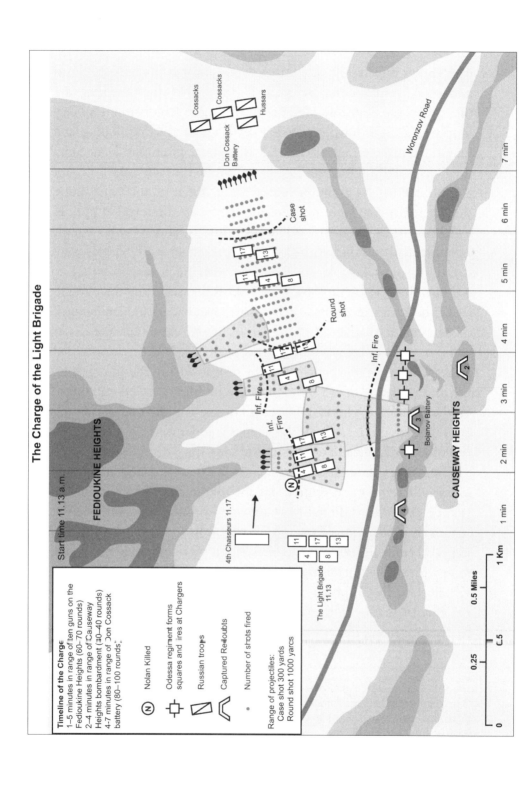

Start time 11.13 a.m.

FEDIOUKINE HEIGHTS

Cossacks
Cossacks
Hussars

Don Cossack
Battery

Case shot

Round shot

Inf. Fire

Inf. Fire

Inf. Fire

4th Chasseurs 11.17

Bojanow Battery

CAUSEWAY HEIGHTS

Woronzov Road

1 min   2 min   3 min   4 min   5 min   6 min   7 min

Timeline of the Charge
1–5 minutes in range of ten guns on the
Fedioukine Heights (60–70 rounds)
2–4 minutes in range of Causeway
Heights bombardment (30–40 rounds)
4–7 minutes in range of Don Cossack
battery (80–100 rounds)

(N) Nolan Killed

Odessa regiment forms
squares and fires at Chargers

Russian troops

Captured Redoubts

• Number of shots fired

Range of projectiles:
Case shot 300 yards
Round shot 1000 yards

The Light Brigade
11.13

0   0.25   0.5   1 Km
0   0.5 Miles

meaning he would be shot. 'Here goes for victory!' some muttered, 'while others declared they would have Russian biscuit for dinner'.

Lord George Paget, Conner's Commanding Officer, was irritated by Lord Cardigan's over-loud pompous insistence that 'I expect your best support – mind your best support.' Paget as second in command bringing up the second main echelon in support suspected it was bravado on Cardigan's part, but the tone and repeated insistence was unfortunate. What on earth did he expect in any case? His support was self-evident. Cardigan was treating the advance like a parade revue. Paget repeated just as loudly, to make the point, 'You shall have it, my lord.' Actually, this was the first indication he had received that there was going to be an attack. Paget still had his expensive cigar clenched firmly between his teeth and would finish it whatever happened. Connor was reassured by his Commanding Officer's bravado, which he found charismatic. 'There was no sign of flinching,' he remembered; 'he made us laugh as he kept drawling out in his own distinctive tone: "Now, then, men, come on", and on we went certainly.'[2]

Cardigan 'Walked' the Brigade at rulebook speed, not exceeding 4mph. 'Here goes the last of the Brudenells,' he was alleged to have muttered as his trumpet call was taken up by the regimental trumpeters, to right and left behind him. When the first line cleared the second, bugles sounded again to 'Trot' and the troopers increased pace to about 8mph. They began to bob up and down with the rhythm of the pace, pennants fluttered above the 17th Lancers to the left as the successive wave lines of animated movement began to flow down the North Valley, forming into three echelons. There was a long way to go, about 1¼ miles, so Cardigan had to pace the advance. The drill was to move at a brisk trot until 250 yards short of the enemy when

---

The Light Brigade was hit sequentially by fire from three directions, left, right and ahead, also including infantry musket fire, but not all at once. Punishing fire came from each direction for just a few minutes, before entering yet another cone of fire further along. Analysis of the regimental casualty returns reveal more men were killed and wounded to the left of the valley, compared to the right.

they would break into an 11mph gallop until at 40 to 50 yards away the 'Charge' would sound.

Up on the Heights the onlookers were increasingly mystified at the direction the brigade was taking. They seemed to be heading straight at the mass of Russians and guns at the far east end of the North Valley. 'We could scarcely believe the evidence of our senses!' Russell recalled. 'Surely that handful of men are not going to charge an enemy in position? … Alas! It was but too true – their desperate valour knew no bounds, and far indeed was it removed from its so-called better part – discretion.'

'What on earth are they going to do? Surely they are not going to charge the whole Russian Army?' the audience around Sergeant Gowing exclaimed; 'it's madness!' Cardigan clearly was going the wrong way. 'They are lost! They are lost!' shouted out more than one spectator. Lord Raglan was quietly succinct: 'those men are going to utter destruction,' he pronounced.[3]

Colonel Brombeuss's Russian battery on the Fedioukine Heights to the left of Cardigan's advance had been watching the British cavalry at the head of the valley sitting motionless for some forty minutes. If they moved, he could subject them to flanking fire. They were about 1,000 yards away, just within range of his 12-pounder guns, but there was no point engaging before they became a threat. Suddenly they began to advance at an unconcerned trot. It took barely a minute to order the gunners into action. The nearest guns banged out and jerked back with the recoil as gunners tried to iden-tify the first strikes through the obscuring smoke.

At 11.11 a.m. Captain Nolan abruptly spurred forward from the left of the line and galloped towards Cardigan at the head of the brigade. 'That won't do, Nolan,' Captain Morris leading the 17th Lancers rep-rimanded the etiquette breach, 'we've a long way to go and must be steady!' Why Nolan did this has since been shrouded in mystery. One of the very first shells to explode resoundingly cracked 20ft above him in a lethal star-shaped airburst, 50 yards ahead of the brigade line. Nolan's chest was lacerated, allegedly exposing his heart, a horrifying precursor of what was to come. The black puffball of smoke seemed to hang motionless in the air. Private James Wightman with the 17th saw the impact of the blast on this lone rider:

> The sword-arm remained upraised and rigid, but all the other limbs so curled in on the contorted trunk as by a spasm, that we wondered how for the moment the huddled form kept the saddle. It was the sudden convulsive twitch of the bridle hand inward on the chest that caused the charger to wheel rearwards so abruptly.

It was an awful spectacle. Did Nolan attempt to force the pace, sensing the disaster to come, or was he trying to retrieve an emerging blunder? It is conceivable he attempted to redirect the advance Raglan intended towards the captured British guns to their right, on the Causeway Heights. Whatever motivated his precipitate rush up front will never be known. 'I shall never forget the shriek that he gave,' remembered Private Henry Naylor with the 13th Light Dragoons riding to the right. 'It rung in my ears above the roaring of the cannon.' Nolan's agonising death was inglorious. Wightman, who had seen him ride out, recalled 'the weird shriek and the awful face as rider and horse disappeared haunt me now to this day'. Cardigan thought Nolan's impetuous behaviour disgraceful, an ADC trying to usurp his position at the head of *his* brigade and then 'riding to the rear and screaming like a woman'. It was an uncharitable comment. Wightman never forgot the episode, 'the first horror of that ride of horrors'.[4]

As they broke into a trot, Cardigan immediately checked his 'Direct' squadrons, the 17th Lancers (leading the attack angle), in a parade manner. 'Steady, steady, Captain Morris!' the Commanding Officer was admonished. Nolan's horse, no longer under rein, turned sharply right and headed for home, tossing his lifeless body to the ground. He had barely got beyond the start.

There was a deafening silence as the Russians, who habitually fired by salvos, reloaded. They had the range, and elevation was a minor adjustment of a few degrees with a one-second fuse, a moving target compensation was required for the loft and drop of projectiles travelling at 1,000ft per second. They aimed slightly ahead. At 11.12 a.m. the second volley boomed out from the left of the advance and a cluster of dirty grey cotton puffs crackled over the top and ahead of the first wave. For three and a half minutes Colonel Brombeuss's battery fired about seventy rounds into the serried lines of the Light Brigade, traversing their front from right to left. Veterans recall the first damaging rounds did indeed howl in from the left. Private Thomas Wroots with the 11th had been pushed out of line by the press of horsemen around him and appealed 'let me come up – let me come up!' 'In half a second there was room enough for an omnibus to come up,' he recalled. 'The charge was a regular "Derby",' he claimed as horsemen collapsed about him. Troop Sergeant Major George Smith was in the second 11th Hussar line and shrank as 'round shot passed through us and the shells burst over and amongst us, causing great havoc.' Every screaming missile had impacts on persons known to all:

> The first man to be struck was Private Young, a cannon ball taking off his right arm, then Private Turner's left arm was also struck off close to the shoulder and Private Ward was struck full in the chest. At the same time a shell burst over us which struck Cornet Houghton.[5]

Many troopers remember the Nolan incident, either because they thought him responsible for their plight, or because it had heralded the Calvary that followed. Private Albert Mitchell with the 13th saw Nolan's horse heading back after his 'fearful cry' and witnessed him fall off as soon as he cleared the squadron file. 'In a few minutes several casualties occurred,' he remembered. Russian gunners sought to 'graze' solid shot at 400 yards at ground level to enable it to ricochet at such a level to plough through the maximum amount of human flesh and bone. A corporal to Mitchell's right 'was struck by a shot or shell burst full in the face,' he recalled, 'completely smashing it, his blood and brains bespattering us who rode near'. His horse carried on alongside them. For three minutes the Russian gunners had a dream target with the pace the brigade was trotting. Whole files of men and horses were caught in enfilade and taken down. 'By this time, the ranks being continuously broken, caused some confusion,' Mitchell recalled. 'Oaths and imprecations might be heard between the report of the guns and the bursting of the shells, as the men crowded and jostled each other in their endeavour to close to the centre.'

Solid shot was clearly discernible, bouncing remorselessly towards them and splattering dirt with each contact with the ground, sounding like ripping canvas as they sped past. Spinning off at unpredictable angles, they wreaked havoc in the ranks. 'Poor old John Lee, my right hand man,' James Wightman in the lead line recalled, 'was all but smashed by a shell.' As his life ebbed away he slipped out of the saddle quietly gasping 'Domino! chum' and disappeared. 'His old grey mare kept alongside of me for some distance,' Wightman remembered, 'treading on and tearing out her entrails as she galloped, till at length she dropped with a strange shriek.'

The angle of Russian fire for these short three minutes was such that the 4th Light Dragoons and 8th Hussars in the third line, and the Heavy Brigade arrayed behind, were still setting off, not yet under fire. Longer-range shells were mixed with solid shot, hollow metal spheres filled with gunpowder timed to explode overhead and shower down white-hot metal shards or lead shot. The effect was discernible as an invisible splash in the ranks when star-shaped dirty grey detonations cracked overhead, shredding shakos and busbies and sweeping men out of their saddles. 'When a shell bursts in the ranks, sometimes bringing down three or four men and horses,' Mitchell explained, the resulting confusion 'made it difficult to avoid an unpleasant crush in the ranks'. Private Robert Grant entered the fire zone with the 4th Light Dragoons and saw a shot decapitate George Gowings' horse 'as cleanly as with a knife'. It was bizarre, 'the horse stood still for a moment then dropped'. Gowings captured a loose horse running by and remounted, and 'in a few minutes this horse's head was also shot clear away'. Gowings bore a charmed life in this action and would eventually be promoted to corporal. On being asked later if he was hurt, he responded 'not a bit of it'.

Maintaining the integrity of the lines became an abiding concern to sergeants, who were the most vocal in getting men to close up. Officers were slightly ahead of the line and intent on setting a good example. Lieutenant Percy Smith with his disabled right arm could carry neither pistol nor sabre, so was obliged to control his horse with his left hand. He shouted encouragement at his men and cursed the enemy. The fearful punishment began to inculcate a form of bloodlust. 'Broken and fast-thinning ranks raised rugged peals of wild fierce cheering,' Wightman recalled, 'that only swelled the louder as the shot and shell from the battery tore gaps through us, and the enfilading musketry fire from the infantry in both flanks brought down horses and men.'

'Close in! Close in!' was the constant shout from squadron and troop officers seeking to fill the gaps torn through ragged lines. Wightman was amazed at the bonding effect of discipline 'in this stress'; orders were hardly needed, he observed. It was not just discipline maintaining formation; 'mechanically, men and horses alike sought to regain the touch,' he recalled. Men sought the emotive reassurance of physical contact with their equally stressed mates. 'We all knew that the thing was desperate before we started' and as one officer remarked, 'it was even worse than we thought'.

Seemingly impervious to all this was Lord Cardigan, riding out in front. Wightman behind could distinguish his 'sonorous command' penetrating the bedlam: 'Steady, steady, the 17th Lancers!' He twice stretched out his sword to check Wightman's squadron commander Captain White from increasing the pace, to escape the murderous fire. 'Cardigan was still straight in front of me, steady as a church,' Wightman observed. Lord Cardigan was an unimaginative man who drew courage simply from the need to maintain a resolute appearance before the men. He conducted the advance as if in formal parade revue order. Despite the intensity of fire, he would not increase the pace to an 11mph gallop until within 250 yards of the enemy. *The Regulations for the Instruction, Formations, and Movements of the Cavalry*, issued thirteen years before, taught drills designed to maintain a cohesive front with which to hit the enemy. Cardigan had no instinctive tactical feel for field operations, but could follow a drill manual, which to his mind, was all that was required. Psychologically it was likely all he could emotionally cope with. It was the junior officers and NCOs that were firmly holding his brigade together behind him.

Sergeant Major George Smith recalled the cannonball that took off Private Young's arm, who was his first casualty. 'Being close on his right rear, I fancied I felt the wind from it as it passed me.' After it shrieked past, 'I found I was bespattered with his flesh.' Young fell out of the line and respectfully asked his sergeant major 'what he was to do' and Smith sent him back to the rear. Turner approached announcing his left arm had been severed and he too was sent back.[6]

Major General Rzyhov, the Russian cavalry commander, had been conversing with Colonel Prince Oboloensky in the Don Battery position, at the far end of the valley. Both had assumed that the battle was likely finished. Lieutenant Yevgenii Arbuzov waited in the rear of two regiments of cavalry drawn up behind the battery. The Ural Cossack Regiment was forty paces behind the guns and the Kiev Hussar Regiment a similar distance behind them. Arbuzov was with the five squadrons of Ingermanland Hussars that had been badly mauled by the Heavy Brigade attack that morning. From Raglan's perspective on the Sapoune Heights they appeared as a distant mass of Russians with guns drawn up ahead of them.

Ryzhov's conversation with Obolensky was interrupted when 'the sharp eyes of the Don men noticed that enemy cavalry was descending the heights.' This galvanised the gunners into action. 'General Liprandi sent his adjutant to tell our battery to prepare to receive a cavalry attack,' a battery officer recalled, but the approaching dust cloud had already been spotted. 'As soon as the adjutant galloped off, the English cavalry passed by the redoubts at a trot in orderly formation,' he remembered, heading straight at the Don battery. Within three to four minutes they opened fire with shot and shell, flailing the front of the Light Brigade as it emerged from its three-and-a-half-minute gauntlet of fire, from Brombeuss's battery from the Fedioukine Heights to its left. Shortly after Bojanov's battery opened up on the other side of the valley. His eight guns would have time to fire some thirty-two rounds in the two minutes it would take the brigade to pass. Rippling salvos of fire were flashing and spitting out from both sides and the head of the valley, pummelling the advancing British in an interlocking fire coming from the left, centre and right.[7]

Corporal Thomas Morley remembered the impact of the Don battery opening up. 'At that instant the Russian artillery in position across the valley, fired a volley into the 17th, which seemed to paralyse it.' Frontal fire swept away a complete section of the line. 'It seemed to me a troop of horses fell, myself and horse knocked over with them.' Morley managed to apprehend a riderless horse 'and followed the shattered line'. Private William Butler's right-hand man was shot out of the saddle. 'He was my comrade for over three years,' he remembered. When the man on his left was bowled over, 'my blood was up, and I began to wish to get near the enemy'. The time was 11.13 a.m. The first line was now virtually halfway down the valley.[8]

The intensity of fire from twenty-one 6- and 9-pounder cannon and howitzers was such that according to Corporal John Kilvert, following up in the second 11th Hussar line, 'it was only the pace of the horses, that carried us through at all.' With 'shot and shell flying like hailstones,' he was convinced, 'I don't think if it had been a body of infantry, that a single man could have reached the bottom of the valley.' Analysis of regimental casualty returns show that more men were killed and injured to the left of the valley than to the right. This could perhaps be explained by the increase in pace as the brigade moved further down the valley. The Fedioukine Hill guns were the first to engage on the left, when regiments were moving at the trot. Accuracy became more questionable by the time Bojanov's battery opened up on the right, because the brigade was cantering, preparatory to the charge, and dust and obscuration from horses and previous artillery strikes was more pronounced.[9]

Some 300 yards behind the first line, Lord George Paget was losing control of the third line, his own 4th Light Dragoons and Shewell's 8th Hussars. Shewell's regiment was remorselessly inclining right as the valley widened. 'Close in to your centre, back the right flank; keep up Private so-and-so,' Paget shouted repeatedly. Ironically, he thought, these were the very commands he might have uttered 'famil-iar to one's ears on the Fifteen Acres, or Wormwood Scrubs [parade grounds], but hardly perhaps to be expected on such a job as ours'. The 'unusual pace at which the first line was leading us was gall-ing,' nevertheless Paget was thankful 'how impossible it was for them [the soldiers], under such circumstances, to forget the rules of parade'. Despite his efforts, the 8th Hussars fell back 'inclining away from us'. '8th Hussars, close in to your left,' he kept shouting and roared: 'Colonel Shewell you are losing your interval.' Paget was mindful of what he had promised Cardigan – 'mind, your best support, my lord' – echoing in his mind, which was clearly slipping away.

Private William Pearson riding with Paget explained one of the hindrances. 'It makes my blood run cold to think of how we had to gallop over the poor wounded fellows lying on the field of battle,' he recalled, 'face up with anxious looks for assistance – what a sicken-ing scene!' When the 8th Hussars inclined right they came under 'a most terrific fire from cannon and musketry', according to Private John Doyle. There 'were three tiers of guns, and the infantry as thick as they could be placed; shot and shell, grape, canister and musketry came upon us like hail'.

Loping and panting alongside was the regimental mascot 'Jemmy', who would be wounded by a splinter in the neck. When she got back to England the dog was awarded a collar with five medal clasps attached to it, for Alma, Balaclava, Inkerman, Sebastopol and Central India.

Doyle was suddenly startled when his friend Heffern to the right was blown clean into the air by an exploding shell, 'but his hips remained for a long time in the saddle' and 'I was covered in his remains'. Private Lennon, who had cared for Jemmy, was struck on the side of the head by round shot, and Doyle recalled, 'I got another splash from him.' His corpse rode in macabre unison alongside Doyle for some considerable time. When his own horse was shot above the noseband Doyle was again deluged in gore: 'Every time he gave his head a chuck the blood spurted over me.' Doyle appeared impervious to injury, five buttons were blown off his dress jacket, as was his right heel and spur shot off his boot and the sling of his sabretache was severed, leaving his sword belt untouched. When he unravelled his cloak that night, 'I found 23 bullets in it.'[10]

By the time Lucan led the Heavy Brigade into the beaten zone churned up by Colonel Brombeuss's ten guns on the Fedioukine Heights, the Russian gunners had their range marks. Private James Prince with the 5th Dragoon Guards remembered 'balls and shells flying about us like hail, and whistling like steam engines'. This was a totally different experience from the cavalry scrap fought two hours before. 'Horses and men fell on all sides,' he recalled, 'swimming in blood.' They had entered an artillery killing area. 'A spent cannon ball struck me in the ribs,' Prince recalled, 'and knocked me off my horse.' 'I scrambled on again and wondered whether I was killed or not, for I could scarcely breathe.'

Another trooper with the 5th recalled the grisly debris they had to dodge in order to keep up with the Light Brigade, now out of sight, deluged in smoke and exploding shells. 'You could see nothing but dismounted soldiers and broken-legged horses,' he remembered. One trooper, 'WB', writing to his brother, described how 'poor J Hill' lost his life, shredded by grapeshot 'an awful cut up', suggesting an awful fate lay ahead. 'I can assure you,' he wrote, 'that it wants a stout heart to meet such an enemy as cannonballs.' Mutilation, with its social consequences back home, was feared as much as an unidentified body, meaning loved ones back home would never know their fate, as they were tipped into unmarked mass graves.

Lieutenant Colonel John Yorke commanding the 1st (Royal) Dragoons rode at their front to the right of the 'Heavies'. Dressing could not be properly maintained because they had to avoid riding over the Light Brigade's fallen and wounded, a 'Via Dolorosa'. 'It was a fearful sight, I can assure you,' he wrote to his sister. 'The appearance of all who retired was as if they had passed through a shower of blood, positively dripping and saturated, and shattered arms blowing back like empty sleeves as the poor fellows ran to the rear.'

He was distracted by the 'constant squelching noise around me', with metal impacting on flesh amid the 'constant squibbling noise' of artillery fire. 'My horse was shot in the right flank,' Yorke later wrote to his wife, and after 'a few fatal paces my left leg was shattered in this fearful manner. You know the rest.' Yorke was swept from his horse with a smashed leg and thigh bone, crippled for life.

'It was not in the charge [earlier that morning] that our men suffered most,' recalled Corporal John Selkrig with the Scots Greys, 'it was when we went down the valley to support the Light Brigade.' For some inexplicable reason they halted, amid 'shot and shell flying about us and bursting among us in a fearful manner'. Stopping made it worse, because 'had we been riding quick through we would not have noticed it so much,' he claimed. A flurry of confusing trumpet calls had sounded out: retire – advance – and then retire again. 'To be halted in it was awful in the extreme,' Selkrig complained. 'A shell burst on a man's horse crop, close to me – tore all the flesh off its hind quarters, cutting through the back part of his saddle and through his valise, and tore off his leg below the thigh.' Selkrig survived, but the man 'has since died'.[11]

Lord Lucan's hesitation was incomprehensible. They had reached redoubt number 4, following the rear of the Light Brigade, clearly being cut to pieces. There was still a long way to go and Lucan was acutely aware that the lead Heavy regiments, the Greys and Royals, were severely cut up. The Royals alone had already lost twenty-one killed, wounded or dismounted and their Commanding Officer Yorke was down. A trooper with the Royals complained:

He would not let us charge, but kept us advancing at a trot, and sometimes at a walk, and even halted us for upwards of five minutes

in the midst of three fires. I did not feel at all comfortable standing doing nothing, and so many 'Russian pills' flying about; shells
sometimes bursting not more than a yard over my head, and sending dust and powder down in my face, but no hard pieces.

Lucan saw seven or eight Greys' horses swept off their feet by a single
shell. His ADC Captain Walker later admitted, 'I would not live over
that moment for a kingdom.' He was badly rattled and remembered, 'I
hope I shall not soon again get such a pelting.' Troop Sergeant Major
Russell with the 5th Dragoon Guards miraculously escaped when a
shell penetrated his horse and exploded, pitching him over the horse's
head. Two chargers alongside with Troop Sergeant Major Franks and
Trumpeter Baker were lifted bodily into the air. Russell amazingly
picked himself up and apprehended a riderless horse to rejoin his men.[12]

Lucan instinctively appreciated Raglan's order was suspect, but
could hardly contradict his superior in the heat of battle. He concluded Cardigan's brigade would be destroyed. 'They have sacrificed
the Light Brigade,' he remarked to Lord William Paulet, his Assistant
Adjutant General. 'They shall not have the Heavy Brigade if I can
help it.' He called upon his trumpeter Joy to sound the halt and then
for the Heavy Brigade to retire. There were hot words from Brigadier
General Scarlett and contradictory bugle calls sounded, but they went
about. The Light Brigade was left to face the enemy alone.

Ironically, at about the same time, Russian gunfire to the left
of the valley began to abate. French cavalry was fanning out and
ascending the slopes of the Fedioukine Heights. This added to the
humiliation and indignation of the more hard-bitten 'Heavies',
who appreciated their withdrawal of close support had left their
Light Brigade comrades in the lurch. Lucan had decided the best
option was to screen any survivors that might come back. He had
written them off, suspecting they might even be destroyed before
they reached the guns. Raglan had precipitated the blunder through
imprecise orders. In a sense Lucan was sacrificing the Light Brigade
to save the Heavy, because the Light Brigade had not yet been

destroyed, but probably would be. In any event, he knew he would attract most of the blame.

French General Pierre Bosquet, commanding the Corps d'Observation, had promised Raglan he would guard the Light Brigade's left flank. True to his word, squadrons of the Chasseurs d'Afrique from the 1st Cavalry Brigade had moved up and occupied dead ground to the left of the valley, out of sight to Russian guns booming out from the Fedioukine Heights. General Canrobert the French Commander and Bousquet had shared Raglan's anxiety, when it appeared the Light Brigade was advancing into the maw of the whole Russian army at the far end of the North Valley. Bousquet, a combat veteran of Algeria, expressed astonishment to his staff, '*C'est magnificent*,' he declared, '*mais ce n'est pas la guerre*' – it is magnificent, but not war.

Lieutenant Henry Clifford with French General Brite heard him likewise exclaim 'Good Heavens! What are they doing?' Clifford, who was ADC to the Light Division Commander, was watching the action from the high ground next to the French. 'I saw shells bursting in the midst of the squadrons and men and horses strewed the ground behind them,' he observed, 'yet on they went.' The rapidity of the fire being poured into them beggared belief, akin to rain drumming on a canvas tarpaulin. Panicked riderless horses were coming back from the smoke that seemed to enfold the scene, while flashes and smoke beyond signified the Light Brigade was pressing on, despite the murderous punishment. The scarlet Heavy Brigade lines had about-faced and were coming back. Clifford, moved to tears, received a reassuring pat on the shoulder from the old French General. 'I am old and I have seen many battles,' he confessed, 'but this is too much.'[13]

Much of the area of punishing fire spitting out from the lower scrub-covered slopes of the Fedioukine Heights had been secured by Russian Major General Zhabokritsky, who was directed to protect Liprandi's right flank. Russian infantry and cavalry held the tops and ends of the re-entrants snaking down into the

North Valley. They covered Colonel Brombeuss's ten-gun battery which was sited in three segments. The Frenchmen of the 1st and 4th Chasseurs d'Afrique waiting in dead ground below could hear and smell the pungent smoke from these guns, lacerating the left flank of the Light Brigade. General d'Allonville, the Commander of the 1st Cavalry Brigade, was directed to clear the Heights to his front of Russian artillery.

The 4th Chasseurs were ordered to mount. Distinctive with tight blue jackets and red baggy overalls with red and blue casquettes, the experienced irregular trained cavalry moved off on fine Arab and Barb horses. They were 532 sabres strong and formed into two demi-squadrons, the lead line led by Major Abdelal, with his senior, Colonel Coste de Champeron, controlling the second. The uneven rocky slope they traversed was covered in a tangle of 3ft- to 4ft-high brush, coming up to saddle-girth height. The Russians regarded it a formidable obstacle for any cavalry to climb. They were in any case totally focused on the Light Brigade advance being played out to their front and not looking to their right or below. There were some 5,000 men with ten guns on top. The veteran chasseurs swiftly negotiated the difficult ground in echelon and then spread out into open order as they neared the top of the Heights. Years of campaigning over the hard and barren foothills of the Algerian Atlas Mountains had prepared them well for such a task. Above them were two battalions of foot Cossacks and two Cossack cavalry squadrons supporting the guns. Nearby were two regular infantry regiments, the Vladimir and Susdal and another two squadrons of Ingermanland Hussars in depth.

The Chasseurs rode at the Russian guns in an extended irregular wave, with 1854 model percussion rifle carbines slung at the shoulder. They imitated the Arab tribesmen they had often confronted, rushing with sabres at the foe before pausing to fire. Russian flankers from No. 6 Rifle Battalion, strung out in skirmish order, were soon outflanked and overrun in the disorientating thick undergrowth. Trumpet calls rang out to up the pace from trot to a canter, and despite some chasseurs pitching from their saddles amid desultory fire, they were swiftly among the Russians and laying about with sabres. Abdelal's unexpected charge through the undergrowth in irregular lines completely unnerved the Russian infantry, who recoiled at the sudden appearance of cavalry on the Heights. They hastily fell back from the edge as Russian guns limbered up in haste and attempted to withdraw, harassed and sabred on their way by pursuing chasseurs. The other battery segments fearing an apparent collapse on their open right did likewise. The artillery fire on the left of the valley therefore petered out as General d'Allonville, observing from behind his line, saw the whole Russian right, Cossacks and all, beat a precipitate retreat before his advancing squadrons.

Major General Zhabokritsky thought the sudden appearance of French cavalry portended a major attack on the Heights and immediately sent three battalions of the Vladimir Regiment at the double towards the enemy. The blue-jacketed chasseurs seemed able to move with impunity over the rugged Heights, snapping off shots from their carbines at the retreating Russians. This intermittent shooting was soon drowned out by rolling volleys, that spat out from the advancing Vladimir infantry columns. They provided the respite that enabled the disordered Cossacks to reform. Retreating artillery could now be safely driven behind their formed squares.

French casualties began to mount: thirty-eight men were knocked down, of which ten were killed, alongside sixteen horses and three were captured. The moment was over. The chasseur squadrons came to a halt and with seeming ease about-faced and flowed back down the brush-covered slopes from which they had appeared. The Russians were shaken. Only gradually did it become apparent in the valley that the fire from the Fedioukine Heights to the left had indeed abated.

THREE MINUTES

11.17 TO 11.20 A.M.

James Wightman's 'ride of horrors' at the forefront of the 17th Lancers was almost halfway through at 11.17 a.m., when, with three minutes to go, they passed redoubts 3 and 2 to their right. They were coming out of Bojanov's battery fire zone but were still under concentrated artillery and musket fire coming from three directions. Prince Obolensky's Don battery up ahead had time to fire eighty-eight rounds of solid shot, shell, case-shot and canister directly at them. The men could see solid shot lazily bounding toward them, 'as large as ordinary Dutch cheeses' according to Sergeant John Baker, riding with the 4th Light Dragoons in the third line. Each languid grazing contact with the ground showering earth and stones. The fast trot was verging on a canter, but Cardigan still held the pace. 'Every man felt convinced that the quicker he rode, the better chance he would have of escaping unhurt,' recalled Cornet George Wombell with the 17th. 'There is a natural instinct to dodge cannon balls,' explained Corporal Morley in the front file. 'In such fire as we were under it changed to an impulse to hurry … There was no time to look right or left.' All eyes focused on the guns ahead. He remembered:

> They were visible as streaks of fire about two feet long and a foot thick in the centre of a gush of thick white smoke, marking every three hundred yards on the way, as they would reload in 30 or 40 seconds.[14]

One Russian Don artillery officer facing them remembered the tension rising among the gun crews when the approaching cavalry passed redoubt number 3: 'At that range the battery started case shot fire managing to fire some 32 rounds, which tore out whole files from the regiment, so that barely a third of the Englishmen reached the battery.'

The action was fast developing into a crisis, and 'last ditch' efforts were instituted to check the cavalry onslaught.

Morley in hindsight had considerable respect for the 'well drilled' professionalism of the Russian artillery, whose impact was lethal. 'There was none of that crackling sound I have often heard,' he explained, intermittent fire going off like 'a bunch of fire-crackers popping in quick succession', when smoke clouds obscured the gunner's line of sight: 'The Russian artillery went off at the word of command, all together. One tremendous volley was heard with flashes through the rolling smoke.'

The 300-yard mark reports going off produced an irresistible desire to shorten the distance to end the torment, because 'every volley came with terrible effect'.[15]

Lord George Paget was under similar galling pressure behind, advancing over an obstacle course hindered with the ugly detritus from those who had fallen ahead. 'One was guiding one's horse so as to avoid trampling on the bleeding objects in one's path,' he recalled, 'sometimes a man, sometimes a horse.' Although the pace was maintained at a brisk trot, the shredding impact of crossfire and the disorientating effect of noise and smoke had broken the symmetry of the parade-ground start. The advance now resembled three irregular lines of horseman, like surf prematurely breaking as it approaches the seashore. The 17th Lancers were shifting left but remained in ragged parity with the 13th Light Dragoons to their right. Paget had closed up just behind the 11th Hussars in the second line, but his right neighbour the 8th Hussars, in the third line, were drifting right, where guns and muskets on the Causeway Heights had swept away whole files. Meanwhile, riderless 'bewildered horses from the first line, rushed in upon our ranks, in every state of mutilation', Paget recalled. At the same time unhorsed troopers, 'some with a limping gait', were trying to desperately apprehend them, and were getting in the way.

Private Joseph Grigg with Paget recalled, 'the lines were about 100 yards apart', because, 'when a man went down with his horse, the man behind had time to turn his horse on one side or jump over the obstacle. Every man thus had all his work to do to look before him.'

The merciful distraction at least meant 'there were not many chances to watch the dreadful work of the shots, shells and bullets, which were showered at us from all directions.' 'So we went on,' Paget recalled: 'Right flank, keep up. Close in to your centre.' But few were able to hear above the din of successive artillery impacts. Paget explained, 'the smoke, the noise, the cheers, the groans, the "ping, ping" whizzing past one's head was disorientating'. Especially ominous was 'the whirr' of shell fragments and familiar 'slush' sound as they struck flesh and bone, 'that unwelcome intruder on one's ears'. The 'din of battle', Paget remembered, produced 'a sublime confusion'.[16]

James Wightman recalled shouted conversations amid the din as friends were swept away by unseen howling projectiles. Private Dudley on his left asked his pal Peter Marsh if he had noticed 'what a hole that bloody shell had made' collapsing a file of five men further left. 'Hold your foul-mouthed tongue,' admonished another, 'swearing like a blackguard when you may be knocked into eternity next minute!' Whereupon Sergeant Edward Talbot suddenly 'had his head clean carried off by a round shot', Wightman remembered, and 'for about a thirty yards further the headless body kept the saddle, the lance at the charge firmly gripped under the right arm'. Wightman was shot through the right knee and seconds later in the shin, and three musket impacts peppered his horse's neck. 'Marsh begged me to fall out,' he remembered, but he opted to carry on, despite crippling wounds because 'in a few minutes we must be into them'.

One sergeant with the 13th Light Dragoons later admitted 'we continued on' despite 'every man feeling certainly we must be annihilated'. An amalgam of factors contributed to this resolve. Ingrained discipline was one, and the community of 'mateship' they might lose if they demonstrated a lack of resolve. 'I could see what would be the result of it,' explained Private Thomas Williams with the 11th Hussars to his parents, 'and so could all of us; but of course as we had got the order, it was our duty to obey.' For the officers, it was about honour.[17]

Cardigan out in front was an extreme illustration of the latter, cocooned in egotism. Lieutenant Henry 'Fitz' Maxse was his ADC and bore him no ill will, but described his ride as being conducted 'in a state of phantasmagoria of self, and never saw or thought of anybody but himself doing his duty as a leader well'. He might well have been distressed if he had allowed himself to look back, but to turn around was to exhibit plebeian curiosity or womanish weakness, which as a natural-born aristocrat he disdained. He was more preoccupied with anger against his detested former brother-in-law, Lucan, putting him in an impossible situation and indignation at the upstart Nolan, riding out at the head of *his* brigade to question his authority. Two affronts in ten minutes had raised his temper to boiling point and done much to assuage physical fear. Not one of his officers would question the blunder for fear of compromising honour within the stultifying confines of a tightly graduated Victorian hierarchy. Catastrophic social implications would follow, inextricably linked to profile and fortune. It simply would not do.

Like influences motivated the men. They could not be seen to be letting their mates down because of fear. Private Samuel Walker with the 8th Hussars had three horses shot from under him and each time caught another to carry on. Private Thomas Wroots with the 11th Hussars saw a man shot in the left side 'and I think he rode 50 yards, then all at once he tumbled to his left and came down on the ground like a lump of clay – just like a lump of clay, that is the only description I can give of it.' Wroots carried on. Private Christopher Fox with the 5th Light Dragoons and 'Butcher Jack' Vahey with the 17th Lancers were risking a flogging by deserting their posts to participate in this desperate charge. They felt impelled to be with their peers.[18]

Bloodlust, arising from the fearful carnage wrought by the Russians' fire, also played a role. Men transitioned from trepidation to a form of 'beserker' rage. At the beginning of the charge one 8th Hussar trooper admitted to acute fear: 'I felt my blood thicken and crawl, as if my heart grew still like a lumpy stone within me,' he confessed. But under such murderous fire: 'my heart began to warm, to become hot, to dance again, and I had neither fear nor pity! I longed to be at the guns. I'm sure I set my teeth together as if I could have bitten a piece out of one.'

Inter-unit 'tribal' rivalry added to the combustion. When Captain Arthur Tremayne's horse went down in the front line of the 13th Light Dragoons just short of the Russian guns, he yelled 'don't let the bastards of the 17th get in front, come on, come on!' Every man had to come to terms with his individual fear. Thomas Dudley with the 17th Lancers remembered, 'when we received the *order*, not a man could believe it.' But they got on with it. 'What each man felt no one can tell,' he explained. 'I cannot tell you my own thoughts,' there was no dissent, 'not a word or a whisper, on we went!'[19]

Paget, ahead of his line, became the focus of attention for swarms of hysterical dismounted horses, 'poor dumb brutes', who had lost riders in the lines ahead, 'galloping about in numbers, like mad wild beasts'. They sought human company in their distressed state, and Paget was in trouble: 'They consequently made dashes at me, some advancing with me a considerable distance, at one time as many as five on my right and two on my left, cringing in on me, and positively squeezing me.'

Round shot tore up the earth under their noses, adding to the terror. Paget's overalls were soon 'a mass of blood from their gory flanks'. Several times he was nearly upset and had 'to use my sword to rid myself of them'. His own horse, despite being hit, showed no signs of fear, 'evincing', as he grandiosely put it, 'the confidence of dumb animals in the superior being!' Cavalry horse and man bonded. At this moment of supreme peril, both depended on each other. A horse and rider could be bodily lifted from the ground on being directly struck by solid shot, the concussive impact bursting open saddlebags. 'I remarked their eyes,' Paget observed, wide with uncomprehending fear, 'betokening as keen a sense of the perils around them as we humans experienced.'

They were nearing the guns. Colonel Prince Obolensky's hotly engaged Don battery relished the opportunity to finally dispatch the madly advancing British. They switched to canister. As the name implied, each projectile was a thin-walled bucket-like container filled with several score 1½oz solid iron balls. On firing, the canister ruptured and spat out a widening stream of balls like a gigantic shotgun. They had been preceded by grapeshot at longer range, which was shot attached like a paper towel holder, wrapped in cloth and laced together. When it was fired a bundle of balls were hurled forward like a bunch of grapes, signifying the name. It had a distinctive sound, like the rattling of hail on rooftops as the balls struck hard objects such as equipment, and eviscerating flesh from bone as it blasted through. 'About half way down the valley we could scarcely see each other,' recalled Private William Nicholson, because 'the ground being at the time very dry, the horse's hooves and shot and shell that were fired ploughed the ground, making the air thick with smoke and dust. In consequence of this we could not see the enemy till we were close to them.'

Fire intensified as they drew nearer the Don Battery. 'Every sound was there,' recalled Cornet Edward Phillips with the 4th Light Dragoons, 'the bursting of the shells, the deep dash of the round shot as they struck the ground, and the whistling storm of Minié balls and grape shot.' Sergeant William Williamson likened the intense fire to 'a person walking through drops of rain' because 'it is the only thing I can compare it to, for the balls of all descriptions whistled like putting your head into a hive of bees'.[20]

Russian crews feverishly worked the guns, sponge men extinguishing burning powder and canvas inside the barrels between each shot. Powder bags and shot were rammed home with a cry of 'Gotov!' 'Ready!' to the vent man, who ignited the powder charge. Eight-gun trails recoiled violently back in unison while sotniks tried to identify the fall of shot through the dispersing smoke. Two men stepped forward to push and lever the trail to roughly realign the gun. Eight men were at work, five crewing and three bringing up ammunition. Two others reassured the horses in their traces attached to the limber just to the rear. Despite the damage wrought ahead, with whole files of cavalry being brought down, ragged waves of horsemen *still* bore down on them.

Doubt and the unsettling realisation they might not stop them became uppermost. The rate of fire had to be stepped up. Experienced gun crews loaded round shot on top of canister. No human being could live through such a storm of solid projectiles mixed with a 10-yard spread of grapeshot, spraying out of each gun. It created an 80-yard no-go beaten zone to the front of the Don battery. Obolensky probably told his men to stop sponging the barrels to save time: dangerous advice, because after firing over seventy rounds, hot fragments from previous shot might well ignite the powder bag when it was rammed home. A barrel explosion could kill and injure several crew, but it did reduce the reloading sequence to twenty seconds. Horse teams were ordered to close in and make ready to drag the guns out in extremis. The gunners could see there were lancers in the first line and the fluttering red and white pennants were lowered. If the last volley did not blow them away, they were finished.

'As we drew nearer, the guns in our front supplied us with grape and canister,' recalled Albert Mitchell, 'which brought down men and horses in heaps.' Cardigan had lost the battle impelled by the momentum behind to up the pace. At the halfway point the tempo had increased to a canter, verging on a gallop, in any case. 'Oh! If you could have seen the faces of that doomed 600 men at that moment,' Private Thomas Dudley with the 17th, closing on him, remembered. 'Every man's features fixed, his teeth clenched, and rigid as death, still it was on – on!' At about 300 yards out he was hit, 'but it did not floor me'. 'We were in the midst of our torture and mad to be out of it,' recalled James Wightman. But still Cardigan sonorously called, 'Steady, steady the 17th Lancers.' 'Come on Deaths! Come on!' Captain Godfrey Morgan never forgot 'the noise of the striking of the men and horses by grape and round shot'; it was 'deafening' he recalled. Private William Pennington remembered: 'To see a fore-arm torn by shot or shell, bleeding and dangling by the tendons which still held it to the upper joint, or brains protruding from a shattered skull would in cool moments have been a soul moving and sickening sight.'

There was no time to reflect, life and death flickered past with alarming rapidity. 'The dust and gravel struck up by the round shot that fell short was almost blinding, and irritated my horse,' recalled Godfrey Morgan, 'so that I could scarcely hold him at all.' Albert Mitchell saw his left-hand man had been unhorsed and suspecting he may well be next, offered up a heartfelt short prayer: 'Oh Lord, protect me and watch over my poor mother.'

Cardigan's trumpeter blew the charge. 'We like bull dogs who had been tied up all day, were too glad to be let loose,' remembered Lieutenant William Gordon with the 17th, 'and off we went at a thundering gallop, cheering more like mad men than like men with common sense.' Private Joseph Grigg with the 4th Light Dragoons recalled, 'away we went at a splendid pace'. His horse 'snorted and vibrated with excitement, and I could hardly keep my seat, for we seemed to go like the wind'. Men spurred to their utmost speed, lances and sabres were lowered to the 'engage'. Frequent mock charges at regulation distance and pace had been drilled into the men, who on finally spotting the guns hardly required any instruction. 'Butcher Jack' Vahey remembered 'setting our teeth hard, off we went across the valley as hard as ever horse could lay foot to ground.' 'Fear was banished from every mind' in the bloodlust of the moment, Gordon recalled. 'On, on we went'.[21]

The 9ft cavalry ash lance was made for the charge, projecting over 3ft beyond the horse's head. It had a particularly adverse and sobering effect on the enemy with the anticipation of its killing blow and awareness of the dreadful wounds it could inflict. 17th Lancer troopers held it firm by a white leather arm strap, attached at the point of balance. It was the momentum of the horse that skewered the lance into the body, invariably causing a mortal wound. In subsequent melees the ash staff became unwieldy, conferring limited stabbing ability and was quickly discarded for the sabre. An opponent impaled too effectively might drag the lancer from the saddle or at minimum bring him to an uncomfortable halt, with a twisted wrist strop anchored to the corpse. The 13th Light Dragoons to the right 'delivering point' had to be equally wary in case the blade became 'locked' inside an opponent's body. The blade could snag in the ribcage or on muscle, and bring the rider to an abrupt halt, straining the wrist or even losing the sword. The 'cut' or 'hacking' with the sabre was the preserve of less cool heads but generally instinctive in a cavalry fracas. Dragoons were well drilled and practised in regulation cuts, which were delivered in sequence, instilled through repetitive drills. The thrust, the preserve of the veteran professional swordsman, was invariably lethal.

'The Russians worked the guns till we were within ten yards of them,' one 17th Lancer officer recalled, which took courage. 'When about a hundred yards from the guns,' Captain Godfrey Morgan remembered, 'I noticed just in front of me, a gunner applying his fuse to the gun I appeared to be riding.' He closed his eyes in anticipation of what was to follow. 'That settled the question as far as I was concerned, but the shot missed me and struck the man on my right full on the chest.' Men had to be quick-witted, canny and responsive in order to survive. Corporal John Penn riding behind Sergeant John Berryman in the 17th saw 'Captain Winter and the whole division on my right' swept away by one of the final discharges of solid shot and grapeshot from the battery. Captain Morris directing the final strike to close the gap called 'Right Incline', but Penn warned Berryman to 'keep straight on Jack', having realised they were opposite one of the gun intervals. Berryman gratefully remembered, 'thus we escaped, for the next round would have swept us into eternity.'

They were virtually there; Albert Mitchell penetrated the smoke cloud hanging in front of the battery. 'I could see some of the gunners running from the guns to the rear,' he recalled, when at that moment 'a shell from the battery on the right struck my horse, carrying away the shoulder and part of the chest', exploding a few yards beyond. He rolled onto the ground and was pinned beneath his horse, dazed with shock. Unable to move, he heard the drumbeat of hooves that heralded the arrival of the next wave. He saw they were 4th Dragoons: 'For God's sake,' he shrieked, 'don't ride over me!'[22]

'The last volley went off when we were close to them,' remembered Corporal Thomas Morley. 'The flame, the smoke, the roar were in our faces' as the 17th Lancers crashed into the Don battery. 'It is not an exaggeration,' Morley claimed, 'to compare the sensation to that of riding into the mouth of a volcano.' 'I saw Captain White go down and Cardigan disappear into the smoke,' James Wightman remembered, at which point he was stunned by an air burst cracking overhead. His horse took a 'tremendous leap in the air; what he jumped I never saw or knew; the smoke was so thick I could not see my arm's length'. Wightman and his horse were seriously wounded. Now inside the battery position he could not see anything, 'no gun or gunner'. 'Before I knew for certain that I had reached it,' he was through and riding beyond. He appeared completely alone, but 'through the [dense] veil' nearby, 'I heard noises of fighting and slaughter'. He reined in his horse thinking, where was everyone?[23]

8

RUNNING THE GAUNTLET

11.20 A.M. TO 11.35 A.M.

RUSSIAN HYSTERIA

11.20 A.M. TO 11.25 A.M.

Lord Cardigan later recalled with satisfaction, 'we reached the battery in a very good line, and at the regular charging pace.' He had done his duty, having virtually conducted a rulebook advance in 'revue order', but did add that 'here, many officers and men were killed.' Cardigan at this point appeared to hand over command of the brigade to his subordinates. Out of his tactical depth, he had focused solely on the execution of the advance up to the charge. On arrival his mind was somewhat blank, possibly a reaction to combat stress. Like Private Wightman with the 17th Lancers, he was totally alone when he emerged out of the smoke surrounding the Don battery. Immediately to his front were masses of steadily retiring grey-clad horsemen. By the time he brought his charger Ronald to a halt, also miraculously unscathed, the Russian cavalry ahead had turned and fronted up. They menacingly regarded this lone horseman. Cardigan had never crossed swords with a live opponent in his life.

When two Cossacks approached to take him prisoner, Captain Percy Smith with the 13th Light Dragoons, nursing his maimed right arm, also emerged from the smoke. He saw Cardigan kept his 'sword at the slope and did not seem to take trouble to defend himself'. More and more British horsemen arrived at the scene. Lieutenant Johnson and Private Keely, also with the 13th, rode up to help, but their horses were badly injured. When he refused to surrender, the Cossacks jabbed at Cardigan with their lances. Johnson thought one thrust went home, but it snagged on Cardigan's pelisse and nearly jerked him from the saddle. This was their last effort to apprehend him because they fell back when more Light Brigade remnants burst through the smoke. Johnston watched as Cardigan, 'cantering quietly', made off in the opposite direction.

Private James Wightman, looking for survivors, nearly rode over Cardigan's badly wounded aide Lieutenant Maxse. 'For God's sake, lancer, don't ride over me!' he appealed. 'See where Lord Cardigan is', he said, pointing at him. 'Rally on him!' But Cardigan was nowhere to be found.[1]

The scene inside the smoke around the battery presented a version of Dante's vision of hell. 'I cut clean off the hand of a Russian gunner who was holding his sponge [staff] against me,' recalled an 8th Hussar trooper. 'He fell, glaring savagely, but I cared little for that.' Pent-up emotion and adrenalin consumed survivors with a berserker desire to exact revenge for their suffering and fallen comrades. 'Bodies and limbs scattered in fragments,' the trooper recalled, 'and blood splashed into my face were now no novelty.' 'Butcher Jack' Vahey rode into the battery and 'what with the drink in me and the wild excitement of the headlong charge, I went stark mad'. He was lucky to be alive. 'The hot air of the cannon's mouth' had scorched one side cheek on entry, he remembered, and 'half a dozen of us leaped in among the guns at once'. He brained a Russian gunner with his axe and 'split open the head of an officer who was trying to rally the artillery detachments in the rear; and then what of us were left went smack through the stragglers cutting and slashing like fiends'.

Private Edward Woodham smashed into the guns with the second 11th Hussar wave. His friend Wootten, who had assured him that the reckless charge order would never be executed, did not make it. 'As soon as we reached the guns, the men [Russians] began dodging by getting under them,' he recalled, 'and for a time they defended with rammers.' 'But it was no contest,' their blood was up. 'They had no chance with us, and we cut them down like ninepins'.[2]

The first man accosted, Joseph Grigg with the 4th Light Dragoons, was a mounted gun carriage driver:

> He cut me across the eyes with his whip, which almost blinded me, but as my horse flew past him, I made a cut at him and caught him in the mouth so that his teeth rattled together as he fell from his horse. I can fancy I hear the horrible sound now.

He hacked and slashed away at the back of the neck of the second driver until he also fell off.

'Clash! And oh God! What a scene!' Private Thomas Dudley described when he got into the battery with the 17th Lancers. 'I know it is not to your taste, what we did,' he later wrote home, 'but we were Englishmen, and that is enough.' He went berserk. 'I believe I was as strong as six men,' he claimed. 'At least I felt so; for I know I had chopped two Russian lances in twos as if they had been reeds.' James Olley with the 4th Light Dragoons cut down a Russian gunner but 'received a severe wound on my forehead, which went through the skull bone'; he continued hacking and cutting until 'a bullet from the enemy took away my left eye'. William Spring with the 11th Hussars saw his friend Tom pinned beneath his fallen horse repeatedly shot by a Russian officer, who 'in the most dastardly manner fired every chamber of his revolver at the prostrate and helpless Hussar'. Remarkably he survived and, months later, 'Tom showed me the deep indentation from these bullets directed at his breast.' He was saved by the thick woollen padding of his Hussar jacket.[3]

Most troopers in the excitement of the melee cut and slashed at their opponents, inflicting disabling injuries, but not fatal. Captain Alexander Low with the 4th Light Dragoons was, however, an exceptional swordsman and used the point. The Homeric-proportioned 15-stone warrior was an imposing fighter and dispatched eleven Russians 'at the point' in the battery with Achilles-like intensity. On arrival at the gun line he was attacked by three Cossacks, two of whom he shot from the saddle with his revolver and sabred the third. Private Robert Grant with the same regiment recalled the effectiveness of the officer's revolvers. 'Many of the Cossacks got shot foolishly, for after a discharge, they thought it was all over, but the revolver had several barrels.' Low 'became afflicted, if so one may speak, with what has been called the blood frenzy', one witness alleged; 'much gore besmeared him'. He 'raged wildly against human life, cutting down, it was said, very many of the obstinate Russians with his own reeking hand'. Low was not only aggressively lethal in a fight, he was also a tactically adept thinking officer. Lieutenant Henry Adlington, a regimental contemporary, thought him 'perhaps the best cavalry officer in the service'. When the blood-bespattered Low paused, during a brief respite, an emotional reaction set in and he wept.[4]

It was the eighth minute since the charge began. Two more waves crashed into the battery, the overspills completely enveloping the guns, with some men completely missing the battery in the smoke. 'We were all higgledy-piggledy' when they hit the guns, recalled Corporal John Buckton with the 11th Hussars, 'fighting more like devils than men'. Lieutenant Percy Smith with his crippled right hand could do little more than encourage his men. Three Russian Cossacks surrounded him on three sides but he managed to save himself by swerving horsemanship, receiving a slight flesh wound. His only recourse to avoid being lanced from the front was to jump his hunting horse on top of his slighter Cossack adversary. The lance tip glanced off his bone before a group of 11th Hussars intervened.[5]

The Don battery stood its ground, firing double shot and canister to the last, but was unable to stop the mad British charge. Its gunners now faced the consequences of failure. Some guns managed to get attached to limbers, recalled a battery officer, but many were mired in confusion. Gun trails ploughed the ground on the order 'pull back' instead of 'limbers back'. 'Surrounded by the English, the battery defended itself as best it could,' he remembered. One intrepid gunner, Cossack Studenikin, felled some horsemen with his ramrod as gun teams tried to resolutely disengage from the melee. The rear driver of one gun, Cossack Nikulin, was impaled through the throat with a lance; 'he lost his voice,' the officer explained, 'but is still alive today.' Gunners attempted to cower beneath their limbers where they were repeatedly stabbed with lances. Gun number five's horses became entangled with their harnesses. 'I was with the gun,' the officer recalled, which managed to make 100 yards before being 'surrounded by enemy cuirassiers'. He described the desperate fighting to get away: 'A ramrod number wounded my attackers in the arm with a pistol shot. I picked up the wounded man's sword and struck his horse's nose so hard it reared up and threw its rider onto the ground, where the Cossacks ran him through.'

The official battery account dwells on successes rather than failures and is inaccurate in many respects, claiming that Cardigan was killed for example. Clearly many battery men were killed on the move trying to extricate the guns and 'a desperate hand to hand fight ensued' the officer claimed, admitting it 'was at great cost'. His report records 'one officer, 32 crew numbers and many riding and draft artillery horses' were lost.[6]

Lancer Lieutenant Koribut Kubitovich had watched the seemingly irresistible progress of the British cavalry from the Kadikoi Heights with increasing anxiety. 'Nothing could stop the Englishmen,' he recalled:

Not canister fire that wiped out entire files of soldiers, nor the bullets that flew about them like flies. The Don Cossack gunners saw that there was no time to save their guns, and withdrew in order to save themselves. But the enemy rode on at their backs and cut them down without mercy.

Lieutenant Stefan Kozhukhov with the guns of the 12th Artillery Brigade, on the high ground near the Tractir bridge, covering the far end of the North Valley gorge, had a grandstand view: 'Once through the guns the enemy moved quickly and bravely at a gallop towards our cavalry.' After the debacle at the hands of the Heavy Brigade that morning, there was reluctance to confront these new mad Englishmen. Swarms of British cavalry emerging from the smoke covering the Don battery 'was so unexpected,' Kozhukhov admitted, 'that before anyone realised it, our cavalry had broken'.[7]

When Captain William Morris leading the remnants of the 17th Lancers emerged from the battery smoke at the head of about twenty men, he found himself confronted by two squadrons of motionless Russian cavalry. The Russians were just as surprised at their abrupt appearance, assuming no man could have survived a head-on rush against an artillery battery. 'Remember what I have told you,' the veteran cavalry commander shouted at his men, 'and keep together,' whereupon they launched themselves at the enemy. The Russians were psychologically unprepared for such a reaction. 'What happened then, say you?' asked 'Butcher Jack' Vahey rhetorically: 'They were round us like a swarm of bees, and we, not more seemingly than a couple of dozen of us to the fore, were hacking and hewing away our hardest!'

Morris transfixed the lead Russian squadron commander riding full tilt at 'the point'. The sword blade protruded halfway beyond the man's back. Locked in muscle and bone, the Russian's body weight pulled Morris from his horse, dragging him down to almost ground level. As he sought to extricate the blade, a Russian sabre cut sliced away a substantial piece of bone above the left ear; the next slash dug into the top of his head, penetrating both skull plates and splitting his forage cap in half at the peak. He fell momentarily senseless from the saddle, which released his sword. Several Russians jabbed at him with lances, but he kept them at bay by whirling his sword about, cutting some in the thigh. A lance point stuck in his temple, splintering bone, and only the actions of a chivalrous Russian officer, striking up Cossack lances, saved him from further injury and induced him to surrender. Once the officer rode off the Cossacks plundered his possessions, clearly intending to finish him off. Somehow in all the confusion Morris managed to lose them in the smoke cloud. Nobody pursued, his wounds looked mortal.[8]

Vahey remembered each man at 'the centre of a separate melee'. His whirling butcher's axe bit flesh here and there and intimidated 'the Russkies' who 'gave ground a bit, only to crush denser round me a minute after'. He had a charmed life: 'They dursn't come to close quarters with the sword for the axe had a devil of a long reach; and they dursn't use pistols, for they were too thick themselves.'

Two groups of English cavalry had charged beyond the battery smoke, straight into the assembled but unprepared Russian cavalry. 'Beyond the guns,' Private Joseph Grigg remembered, 'the Russian cavalry, who should have come out to prevent our getting near the gunners, were coming down upon us howling wildly, and we went at them with a rush.'[9]

'It was the maddest thing that was ever done,' Russian Hussar officer Ivan Ivanovich, who had been wounded in the Heavy Brigade charge that morning, remembered. 'They broke through our lines, took our artillery, and then, instead of capturing our guns and making off with them, they went for us.' It was an intimidating charge; 'they came on magnificently,' he recalled, thinking they had to be drunk because they were even brandishing lances in the air like spears in their frenzy. 'The men were mad sir,' he explained, 'they dashed in among us, shouting, cheering and cursing. I never saw anything like it.' Lieutenant Kubitovich watched the Russian cavalry squadrons behind the guns unravel:

They panicked and wheeled to their left to escape. Some of the men fired on their own comrades to clear a passage for themselves.

In their flight the Cossacks rode straight into the regiment that was supporting the guns, and caused great mayhem, and this regiment fell back on the next.

It was hysteria. 'Chaos', artillery Lieutenant Kozhukhov agreed: 'our cavalry outnumbered the enemy five times over, and yet it fell back in total disorder to the [River] Chernya, with the English coming hotly forward at the hooves of our horses.' 11th Hussar Troop Sergeant Major George Smith even recalled seeing 'one of their leading Cossacks fall from the bridge, there being no parapet'. The mass of cavalry was so compressed in front of the narrow Tractir bridge that both bodies of horsemen came to an involuntary halt. 'Here and there inside this great mass, were the English,' Kozhukhov recalled, 'probably as surprised as ourselves at this unexpected circumstance.' 'Our fellows were quite demoralised,' Ivanovich remembered, but the pause signalled the impasse was over. The face-off revealed the gross disparity of English numbers in the puny pursuing force. Russian officers reasserted control; there could now only be one outcome. Vahey, in the thick of the congestion at the end of the North Valley, heard 'above the din a trumpet somewhere far in the rear sound *Threes About*'. The hunters were about to become the hunted.[10]

Onlookers, clinically detached from the viscera in the valley below, realised they had witnessed a remarkable event. Less than 600 British cavalry had charged the length of the North Valley and bottled up an apparent mass of Russian cavalry at the far end. 'We could scarcely believe in the evidence of our senses!' war correspondent 'Billy' Russell on the Sapoune Heights remembered. 'Surely that handful of men are not going to charge an army in position.' But they had. The Light Brigade had been subjected to withering artillery and musket fire from three directions, for seven minutes, charging headlong into an eight-gun battery. Artillery Lieutenant Stefan Kozhukhov was deeply impressed: 'The English chose to do what we had not considered, because no one imagined it possible,' and had put the Russian cavalry to flight again. 'These mad cavalrymen were intent on doing what no one thought could be done,' he concluded. 'A more fear-ful spectacle was never witnessed,' Russell claimed in his subsequent dispatch. The Russian commander General Liprandi described it as 'a most obstinate charge', only explicable, he suspected, because the English had been plied with drink; a view shared by Russian cavalry commander Ryzhov, who sought to justify the dismal performance of his men.

'Every man's heart on that hill side beat high,' recalled Sergeant Timothy Gowing, watching from the Heights. It was an iconic spec-tacle that would stand in history. 'The excitement was beyond my pen to express,' he admitted. Cavalry stock among the infantry was high again: 'Big briny tears gushed down more than one man's face that had resolutely stormed the Alma. To see their countrymen rush-ing at a fearful pace right into the jaw's death was a most exciting scene to stand and witness!'

Russell's claims of 'a halo of flashing steel above their heads' as they reached the battery are inflated. Such detail was not visible at that distance, but it was clear the British cavalry had ridden through and gone beyond the guns. This epic in the making had yet to be immor-talised in Tennyson's verse. However, apart from it being remarkable, nobody on the Heights or in the chaos of the valley below could really work out what was happening.[11]

As Lord George Paget's third wave hit the Don battery he remem-bered 'the first objects that caught my eyes were some of these guns, in the act of endeavouring to get away from us.' He had nearly caught up with the 11th Hussars in the second wave, of whom forty to sixty had passed to the left of the guns without even engaging them. Colonel Douglas, their commander, spotted Russian cavalry beyond and bore down on them, following Captain Morris's small 17th Lancer group of about twenty up ahead. Another band to their right under Colonel Mayow, the brigade second in command, was also pursuing the Russian cavalry with thirty or so men from the first wave. Two groups of British survivors were coalescing at the far end of North Valley. One group was mauling the gun battery while the second had taken up the pursuit of the Russian cavalry beyond. Paget, still intent on closely supporting Lord Cardigan, was looking for him, as were the regimental commanders. 'We are in a desperate scrape,' Paget remarked to an embattled Captain Low fighting alongside; 'What the devil shall we do? Has anyone seen Lord Cardigan?'

As the second and third waves were crashing into the battery, one officer and six soldiers from the 8th Hussars and 4th Light Dragoons saw him cantering back, even before they had reached the guns. Private Albert Mitchell had gone down with the 13th just short of the battery, narrowly escaping being trampled by subsequent waves. Mitchell was accosted by Cardigan as he made his way back on foot. 'Where is your horse?' he was sternly asked. 'Killed, my Lord,' he responded. 'You had better make the best of your way back as fast as you can go, or you will be taken prisoner,' he said as he rode off, leaving him to his fate. Cardigan made no attempt to rally his men or tell them what to do on reaching the guns.[12]

Wellington had time and again been frustrated by the 'derring-do' of his cavalry during the Napoleonic Wars. They had often overreached themselves on blown horses, such as at the celebrated charge of his Heavy Brigades at Waterloo, and then suffered the consequences. Raglan had carefully husbanded his cavalry throughout the Crimean campaign thus far, and now the Light Brigade appeared to have dashed itself to pieces at the end of the North Valley. The charge had overextended itself, with remarkable results. The rush at the Russian cavalry at the gorge end of the valley was not totally impetuous. The men had every reason to anticipate they were closely supported by the Heavy Brigade, whose arrival was anticipated at any moment. Then 'to our horror' Captain Edwin Cook with the second 11th Hussar wave realised, 'the Heavy Brigade had not followed'. It was a psychological tipping point. 'Seeing there were so few of us, and without supports,' Troop Sergeant Smith facing the Russian cavalry at the end of the valley recalled, 'they turned about.' It was a tense stand-off, because 'we sat face to face, our horse's heads close to theirs.' There was a lot of involuntary counting. 'The stillness and suspense during those moments was terrible,' Smith remembered. It was broken by Russian officers urging their men forward with pistol shots as 'the Cossacks began to double round our flanks and get in the rear'. The moment had passed. 'Had a few more of our squadrons came up at this time, I am of the opinion that this body of cavalry would have surrendered to us,' Smith claimed. Another 17th Lancer officer echoed Smith's opinion: 'It was a bitter moment after we broke through the line of cavalry in rear of their guns, when I looked round and saw there was no support beyond our own brigade.'

Backward-looking troopers could only see the debris of their advance and bedraggled groups of wounded making their way back on foot, amid riderless horses and dispersing smoke. 'When I saw them form four deep,' the officer admitted, 'I knew it was all up.' He called upon his men to rally.[13]

A withdrawal in contact with the enemy is the most difficult phase of war. Private Edward Firkins with the 13th 'could not see three men of our regiment' and in breaking clean 'saw two Russian lancers coming towards me with clenched teeth and staring like savages'. He struck down one heavy Cossack lance, following up with a thrust 'through the fellow's neck'. 'He fell from his horse with a groan,' but the shock of the momentum 'nearly brought me from my saddle'. As the other Cossack wheeled around his dying comrade and thrust at him with his lance, 'I had not the strength to strike down the blow.' His sword slipped from his grasp just as a British lancer 'thrust his lance clean through the fellow's body'. Private James Wightman saw Corporal Morley, long hair streaming in the wind, rallying 17th Lancers still inside the battery. 'Coom 'ere! coom'ere!' he shouted with his broad accent, 'Fall in, lads, fall in!' Twenty or so troopers attracted to the stream of invective and oaths rallied around him and they went through a body of encircling Russian hussars 'as if they were made of tinsel paper'.[14]

THE RETREAT

Four British groups were now rallying left and right of the valley. On the west side were two groups led by Colonel Paget and Douglas, while to the east there were remnants led by Colonel Mayow and Shewell. 'Halt, front,' Paget had shouted. 'If you don't boys, we are done.' This was the genesis of his group, momentarily checking Russians trying to recover the battery from the north. He then heard a cry: 'they are attacking us, my Lord, in our rear!' A large body of Russian lancers was forming across their direct line of retreat. 'Threes about,' he ordered, adding, 'we must do the best we can for ourselves.' Pursued by Russians in their rear, 'helter-skelter then we went at these lancers,' Paget recalled. With blown horses, they had now to run the gauntlet through the 'Valley of Death' again in reverse. As the four groups headed home, they found the valley filling with increasing numbers of Russian horse. In between the four bands were other smaller parties of men and knots of desperate stragglers, all part of a developing epic odyssey to get back to the British lines.

Only a few of Corporal Morley's small contingent made it back. James Wightman's injured horse finally went down 'riddled with bullets'; he was shot in the forehead and through the top of his shoulder. Pinned beneath the horse, Cossacks closed in to finish him off. 'Those vermin are always prowling about and act independently,' remembered one soldier. The retreating remnants were an attractive target for the irregular Russian cavalry, on the lookout for loot. Private William Pennington with the 11th had already seen them 'lancing our dismounted men'. 'The demons,' he recalled with some venom, 'give no quarter when you are down.' Anybody unhorsed was exposed. Private William Cullen with the same unit recalled going 'through the crossfire to reach our lines, and on my way I saw poor Bob Lazell lying wounded with his horse beside him and several Cossacks murdering him'. The helpless Wightman had few illusions about what to expect: 'While struggling out from under my dead horse a Cossack standing over me stabbed me with his lance once in the neck near the jugular, again above the collar bone, several times in the back, and once under the short rib.'

He was still alive, taken prisoner and 'very roughly used'. The Cossacks dragged him along by the tail of his coat until he gained his feet, and then brutally prodded him along with lance butts. With his shattered knee, numerous wounds and a bullet to the shin, 'I could barely limp.' His friend Fletcher, unhorsed at the same time, managed to save him. 'Get on my back chum!' Wightman was urged, only to find when he climbed aboard that Fletcher had a gaping bullet wound at the back of his head. 'Oh never mind that,' he assured him, 'it's not much, I don't think.' Wightman was immensely moved by his unselfish behaviour, suspecting the hideous wound was probably fatal. 'Here he was,' he recalled with admiration, 'a doomed man himself, making light of a mortal wound, and carrying a chance comrade of another regiment on his back.'[15]

Russian Lieutenant Yevgenii Arbuzov's regiment of Ingermanland Hussars had been worsted twice that morning by British cavalry: first by the Heavy Brigade, and again by the impetuous Light Brigade attack beyond the guns. 'We were overturned since we were standing with an extended front,' he explained, 'and so forced to retreat to the canal [Tractir bridge] whether we wanted to or not.' Looking up the valley: 'With no breeze blowing at all, between the hills there was a dense cloud of gunpowder smoke and dust raised by the galloping cavalry, so impenetrable that nothing could be observed even at close distances to oneself.'

On the high ground to his left between redoubts 2 and 3 he saw with mounting satisfaction Colonel Yeropkin's Composite Lancer Regiment emerging from the brush-covered slopes to attack the withdrawing British cavalry in the right flank. On the valley floor 'the Ural men and Hussars turned around and charged the English to the front.' English survivors would have to re-run the gauntlet of Russian fire back the way they had come. 'Almost all were hit,' he claimed, 'and no more than ten or twelve men were able to return back and save themselves.'

The order to attack the withdrawing enemy 'made us happy' remembered Lieutenant Koribut Kubitovich, commanding Yeropkin's 2nd Squadron. His newly trained recruits had been itching to get into action all day, after being checked earlier that morning from intervening in the Heavy Brigade fight. 'We were finally getting our turn,' he recalled; 'from being just onlookers we were active participants.' It was not an auspicious start, because they were fired upon by a battalion square of nervous Odessa infantry. 'We cried out with all our might,' he recalled with frustration, 'so that they would see their mistake, but they did not stop shooting.' The Odessa regiments had witnessed many unexpected cavalry actions that day and were taking no chances. Three of Kubitovich's horses went down with two men wounded; nevertheless, they reached the valley floor and began to deploy to block it in extended line. They were nervous. 'Justice must be done to the Englishmen,' he admitted. 'This was not a flying retreat'; they may have been wounded, but they could still bite. When the English approached, they exuded 'the peak of perfection at a trot and in good order, as if on an exercise'. The new recruits felt queasy.

Lieutenant Colonel Shewell heading the approaching 8th Hussar survivors was still the dispassionate and intense disciplinarian. On the order 'form threes' to break through, Sergeant Reilly was chewed out for being out of place. But according to one of the other troopers, Reilly's 'eyes were fixed and staring, and his face as rigid and white as a flagstone'. Reilly was dead in the saddle, unnoticed by the others, when his horse tagged alongside and joined the formation. His fate paralleled the hapless Sergeant Williams, whom Shewell had arrested at the start line for smoking. Having been disarmed he was caught up in the charge and defenceless when he reached the battery, where he was promptly surrounded and cut down by Russian gunners. '*Threes about!*' Shewell shouted in response to the new threat, 'and the 8th responded as if on home parade', recalled William Pennington. The colonel was no swordsman; he simply put his head down, gripped both reins and rode directly at the Russian commander ahead.[16]

Captain Verzhbitskii's squadron hit the British first, followed successively by Kubitovich and then the 3rd Squadron under Major Lavrenius. One lone Russian, Cornet Astaf'ev, recklessly tore into the British line ahead and was cut down. 'The enemy was stunned by our appearance,' Kubitovich claimed, as they plunged into their flank, 'which was completely unexpected by them, and a desperate slashing fight ensued.' 'Of course with our handful, it was life or death,' Private Pennington recalled, 'so we rushed at them to break through.' One trooper likened the desperate slashing and hacking to 'cutting through a thickset hedge with a billhook'. Pennington fought 'with the determination of one who would not lose his life', snapping off lances and 'occasionally catching one a slap with the sword across his teeth, and giving another the point on his arm or breast'. Lieutenant Edward Seager with the group, with his wife and child's portrait in his sabretache, severely cut a Russian over the head and then narrowly escaped a massive lance thrust that snagged against the bars of his sword hilt. It took the skin off the top of the knuckle of his second finger, which was the only wound he suffered in the battle.

The group burst clear of the Russians and emerged in the open where it was 'severely peppered in grand style' by Russian artillery again, losing a great number of men and horses. They dispersed 'in a scattered manner', Seager recalled, 'so as not to give them so great a chance of killing us'. Jemmy the terrier kept up, panting alongside, despite a slight neck wound. On riding to the right, they benefitted from the neutralised fire zone that the audacious French Chasseur attack against the Fedioukine Heights had created. 'Through all this fire I returned,' Seager remembered, 'sometimes galloping and sometimes walking my horse.'[17]

Part of their luck, Kubitovich pointed out, came from Russian artillery and infantry fire from the Causeway Heights, which was indiscriminately sweeping the valley floor below, 'so that a large part of our own horses were wounded and killed by our own bullets'.

It had not been easy, but the British column 'was almost completely destroyed, and there were only a few of the enemy who returned to their camp'. His own recruits were chastened: 'The Englishmen fought with amazing bravery, and even the unhorsed and wounded did not want to surrender and continued to fight back, as they say, to the last drop of blood.'

His men were relieved it was over and they remained 'stood in extended line' across the valley, 'awaiting the order to dismount, supposing that we were all done with the enemy.'

'I say Colonel,' one of Lord George Paget's retreating group of lancers asked him, 'are you sure those are not the 17th?' They were the next group of Englishmen to ride up. 'Look at the colour of their flags,' Paget responded dismissively. 'When we first saw them, the formation of the lancers in our rear appeared to be that of a contiguous column,' he remembered. To their front was a compact body of Russians, two to three squadrons deep. The only option was to attack and break through, 'we being little more than a rabble of 60 to 70 men'. Paget ordered his men to 'front to the left' but his voice did not carry across the din of artillery and musket fire, so the best they managed was to 'edge away to the left'. Bizarrely, the Russians appeared not to decisively react. As Paget's group closed 'they came down on us at a sort of trot', not purposefully, and then paused, 'evincing that same air of bewilderment' he had seen opposite the Heavy Brigade that morning. Paget did not hesitate.

Yeropkin's lancers appreciated the approaching dust cloud signified 'a mass of cavalry' but 'it was too far back to be able to make out whether it was our own or the enemy'. Kubitovich saw they were 'hussars in black pelisses' looking 'just like our Leuchtenbergers', confirmed by a Russian staff officer, who had just rode up. He agreed that they were reinforcements. It was only when the horsemen were upon them that 'we saw our suppositions were mistaken,' Kubitovich admitted; 'it was another enemy column retreating in the footsteps of the first.'

Paget bulldozed ahead, bouncing off the Russian right flank, as they sought to edge past. The Russians 'did nothing', he recalled, which was totally unexpected. They 'actually allowed us to shuffle, to edge away, by them, at a distance of hardly a horse's length'. There was no check in the pace, the British simply flowed on. 'I can only say,' Paget remembered, 'if the point of my sword crossed the ends of three or four of their lances, it was as much as I did … Well, we got by them without I believe, the loss of a single man – how, I know not!'

The Russians were nonplussed. 'The loss of the right instant is absolutely irrecoverable' during a fast-moving cavalry engagement, Kubitovich recalled, and 'we lost such a favourable moment'. If they had charged they could have driven the English into the path of the pursuing Russian Hussars. 'Now it was already too late'. They had been completely wrong-footed.

Private James Herbert with the 4th Dragoons group saw Russian officers waving swords to get the lancers to hem them in from the flanks, 'but they seemed to me either to be afraid to move, or not to know what their officers were driving at.' They were thankful; 'it was of course a disgraceful thing that they allowed a single man of us' on 'utterly winded, and distressed horses' to 'get back again down the valley'. The British took no chances and as Herbert recalled, 'rushed in amongst them, cutting, slashing, pointing, and parrying'. 'There was no fancy work,' he commented, 'just hard useful business.' Nothing was going to stop them getting home. Paget was as contemptuous as he was incredulous: 'It is a mystery to me! Had that force been composed of English *ladies*, I don't think one of us could have escaped.'[18]

Contrary to the Russian claims of a desperate fight, there was no immediate pursuit. 'They knew too well the sort of reception they would share with us,' Paget claimed. The first engagement for Yeropkin's recently trained recruits had been painful. They felt intimidated at the second British approach and were placed on the back foot with a maldeployment by unalert or inexperienced officers. The opportunity was missed.

The British ordeal was still far from over because as Paget appreciated, 'they had a ride of a mile or more before us,' picking their way across the Via Dolorosa of the original advance:

And what a scene of havoc was this last mile, strewn with the dead and dying, and all friends! Some running, some limping, some crawling; horses in every position of agony struggling to get up, then floundering again on their mutilated riders!

Private Edward Woodham with the 11th had been unhorsed and was running back when he heard a plaintive cry from an 8th Hussar trooper pinned beneath his horse. 'For God's sake man, don't leave me here,' he appealed. Woodham recalled they were still under 'murderous' fire, because 'at this time the firing from the guns was incessant'. He pulled and tugged but could not release the man from under the dead weight. He saw 'the enemy at this time coming up the valley, and killing the wounded on their march'. Reluctantly he decided to leave him. 'The poor fellow said something in reply, but I don't recollect it now.' He would probably not wish to. He caught a free-running 17th Lancer horse and made his way out of the valley, which 'presented a fearful scene at this time. Our poor fellows lay moaning and groaning everywhere.' 'It's no use my stopping here,' he appealed to the trooper he abandoned. 'We shall both be killed.'

Cornet Edward Phillips with the 8th had been unhorsed. Delirious and exhausted as he moved back, he came upon another mount standing by his dead or dying master. The saddle, however, was upside down and 'what with the excitement and running for one's life, I was so done, that I had not the strength to right it.' He released the girths and standing on the discarded saddle managed to mount bare-back; 'never was I so happy as when I felt a horse under me again.' He remembered, 'I passed lots of poor fellows wounded or dying, and after an anxious gallop of nearly a mile, at last got out of fire.'

Paget overtook Captain Thomas Hutton, who had been shot through the thigh before reaching the guns. His squadron commander Captain Low had told him: 'If you can sit on your horse, you had better come on with us, there's no use going back now, you'll only be killed.'

Hutton reached the guns and in the melee was shot through the other thigh while his horse was hit eleven times. Paget saw he was hurt and faint and passed over his rum flask. 'I have been wounded Colonel,' Hutton quietly informed him; 'would you have any objection to my going to the doctor when I get in?' Hutton did get back but his horse had to be destroyed on arrival.[19]

After Cardigan left him, Albert Mitchell trudged on through a recently cultivated strip of farmland, which made very heavy going. He felt that everyone else seemed to be getting rescued by retreating stray horsemen except for him. Whenever a group of stragglers banded together, Russian batteries on the Causeway Heights sent a shell their way. Mitchell eventually came across an abandoned trooper, standing alone. 'Is that an Englishman?' came a plaintive appeal. The man, bleeding profusely from the head, had been blinded by shrapnel, which had hit him between the eyes. Mitchell bound him up with a handkerchief and took him along. Before long they came across a man that had been shot out of his saddle on his left during the charge. He lay on his back, 'labouring very hard for breath', with a wound that appeared terminal: 'Every breath he drew brought up a quantity of blood, which as he lay on his back, he could not clear from his mouth, and was almost choking.'

He turned him over and placed his arm beneath his forehead to clear the blood from his airway. 'I could see death in his countenance,' Mitchell observed, so they left him. When they came level with redoubt 4, to their relief, a British infantry officer from the 68th Light Regiment appeared. 'Have you a drop of water, sir, if you please, you can give this man?' he respectfully asked him. They did better, and readily offered a cup of half water and rum. His wounded companion greedily downed 'a good half', with Mitchell noticing how much his 'moustache and mouth being covered with blood had dipped into it'. But he was not squeamish; 'I emptied the cup,' he recalled.

Cornet Denzil Chamberlayne with the 13th walked almost the entire length of the valley with his saddle on his head. His beloved horse Pimento had been killed during the charge and Lieutenant Percy Smith found him sitting beside the carcass. Chamberlayne asked what he should do. 'Another horse you can get,' Smith told him, 'but you will not get another saddle and bridle so easily.' At this the young cornet hefted the equipment onto his head and walked back. He was ignored by Cossacks looting and murdering the wounded on the way, because he looked like another one of them.[20]

Lord Cardigan was among the first to get back, and rode in alone. He studiously ignored Lord Lucan, who watched him pass 200 yards away. Later Captain Lockwood, Cardigan's Aide-de-Camp, rode up to the staff group and asked, 'My Lord, can you tell me where is Lord Cardigan?' Lucan replied he had just passed but Lockwood misinterpreted the direction, assuming he meant he was still down the valley at the guns. He rode off urgently to locate him and was never seen again.

Exhausted and bleeding men stumbled in, each group greeted with cheers and handshakes. On the Sapoune Heights Fanny Duberly, having lost sight of what was going on in all the smoke and dust, noticed the small groups coming back. 'What can those skirmishers be doing?' she asked, 'see they form up together again.' 'Good God!' she exclaimed when the realisation dawned, 'it is the Light Brigade!' The unhappy 'Heavies', racked with guilt at having denied their support, gloomily watched them pass by. They came 'by one's and two's' recalled a witness; 'such a smash was never seen.' A wounded horse cantered by, adding to the poignant scene, with its broken hind leg swinging round and round.[21]

Cardigan, on hearing the 'Heavies' cheer the return of Mayow's and Shewell's groups, positioned himself at the front of the rally line, so as to lead them in at the walk. Behind his back Mayow was seen shaking his head and indicating Cardigan, clearly disgusted. Many troopers in the second and third waves of the charge had seen him heading back alone into the smoke around the guns, getting back well before them. Men pointed him out making jeering signs to the Heavies with muttered oaths that suggested the Brigade Commander may not even had been at the guns. Cardigan self-importantly smiled and waved his sword, blissfully unaware of the ridicule behind, acknowledging cheers that were actually for the benefit of the 8th survivors. All this was acutely embarrassing to the onlookers. Trumpeter James

Donoghue with the 8th remembered that 'after the battle I heard of the fact of Lord Cardigan going back much spoken of and commented upon by the men in the regiment.' There was elation they survived and indignation that the Heavy Brigade had not supported them. 'And who, I ask, was answerable for all this?' reminisced Troop Sergeant Major George Smith with the 11th Hussars. They were a 'forlorn hope' left to fend for themselves after taking the guns: 'We cut their army completely in two, taking their principal battery, driving their cavalry far to the rear. What more could 670 men do?'

All Cardigan had to say when he eventually deigned to approach Lord Lucan was to admonish Captain Nolan 'in a very vehement manner' for 'insubordination' for placing himself in front of his squadrons, 'and his gross misconduct in shrieking and turning away'. Perplexed, Lucan recalled having 'difficulty in making him understand' that Nolan's screams 'had been occasioned by his being shot through the heart'. Dissatisfied, Cardigan rode across to Brigadier General Scarlett, his fellow Heavy Brigade commander, and continued the tirade, still in Lucan's hearing, of what Scarlett thought of Nolan 'riding to the rear and screaming like a woman'. 'Do not say any more,' Scarlett hushed him, 'for I have ridden over his body.'[22]

Lord George Paget finally rode up on his wounded horse recalling 'the shouts of welcome' that greeted every returning officer or group, struggling up the incline, 'telling us of our safety'. He reported to Cardigan that he could not account for any survivors of the first wave, until with relief he saw a cluster of 13th and 17th troopers 'standing by their horses, on the brow of the hill, in my front'. Cardigan ordered the first count by the Brigade Major, who reported 195 mounted men out of about 670. His men managed to raise three cheers. 'This is a great blunder,' Cardigan responded defensively, 'but no fault of mine.' 'My Lord,' replied one of the troopers, 'we are ready to go back again.' Cornet George Wombwell's letter home that night was more honest: 'I want to see no more fighting, it has pleased God to keep me safe through what I have seen, and I am now anxious to get home.'[23]

The whole affair had lasted little more than twenty minutes.

9

STAND-OFF

11.35 A.M. TO MIDNIGHT

POSTURING

11.35 A.M. TO 6.20 P.M.

'At 35 minutes past eleven,' reported war correspondent William Russell, 'not a British soldier except the dead and dying, was left in front of these Muscovite guns.' Ten minutes later he watched as seven of the nine captured British cannon – the whole point of the charge – were taken away. 'There is no concealing the thing,' concluded a 17th Lancer officer. 'The Light Brigade was greatly damaged, and for nothing!'[1]

Captain William Morris's group of twenty or so 17th Lancers, that attacked beyond the guns, was virtually annihilated. Hacked about the head to the bone, Morris managed to grab a passing saddle when he blindly stumbled into thick smoke. The horse dragged him along some distance before he lost his grip. Picking himself up he mounted another loose horse and managed to elude predatory Cossacks in the smoke and confusion. When he cleared the smoke, he came under tremendous crossfire in the open and his horse was felled again, pinning him beneath, where he lost consciousness. Later, after considerable effort, he freed his leg and wobbled off on foot. Sergeant Major Loy Smith briefly glimpsed him passing by, recalling, 'his face was covered in blood and he had a very wild appearance.' Smith did not rate his survival chances at all. Morris exhausted himself by his efforts and sank to the ground. Nearby was the body of his friend Captain Nolan, signifying he had almost made it back. Captain Ewart, Raglan's ADC, came across him, having been warned by survivors that there was a severely wounded officer lying further back. Morris was 'almost insensible', he remembered, bespattered in blood still flowing from his grievous head wounds. Surgeon James Mowatt came up and roughly bound Morris's head, over-watched by Sergeant Charles Wooden. Between them, they managed to keep the Cossacks at bay, for which both were awarded the Victoria Cross.

Captain Nolan's body was recovered by artillery Captain Brandling, who, with five accompanying gunners, rolled him into a hastily scraped shallow grave. It was a hurried affair, conducted under fire. Nolan had been one of the first to be killed in the charge. One of the bombardiers observed 'the poor fellow's chest had been quite broken away', torn apart with his heart exposed. The gold lace and cloth on his jacket was 'very much burnt by the shell which killed him, and which must have burst close by'. Lucan was unsympathetic. 'He met his deserts [sic] – a dog's death,' he insisted, 'and like a dog let him be buried in a ditch.' Nolan and Morris had been close friends; Nolan's letter to his mother was found on Morris, and a letter written by Morris to his wife Amelia was discovered in Nolan's sabretache. Both letters were sent on to England because it was assumed Morris was unlikely to survive. Nolan's pauper's grave was probably near redoubt number 4, but his remains were never recovered.

Lord Raglan was white with anger when he confronted Cardigan. 'What do you mean, sir, by attacking a battery in front, contrary to all the usages of warfare?' he demanded. Russell noticed that 'he shook his head as he spoke, and jerked the armless sleeve of his coat.' Cardigan, unperturbed, blandly responded, 'My Lord, I hope you will not blame me,' disingenuously remarking, 'I received the order to attack from my superior officer in front of the troops.' Lucan later attempted to explain, but was met with the cold, and not unexpected accusation, that 'you have lost the Light Brigade!'[2]

There is some controversy about the numbers who rode, varying between 666 to 676 and casualties. The most reliable figures based on returns made the following day reveal 271 killed and wounded with 32 taken prisoner. Remarkably, and contrary to Tennyson's later epic verse, 395 men, or 60 per cent of the brigade, made the epic ride 1¼ miles down the valley unscathed. They were fired at from three sides, attacked and pursued superior numbers of Russian cavalry and retired under fire again, losing just 17 per cent of their men. The brigade was rendered ineffective because they lost 375 horses or 56 per cent of their mounted strength. In all, 75 per cent of the officers and men that rode were untouched or recovered from their wounds. Cardigan had 195 men still mounted just after the charge. The ensuing winter, not Russians, destroyed the brigade's irreplaceable mounts, more difficult to replace than men.[3]

The Light Brigade was, however, badly mauled, with even deeper psychological and emotional damage. Wounded men were left behind. Robert Duke with the 13th Light Dragoons was wounded fourteen times, in the head, two sword cuts to the knee, a gunshot wound to his right wrist and ten lance stab wounds on his arms and torso. Fragmentary survivor reports give some clue how traumatic the experience on the valley floor must have been. Nurse Sarah Anne Terrot at Scutari was so affected by the experiences she heard that she wrote some down. Nearly all were young men and mostly hit by cannon fire. One provided a snapshot of his experience:

Ward in front of me was blown to pieces. Turner on my left had his right arm blown off, and afterwards died, and Young on my right also had his right arm blown off. Just then my right arm was shattered to pieces. I gathered it together as well I could, and laid it across my knees.[4]

When Lieutenant Seager with the 8th Hussars got back, he 'found the remains of the regiment collecting gradually and counting over the missing'. They had lost twenty-seven killed, seventeen wounded and thirty-eight horses killed. 'The Light Brigade is now a skeleton,' he recalled, 'as all the regiments suffered more or less.' Survivors 'shook hands and congratulated each other on escaping'. He sat with five men on the grass 'and fared sumptuously on salt pork and biscuits, washed down by rations of rum'. Many men had not eaten for twenty-seven hours. Albert Mitchell got his blind companion back and into the back of a wagon. He was discharged blind, with a shilling per day pension, and unexpectedly later regained his sight. Mitchell found his tent and 'soon dived into the biscuit bag', chewing his way back to the start line where the regiment was gathering. Only thirteen of them were still mounted.

Psychological post-combat stress disorder soon set in. Sergeant Major George Smith got back to his tent and shook hands with the orderly room clerk he shared it with. 'How glad I am you have escaped George,' the clerk said. Smith told him, 'I had lost my beautiful horse'; they had been inseparable for three years. 'What is this on your busby and jacket?' the clerk asked him while he was explaining 'how fearfully the regiment had been cut up'. They found he was peppered with small pieces of meat. 'On picking it off I found it to be small pieces of flesh that had flown over me when Private Young's arm had been shot off.' Smith sat down, admitting that the 'feelings that came over me are not easy to describe' and as memories of what he had endured in the valley came flooding back, he wept.[5]

One 5th Dragoon bandsman acting as a medical assistant wrote down snatched survivor conversations from the men that returned – 'all of them wounded, little or more,' he recalled, 'others cut and mutilated in a shocking manner.' Some came in without horses and often horses without riders. Dead men toppled from the saddle while other horses sank to the ground and expired on arrival in the midst of the survivors. The bandsman remembered men reminiscing about lucky escapes:

> Bill, did you see my poor mare shot? Ah poor beast, I was so sorry. My poor horse had [its belly] shot right away by a cannon ball, but I saw Jack so-and-so shot dead, so I took his horse and I mounted him, when both its hind legs were taken away by another shot.

Men unloaded distress among friends with like experiences, a common occurrence among veterans after a hard-fought engagement. Combat stress was neither recognised nor acknowledged at the time. Distant Napoleonic war memories evinced a certain 'craziness' and odd behaviour after battles, which remained untreated.

The bandsman, in aprons covered with dirt and gore, treated 'frightful looking articles' on their stretchers. 'Oh it was dreadful to look on,' another witness recalled. 'It was our turn next to attack them – there they stood and there we stood facing them.' All were agreed: 'great damage' would have been inflicted on them if the Russians had reacted differently on reaching the guns, 'but their soft hearts failed them'. 'Damned Cossacks got around me,' described another survivor:

> But I managed to send two of them to pay their reckoning with the loss of their heads. At least one, the ★★★★ made a slapping cut at me, and took away my trotters, so I must hop to old England with a wooden leg. No matter doctor, I shall soon be well.

There would be future difficulties for these men, unemployment and the workhouse beckoned for the unfortunate, and social rejection for others unable to fend for themselves. 'That was the sort of conversation,' the bandsman explained, 'these brave fellows were using in front of death.'

Fanny Duberly recalled 'many had a sad tale to tell' when she rode down with her husband to see how the regiment had fared. Although the 8th Hussars had been in the second line, 'all had been struck with the exception of Colonel Shewell, either themselves or their horses.' Some of the men thought her morbid fascination with death to be a little vulture-like for their liking; they had lost twenty-eight killed and nineteen wounded.

> Poor Lord Fitzgibbon was dead. Of Captain Lockwood no tidings had been heard; none had seen him fall, and none had seen him since the action. Mr Clutterbuck was wounded in the foot; Mr Seager in the hand. Captain Tomkinson's horse had been shot under him; Major De Salis's horse wounded. Mr Musenden showed me a grapeshot which had 'killed my poor mare'. Mr Clawes was a prisoner. Poor Captain Goad, of the 13th, is dead. Ah what a [catalogue]!

These were friends and acquaintances of seven years' standing in the Duberly regimental family community. Her maid, Mrs Letitia Finnegan, lost her husband Francis, serving in the regiment.[6]

Private Christopher Fox, the inveterate hardcase with the 4th Light Dragoons, got safely back but was re-arrested for leaving his post without orders. He was sentenced to fifty lashes.

'Butcher Jack' Vahey dropped off the wounded 11th Hussar man he saved and gave the detention tent a wide berth when he got back, and fortunately 'there was no notice taken of me,' he recalled. He too was re-arrested for breaking out of the guard tent. Vahey and his butcher's-axe exploits were to become something of a legend, but the cleaver may well have been a colourful exaggeration. Private Anthony Sheridan in later years certainly claimed to have seen him wearing a 'blood bespattered smock front', but Vahey's personal account likely played fast and loose with alleged facts. Sergeant Joseph Pardoe with the 1st Dragoons saw him briefly with the Heavy Brigade but does not recall an axe, claiming 'he had one sword in his hand, one in a scabbard buckled around his waist'. He did, however, look like a butcher with his rolled-up shirt sleeves.

Pardoe also heard from a 17th Lancer colleague that contrary to Vahey's account he 'was not seen or heard of for three days' after the charge and was assumed killed, before being discovered and arrested. 'When he found out by some means that he would be pardoned for breaking his arrest, he turned up.' Vahey, unlike Fox, was considered a bit of a character by the officers and well-liked, as well as being useful when sober. Lucan told him, 'he had a good mind to try me by court martial,' and deservedly so, 'but he would let me off this time, in consideration of the use I had made of the liberty I had taken.' The incorrigible Vahey was let off and promised by Lucan that 'perhaps he would do more for me if I kept sober'; in fact, he received a Distinguished Conduct Medal.[7]

Major General Cathcart's 4th Infantry Division came up on the British right moving south of the Causeway Heights. Afterwards, it began to advance steadily on the Russian-occupied former Turkish redoubts. Redoubt number 5 was found to be empty. It was only when they moved on that they discovered the cavalry had already conducted a charge on the other, blind side of the Causeway ridge. This was their first intimation of the tragedy. Lucan had been told to await the infantry, but Cathcart had not been informed by Raglan that he was supposed to support the cavalry. Massive thumps and bulbous clouds of smoke rising over redoubts 2 and 3 signified the Russians had blown the powder magazines as they retired further along the North Valley. On the other side of the valley the Duke of Cambridge's 1st Division was told to lie down to avoid the shot and shell being fired at them from the occupied redoubts further along the Causeway Heights. Three British scarlet lines remained along the Woronzov road. After the events of the hour before, both sides warily regarded each other as they decided what to do next.

At 12.28 p.m. Russell, observing from the Sapoune Heights, discerned a general Allied forward move, with the 4th Division edging along the Causeway Heights to the right and the 1st Division moving in echelon against the Fedioukine Heights on the left. Russian infantry slowly retired towards the gorge end of the North Valley and redoubt number 1 on Canrobert's Hill. This posturing by both sides was accompanied by intermittent exchanges of artillery fire. 'I cannot conceive a more splendid sight than what was witnessed during this afternoon,' remembered a Scots Greys officer: 'the two armies, the Russians being enormously strong, and our own, waiting for one or the other to advance, with an occasional shell by way of invitation or challenge.' He watched rifle-brigade sharpshooters creeping to within 300 yards of the Russian positions, where they lay 'on their bellies till a chance offers, when crack! goes a Minié, and down falls a Russian'.

There was a feeling the battle was over. The Russians held the more strategically important redoubts 1 to 3 and Cathcart's infantry, up all night in the trenches, and having to march down to the plain, were exhausted. He had no intention of mounting a costly assault on the remaining redoubts, some distance away, unless he was specifically ordered to do so. Raglan wanted to, but was dissuaded by the French, who considered further action to recapture the overextended line a diversion of experienced troops away from the greater imperative, which was to capture Sevastopol.

Russian artillery Lieutenant Kozhukhov, observing from the high ground near the gorge, also suspected the battle was over. The Cossacks on the valley floor below certainly did; 'when all this madness ended' he recalled, they had begun horse-trading and selling loot. 'They rounded up the English horses and right there opened up a horse market', attracting considerable interest. 'Valuable pure-blooded horses sold then for 3½ imperials, many for 4, and some could be had for even 2 or 1.' Now and again cannon boomed out across the desolate valley. 'We of course paid them back with the same coin,' a 5th Dragoon bandsman recalled, 'shot after shot; and there we stood, balls flying over our heads, as firm as if we feared no death.'

The Russians clearly hoped to attract British infantry assaults against the furthest three redoubts they held in force. 'We expected to have to storm them that night, but little did we know the extent of the reverse which had befallen our cavalry,' remembered a 4th Division infantry officer, 'which made our chiefs tired of fighting for the moment.' Despite losing the only metalled road between Balaclava and Sevastopol, the secondary track that led across the southern col to the Sapoune Heights was deemed sufficient for the moment. After all, Sevastopol would soon be ready to assault. The subsequent winter proved this premise false. Cannon fire petered out at 1.15 p.m., Russell reported, 'and the two armies retained their respective positions'. The battle was as good as over. 'Our men and horses alike tired and hungry,' he remembered, 'and the French were no better.' It was an impasse.[8]

Fifty-eight British cavalrymen were captured by the Russians in the valley, of which twenty-one would die of their wounds. Private John Dryden was surrounded by twenty Russian lancers and dragoons and repeatedly stabbed, and when he fell off his horse was stuck again and again and left for dead. About an hour later Cossacks on foot searching for loot found him and speared him again. Dryden 'made signs of life' but to no avail, 'they would not desist'. At nightfall he was picked up and slung on the back of a bullock cart. Remarkably, he survived capture. When examined by British surgeons on return he was found to have six sword wounds about the face and head and twenty-four lance thrusts, of which fifteen were in the trunk and spinal region. The equanimity with which men endured wounds is striking by modern standards. 'I had a pretty narrow escape,' Cornet George Clowes wrote to his father from Russian confinement, 'being hit hard in the back by a grape shot, but it only skimmed across, taking a few splinters of bone off my right shoulder blade.' 'However,' he reassured his parents, 'I am nearly all right now.'[9]

Private James Wightman with the 17th Lancers offers the only fully documented account of the experience of capture on the valley floor to eventual release a year later. Beaten while wounded and dragged by Cossacks, he was carried to safety on the back of mortally wounded Private Fletcher: 'When we reached the Chernya [River, at the end of the North Valley] the Russians were as kind to us as the Cossacks had been brutal before.' A Russian surgeon extracted a bullet from his knee and placed it on a window ledge. When his Russian guard picked it up, having been informed by sign language where it had come from, he spat on it and hurled it out of the window, exclaiming '*Sukin sin!*' ('Son of a bitch!').

The moment of capture is humiliating for the soldier, who is acutely vulnerable and from that moment on completely at the whim and mercy of his captors, for survival. Tension arose when a wounded Russian cavalryman sitting opposite Wightman, nursing two severe sword cuts across the head and minus three fingers, recognised Private John Bevin from the 8th Hussars as being responsible for the mess of his face. Bevin cheerfully owned up and pointing to the grisly fragment of the Russian's right ear, led him to understand 'it was he who had played the part of Saint Peter'. Thereupon, the two got on famously, with the embarrassed Bevin having 'to resort to much artifice to avoid being kissed by the battered Muscovite'.

General Liprandi put in an appearance according to Wightman, convinced these mad cavalrymen had to have been drunk, to attempt such a charge. Private William Kirk, an unwounded 17th Lancer who 'had been punishing the vodka a bit', assured him that 'if we had so much as smelt a barrel, we would have taken half Russia by this time!' Liprandi smiled at this apparent confirmation of his theory, until Sergeant Major Fowler of the 4th Light Dragoons rose in considerable pain from a corner. He 'had been run in the back by a Cossack lance' and admonished Kirk for his 'impertinent forwardness'. Coming to attention, the sergeant major assured Liprandi, 'except for the vodka that your men have given to some of them, there is not a man of us who had tasted food or drink this day.' Adding, they got 'a mouthful' of rum with the ration per day 'and, believe me, sir, we don't hoard it'. Wightman thought Fowler 'a fine dignified soldier, a gentleman born I believe, and one of the handsomest men in the Light Brigade'. Liprandi was left with food for thought. Fowler was much admired, and later walked every step of the 50 miles to Simferopol, the capital of the Crimea, to make more room for the seriously wounded in the carts. The effort virtually killed him; he was dead within a week.

There was a bleak side to Wightman's first afternoon in captivity. When Liprandi left, the surgeons came in and 'set about amputating a leg of each of four men'. Chloroform was not available, they 'simply sprinkled cold water on the poor fellows' faces', Wightman recalled. 'It seemed a butcherly job, and certainly was a sickening sight,' adding to the collective depression of captivity. 'Nor was any good purpose served,' he remembered, 'for each of the sufferers died immediately on the removal of the limb.' Fletcher, his mortally wounded saviour, was also dead within days. 'I can write this,' the visibly moved Wightman explained, 'but I could not tell of it in a speech, because I know I should play the woman.' Thirty-seven of them would eventually survive to be repatriated to their regiments.[10]

The Light Brigade wounded received their first treatment in the small Orthodox church at Kadikoi, employed as a field hospital. Serious cases were transported by cart to the general hospital at Balaclava. Unable to cope with the number and severity of wounds, the troopship *Australia* was dispatched the next day with over 100 of the worse cases on the four-day journey across the Black Sea to the barrack hospital at Scutari, in the suburbs of Constantinople. Private Albert Mitchell managed to locate his friend Nicholson before he was taken on board. 'He had a lance wound in the side, and had received a blow in the mouth from the butt of a lance.' He did not consider himself seriously wounded 'and did not want to be sent away'. Men instinctively knew from experience that hospital could be every bit as lethal as the battlefield. Private James Cameron with the same regiment was loaded on board ship to Scutari without even first being attended to by a surgeon. Surgeon Scott with the 57th Foot treating the wounded explained conditions were not as bad as salacious press accounts alleged. High rates of subsequent mortality was due less to incompetent medical staff, more because the sick were 'already dead'. They were 'mere skeletons' from exposure and starvation before they went aboard, victims of commissariat incompetence in the 'Crimea – that land of death'. Lieutenant Colonel John Yorke from the Heavy Brigade was taken on board after writing to his sister Ethel that he 'feared the voyage would do one last injury', but he survived the ordeal.[11]

A DESOLATE NIGHT

6.20 P.M. TO MIDNIGHT

Sunset was at about 6.20 p.m. with last light twenty minutes later. Lord Raglan stayed on the Sapoune Heights for the rest of the day. At dusk Cathcart's 4th Infantry Division and the Brigade of Guards began to thread their way back to the camp and the trenches on the plateau. 'With the last gleam of day we could see the sheen of the enemy's lances in their old position in the valley,' Russell reported. Russian infantry still held the key high ground at redoubt 1 on Canrobert's Hill. Campbell's 93rd Regiment of Highlanders, the 'thin red line' that morning pulled back 500 yards to their rear, near the British battery positions, holding a reduced perimeter around Balaclava with the 42nd and 79th regiments. Lieutenant Colonel Anthony Sterling heard melancholy rumours that 'the abandonment of Balaclava is mooted'. 'We may, indeed, abandon the harbour, and occupy the heights on its west side, nearer the besieging [Allied] armies,' he recalled.

The British were unsettled. Russian General Liprandi may have failed to take the harbour, but by hanging onto the easterly former Turkish redoubts, he controlled the Woronzov road. From now on all logistic traffic would have to use the non-metalled Col track running between Balaclava and over the Sapoune Heights. It would become virtually impassable that winter. Losing the outer defence ring was a blow to the Allies. The Russian army outside Sevastopol was now closer and more numerous, restricting the British to a very narrow area between Balaclava and Sevastopol. Russell described the preoccupied Raglan's return to headquarters: 'all our operations in the trenches were lost sight of in the interest of this melancholy day'.

Colonel Sterling felt obliged to quickly post his mail home 'because I know not if it will be possible to write up to the moment of post, as we may be attacked in an hour for what I know.'[12]

On balance General Liprandi had a good day and began composing a dispatch to Prince Menshikov and the Tsar. It would offer the first glimmer of success since the British had landed in the Crimea. There was great rejoicing inside Sevastopol's walls that night when the captured English cannon were triumphantly paraded through the streets. Russian morale rose, a tremendous cannonade was opened on the British lines at 9 p.m. and a glorious *Te Deum* chanted in the city. Much bolstered by this success, Russian infantry moved forward during the night to be ready for a major sortie against the British trenches the next day. Liprandi made the most of the opportunity to curry favour with the Tsar, writing eight guns were captured compared to seven the Allies admitted lost. The underwhelming performance of the Russian cavalry was glossed over, aided by Major General Ryzhov's spirited declarations of success in subsequent written accounts. The insane charge by the Light Brigade, which Liprandi concluded was 'impetuous' rather than alcohol-driven, was magnified to a force of 2,000 strong. British cavalry was notoriously unpredictable and seemed composed of reckless fanatics. The Russian scoresheet undisputedly showed success, even if at an underestimated cost of 300 men and perhaps only partial.

The exuberance that spilled over from the walls of Sevastopol was not matched by the atmosphere around Russian campfires outside the city that night. Artillery Lieutenant Stefan Kozhukhov, who had witnessed the entire battle from the high ground outside Kamara, felt uneasy about inflated reports, which did not reflect what he had clearly seen. He found it incomprehensible that the British cavalry, caught between two fires, pursued by Russian cavalry and enveloped by Cossacks from the flanks, could possibly have escaped. It led him to conclude 'there was no effective pursuit on the part of the hussars and lancers.' 'This is how the affair appeared to us,' watching from the slopes, 'who were calm and objective observers.'

'When we gathered around the campfires that evening, there was no end to the stories,' remembered lancer Lieutenant Koribut Kubitovich. 'Everyone interrupted each other in trying to tell the deeds they had witnessed.' All this was in stark contrast to the innocent banter they had exchanged the night before, prior to setting off. 'This evening was not so noisy and jolly as the preceding one,' Kubitovich reflected. His cavalry recruits had been severely bloodied in the ill-directed attempts to head off the remnants of the escaping Light Brigade. The 'many frightening brushes with death' had proved chastening and had 'left a heavy feeling in the heart'. He summed up the prevailing atmosphere as men bonded after haunting experiences: 'Many of us were no longer present. Some were maimed, the bodies of the dead lay everywhere – all this together worked to depress all of us and we fell asleep in the most sombre mood.'

Russian cavalry were deployed to support cordons of infantry positioned around the newly captured redoubts. It was dark and 'we ourselves, who had hardly been off our horses for almost 24 hours, were completely exhausted and settled down to rest,' recalled Ingermanland Hussar Yevgenii Arbuzov. The respite did not last long, because at 10 p.m., in the midst of preparing Kasha porridge, 'the command "saddle up!" was shouted through our camp'. They heard the rumble of cavalry in the distance and heavy cannon started to bang out from the Fedioukine and Causeway Heights, both sides of the North Valley. But they could not see a thing. It was a false alarm, a box crashing to the ground in the Kargopol Dragoon Regiment lines had set off a stampede of ten squadrons' worth of horses. 'The enemy in turn, thinking that this was an attack from our side, also opened up with a very heavy bombardment from the Sapoune Heights,' Arbuzov remembered. The horses penetrated as far as the Sevastopol trench lines, lashed by heavy artillery fire to their right, which brought down 250 stampeding horses. The Kargopol Dragoons lost two and a half squadrons of horse without even being in action.

The events of that day magnified the fearsome reputation of the English cavalry. 'We did not expect this night to be a quiet one,'

Lieutenant Kozhukhov explained. They were already much 'subdued' by what had happened and the 'dull roar of gunfire' the celebratory cannonade that had spat out from Sevastopol 'made us take care to be vigilant'. 'In truth, the enemy was in front and the pitch-black night, with saddled horses, and guns loaded with canister, were an uncomfortable reminder of the recent mad attack by the English.'[13]

For the British it had been a roller-coaster of a day, full of contradictions. At first the senior British commanders had been completely surprised by the dawn Russian attack. Iconic high points at the 'thin red line' and the stirling success of the Heavy Brigade rout of the Russian cavalry that recaptured the initiative were eclipsed by the reckless charge by the Light Brigade. Ironically, this epic disaster was to endure generations after the success of the Heavy Brigade was long forgotten.

Recriminations were just beginning in the small hours leading up to midnight. Cardigan was uncharacteristically checking on the health of his wounded aide Lieutenant Maxse, before wrapping himself in his cloak beside Maxse's campfire. He was not at all phased by Raglan's admonishment for losing his brigade, insisting he clearly followed orders. Raglan, accepting that guilt could not reasonably be pinned to the brigade commander, went for Lucan, with whom he had a more difficult relationship. Cardigan's proximity to the campfire was likely a combination of exhaustion and stress, coupled with a defensive appreciation of the murmurings in the ranks about his precipitate return from the guns. Some troopers alleged, but not publicly, that he had not even reached them. If he had, then afterwards he abandoned his men. Lord George Paget never forgave him. 'Holloa, Lord Cardigan!' he had involuntarily called out on his return, 'were not you there?' Cardigan grandly responded, 'Oh, wasn't I, though!' turning to one of his men, 'Here Jenyns, did you see me at the guns?' Paget confided to his journal that night that the day 'will be the cause of much ill-blood and accusation, I promise you'. Cardigan, unlike his more Spartan superior Lucan, did not usually share the discomforts with his men, but he felt the need to bond with their emotional pain that night. Many allege that he later took himself off to his yacht in Balaclava harbour.

Bickering came to the fore between Raglan and Lucan that night. Raglan as commander had some explaining to do. The army had been caught napping that morning. He had also composed the fateful order to the Light Brigade. Even its intended meaning, an uphill advance over rough ground unsupported by artillery or infantry, was questionable. It is conceivable that after the moral success of the Heavy Brigade episode, he anticipated the Russians would beat a precipitate retreat. The unclear order, in both written and oral form, demanded immediate action. Raglan was already irritated with Lucan for ignoring the previous – also imprecise – order, and wanted swift action. Raglan's later carefully composed official written dispatch suggested Lucan had 'some misconception of the order to advance' and 'fancied he had no discretion to exercise' but 'was bound to attack at all hazards'. Lucan immediately saw this to be disingenuous. If Cardigan was not to be blamed for obeying an order why should Lucan be? Raglan never allowed any discretion over orders with any of his division commanders in the Crimea. Indeed, slavish adherence to instructions was expected in the Victorian army.

Although Raglan blamed Lucan, he had no intention of taking it any further beyond this loose reprimand. Lucan was convinced he had a case and wrote in his tent that night that: 'I do not intend to bear the smallest particle of responsibility. I gave the order to charge under what I considered a most imperious necessity, and I will not bear one particle of the blame.'

In the obsequious world of the Victorian military, this would be an uphill climb. 'Lucan is much cut up,' Paget observed that night, 'and with tears in his eyes this morning he said how infamous it was to lay the blame on him.' Both Lucan and Raglan spent an uneasy night.[14]

Night fell on the British cavalry camp against a backdrop of flickering artillery fire silhouetting the western skyline. An order was issued forbidding fires and noise as further attacks from the Russians were considered possible. The exhausted and overwrought survivors of the Light Brigade stood about in groups, discussing the dead, wounded and missing, and the events of the day. It was bitterly cold. The Heavy Brigade had attacked over their tent lines that morning and soldiers were prevented from returning until 5 p.m., despite their camp being only 500 yards away. 'None of the men or horses had anything to eat since the night before,' Paget recalled. The camp area was in chaos. 'We have lost a good deal of property,' Paget observed. The perennial answer to account for losses was 'Oh, it was knocked over in the attack – I cannot find it' or 'the Turks must have stolen it' – conceivable, because they had fled through the camp.

Colonel Edward 'Little' Hodge commanding the Heavy Brigade's 4th Dragoon Guards saw the camp was completely disorganised when he got back in the dark. 'Both my servants got brutally drunk,' he remembered, 'and I found them lying on their backs, and with difficulty I was enabled to save my baggage.' They had helped themselves to officer's stores, which added insult to injury, and his tent was gone. 'I only wonder that I have any kit left,' he recalled. Hodge hated drunkenness. 'I am most uncomfortable,' he complained, 'with blackguards as these about me.'

An emotional reaction to the horrors of the day now began to set in. 'Well, we have had a fearful day's work,' Paget confided to his journal, 'out of which it has pleased God to bring me harmless.' But they were surrounded by ghosts; 'not an officer of the 4th escaped without himself or his horse being wounded,' Paget remembered.

Poor Halkett, we believe killed. He was struck down in the advance, Sparke missing, supposed to have been sabred in the melee at the end, and Hutton shot in both thighs and his horse wounded in eleven places; my horse was grazed in three or four places, and I had a shot through my holster. My poor orderly was knocked over, as well as my trumpeter, both by my side. Every trumpeter in the regiment and two Sergeant Majors out of three knocked over.

Paget's voice had gone from shouting himself hoarse throughout the action; 'it is like an old crow,' he remarked. Corporal James Nunnerly finally returned to his 17th Lancer tent that he normally shared with nine others; that night he slept alone.[15]

Private Albert Mitchell remembered, 'we did not take our tents that night, but were ordered to let them remain to deceive the enemy.' It was an uncomfortable night for the 13th Light Dragoons, 'for I had nothing but what I stood upright in'. His equipment, jacket, overalls, cloak and blanket were attached to his dead horse lying on the battle-field. He did not get another cloak until after the worst of the winter, at the end of February.

With time to reflect, men pondered on their tenuous mortality. Major William Gray with the 8th Hussars recovered his pipe from his overall pocket, 'broken in a hundred pieces, and the ball left there in my pocket'. Another ball had gone through his horseshoe case and 'took part of my sword belts away from my sword and only left part of my sword remaining'. Private Thomas Williams in the 11th Hussars found his sword scabbard severely dented by shot and very nearly cut cleanly in two at the centre.

'Several men on unrolling their cloaks,' Mitchell recalled, 'found grapeshot and pieces of shell drop from them.' He faced a bitterly cold night and 'laid down with my back against another man for warmth'. He woke several times to find he was covered in white frost, but despite the discomforts continued 'thanking God for His great mercies towards me this day'.

James Wightman, experiencing his first night in Russian captivity, was just as cold. There were no blankets, but the Russians handed out the greatcoats the Turks had abandoned at the redoubts. 'They swarmed with vermin,' he remembered, 'but the night was bitterly cold, and we found them very acceptable.' They were alive, too. Later that night they were put in one-horse carts, 'two men in a cart lying on straw' and departed for Simferopol, 50 miles away. It took four marches with brief halts. When they arrived at the hospital 'most of our uniforms were so stiff with blood that they could have stood on end themselves.'[16]

Fanny Duberly made 'the dreary ride' back to her ship in Balaclava harbour, escorted by Henry, her husband. Her maid Letitia Finnegan was still 'in deep anxiety and distress'. 'When I left last night, her husband had not been seen,' she remembered. Private Finnegan had not returned; 'one man told me he thought he saw him fall but, of course, I would give her no information but *facts*.' At first the rumours suggested he had been wounded, but when her maid checked the hospital 'all she heard was tidings of his death'. Characteristically, Fanny had hardly ever mentioned her maid before in her journal, despite having accompanied her before and after her journey to Balaclava. There is more information about her horse 'Bobs' travels than Mrs Finnegan. To lose a husband when accompanied on active service was little short of disastrous. Finnegan was indeed killed during the charge. There would be no provider unless Letitia quickly developed an intimate relationship with another 'protector'.

'It is a novel office for me to be comforter to the poor broken-hearted woman who is with me,' Mrs Duberly recalled. 'She will not leave me for a moment.' Whether or not she realised it, her maid's physical security and sustenance was at stake. In the short term she was totally reliant on her employer. 'Oh Ma'am it's my heart that's bad,' her maid insisted. 'You seem to give me strength.' 'Fancy me,' was Fanny's reaction, 'from my weakness dealing out strength.' Once on board, with time to reflect, she too felt vulnerable. There were false alarms that night: 'steamers getting up their steam, anchors being weighed'. She slept fitfully; there were fears about the Russians and 'even my closed eyelids were filled with the ruddy glow of blood.'[17]

Sergeant Timothy Gowing's Royal Fusilier fatigue group finally reached Balaclava harbour, to pick up their 'priceless blankets'. As the stores were closed the assistant quartermaster general sent them down to the plain to assist with the recovery of the wounded. On arrival they met with Light Brigade survivors, with whom they patriotically offered 'a warm shake of the hand'. The unasked question, hinted and remarked upon in many veteran accounts was *what had happened?*

Lord George Paget wrote in his journal 'the fact is, we can fight better than any other nation, but we have no organisation.' It had obviously gone wrong with the Light Brigade. 'I have always anticipated a disaster when the cavalry came to be engaged,' he later admitted, 'though I kept it to myself.' Many of the officers did so, but war correspondent William Russell was composing a newspaper report that would electrify Victorian London back home. He hinted at poor decisions but remained circumspect, the facts were speaking for themselves. It was a later *Times* newspaper editorial that coined the phrase 'some hideous blunder' which was to be taken up by Alfred Lord Tennyson's 'some one had blunder'd', reworded to achieve the rhythmic beat that powered short pithy stanzas of verse to echo the pace of the ride.

Sergeant Timothy Gowing recalled asking the:

Sergeant of the old Cherry Pickers [11th Hussars], as he gripped him by the hand amid a group of survivors, 'Has there not been some mistake?' 'It cannot be helped now – we have tried to do our part,' was his response. 'It will all come out some day.'[18]

BEYOND 24 HOURS

The next day the Russians attempted to capitalise on the euphoria accompanying the capture of the guns with a major sortie to the right of the British trench lines. Three columns of Russian infantry, numbering about 4,000 strong, were shot to pieces by cannon and musket fire in the 'Little Inkerman' action. Russian losses were between 500 and 600, with 130 dead left lying in front of the British trenches and some 80 prisoners taken. Two days after the charge Lord Raglan visited the Light Brigade camp to coordinate its move to the Heights by the Inkerman windmill, right of the line, because the French had felt exposed by the sortie. Men rushed out in their shirtsleeves to cheer him, but true to his Wellington demeanour, Raglan remained aloof, giving no indication of being pleased. 'How I longed for him to do so,' Paget subsequently wrote to his wife. 'One little word. "Well my boys, you have done well!" or something of the sort, would have cheered us all up.'[1]

The move to the new camp exposed the badly battered brigade to the bitter winds that swept across the Crimean Peninsula. Within two days the first snow fell. Cardigan continued to dine and sleep evenings on his yacht, appearing each day dressed in an unconventional woollen jacket buttoned down the front, which the men labelled a 'cardigan'.

Forage arrived by ship at Balaclava and was transported by a daily train of cavalry mounts to carry it up the 14 miles to the Heights. Giving up the Woronzov road had not initially been considered significant, after all it was felt the campaign would be over by the end of the year. 'I think they will funk to cross swords with us after their licking,' thought Richard Temple Godman with the 5th Dragoon Guards. 'They have never licked the English yet.' The condition of the rutted track deteriorated daily as did the horses. What happened on 5 November was to change everything, when an estimated 60,000 Russians made yet another surprise attack at Inkerman in mist and fog.

Inkerman was the infantry soldier's battle as much as Balaclava had been the cavalry one. British command and control broke down in the misty conditions of a ferocious close-quarter battle during which landmarks were lost and won in dense fog several times. The British bore the brunt, losing 3,300 men, although it was Bosquet's French Division that finally tipped the balance. Menshikov, having wrong-footed the Allied rear yet again, broke off the action having lost 12,000 men. It was a pyrrhic victory because Raglan appreciated his army was no longer strong enough to storm Sevastopol. The campaign would have to be maintained through the winter.

The depressing sequence of events continued with a hurricane on 14 November that sank twenty-one ships waiting to enter Balaclava harbour, alongside much needed winter clothing, fuel and forage for the animals. The rutted track from the harbour to the Heights became a quagmire, virtually impassable and lined with dead animals. By 3 December constant rain and plunging temperatures reduced the Light Brigade to just 10 per cent of the mounts they had brought out from England. The 13th Light Dragoons was down to twelve of its original 250 horses. In January 1855 the British Army numbered 12,000 effectives alongside 135,000 French; a weak brigade within a French army. Serious operations were delayed until the spring, when improved logistics enabled sustained artillery bombardments to commence in April. A series of bombardments were followed by a succession of failed mass assaults in June, August and September. On 8 September the previously impregnable Malakov feature was taken and the Russians abandoned the city the next day. An armistice was not signed until February 1856. One in five British soldiers who had embarked so confidently in the spring of 1854 failed to return.

William Russell's first report in the *Times* newspaper about Balaclava took three weeks to arrive on Victorian breakfast tables. It was implicitly critical but did not directly label the action a blunder. 'Our Light Brigade was annihilated by their own rashness,' he wrote, attacking too far without infantry or artillery support. The term 'some hideous blunder' came from a *Times* editorial, not Russell's dispatch. The *Morning Chronicle* labelled the event 'brilliant but unfortunate' launched 'by an imbecile command', commenting 'it was not an ambush' because batteries on three sides 'were visible to the dullest eye'. It was an emotional accusatory article that claimed 'never was more wilful murder committed than in ordering an advance against such fearful odds and certain destruction.'[2]

Poet Laureate Alfred Lord Tennyson had watched the fleet gathering at Portsmouth in spring 1854, from his home on the Isle of Wight. He read Russell's newspaper report appearing on Tuesday, 14 November and claimed he wrote his famous poem about The Charge of the Light Brigade 'in a few minutes'. It was based on incomplete information. The first *Times* report spoke of 607 sabres instead of the 664 that painstaking research since suggests actually rode. 'Some one had blunder'd' rhymed with 'six hundred', more than the numbers originally reported. This would have compromised the galloping metre of the poem, which was published in *The Examiner* on 9 December. It captured the imagination of the public and quickly became popular with the troops at the hospital at Scutari and in the Crimea. Lord Cardigan arrived back in England the following month and was received with immediate acclamation, a contrast to the normal opprobrium he attracted in the press. Pictures of him were displayed in shop windows and he was invited to dine with Queen Victoria and Prince Albert. He showed up on horseback at a London Mansion House banquet held in his honour, on his charger Roland, wearing the very uniform worn at the charge. Souvenir hunters plucked hairs from Roland's tail. Lieutenant Colonel Charles Walker, who rode with the Heavy Brigade staff in the charge, had already sent a cautionary note home on 2 November: 'Don't believe any bosh you hear about Lord Cardigan. He showed no head, and beyond riding with his brigade, no greater pluck than others.' 'Old Scarlett,' he insisted, the Heavy Brigade Commander, 'is worth two of him.'[3]

Tennyson's vivid and dramatically paced poem has spawned a large number of narrative and feature film accounts of the charge since. 'Some one had blunder'd' most certainly, but who? The dilemma has never been satisfactorily resolved over sixteen or more decades. Nothing new has emerged.

Lord Raglan bore responsibility for the content of the order that was obscurely composed. Ensconced on the Olympian Sapoune Heights, scientifically based topographical surveys have since revealed how much his three-dimensional view from the top differed from the two-dimensional scene seen by Lucan and Cardigan in the valley below. Captain Nolan was the only officer in the orders chain who had viewed the situation from both perspectives. Raglan had never commanded troops in action before and was separated by time and space from the action on the valley floor. Passage of written or oral information took an average of thirty minutes to deliver each way, during a series of fast-moving cavalry actions that waited for no man. If Raglan had acted upon the intelligence reports ignored the previous evening, his infantry could have been in place to offer support. 'Cry wolf' had happened many times before, and he appreciated overreactions were exhausting his men. If Captain Nolan had survived, more information would have been forthcoming, but not necessarily answers. Alleged insubordination at the point of delivery, prompted by an earnest desire to be included in the coming action, raised the emotional ante on the valley floor. Yet Raglan's order, in both its written and oral form, demanded immediate action. Evidence suggests that Nolan, an experienced staff officer, was neither excitable nor overbearing when dealing with superiors, when obsequious behaviour in the Victorian military hierarchy was more the norm. If Lucan had paused to question Raglan's order, Nolan would have been merely a footnote in history. His influence can be measured in minutes.

Responsibility within the hierarchical military chain of command starts at the top. Raglan composed the command and expressed it badly. Lucan, as the senior cavalry commander, felt unable to question it because he had been intimidated by a whole series of misinterpretations of Raglan's unclear orders in the past. The ire this attracted lessened his confidence. He was indecisive and honour-bound not to question orders in a fast-moving situation, visibly developing by the minute, for which he would be blamed if it went wrong. So at two stages in the command chain, full responsibility was not accepted. Was sacrificing the Light Brigade worth the loss of just seven or eight guns?

Cardigan, with a narcissistic belief in his own infallibility, had no practical field experience at all. He conducted the charge like it was a Hyde Park drill, covering himself by doing what he was simply told. Lacking common sense, but not physical courage, his adversarial relationship with his detested ex-brother-in-law enabled him to revel in a little *Schadenfreude* over what even he realised was a stupid decision. The satisfaction was that Lucan would have to take it, and not himself.

Definitive answers are unlikely ever to be forthcoming. Contemporary comment is tainted with preference for or dislike of all these men. There has been no shortage of revisionist interpretations since, often based on topographical or behavioural theories of what *likely* happened. One fair comment was raised by Major Forrest with the 4th Dragoon Guards, who despite his prejudices claimed:

Captain Nolan may have been, and I believe was, somewhat to blame about that Light Brigade tragedy, but I think my Lord Lucan the most to blame. If a Lieutenant General will not take any responsibility upon himself, a lance corporal might fill his place. He should have waited until the infantry on their way up had arrived, or sent to inquire whether that was not Lord Raglan's intention.

William Russell mercilessly castigated Raglan after Inkerman, claiming he 'is utterly incompetent to lead an army through any arduous task'. Russell was not necessarily infallible as a military commentator himself, according to Private James Auchinloss, with the 4th Dragoon Guards. He wrote home how 'highly amused' he was about Russell's account of the Heavy Brigade action. The 'Special Correspondent,' he teased, claims 'he was an "eye" witness of the heavy cavalry charge; but I much doubt whether he has an "eye" or not, for he says the Greys and Inniskillings Dragoons charged in the first line.' The press, he was insinuating, are not necessarily the purveyors of the universal truth.[4]

Raglan died after the failure of the much-hyped infantry assault on Sevastopol that occurred with heavy losses on 18 June 1855, some said of a broken heart. 'I could never return to England now,' he was alleged to have commented, 'they would stone me to death.' Lieutenant Colonel 'Little' Hodge wrote in his diary that he died 'of exhaustion and dysentery, added to I hear, by worry of mind'. Lucan, publicly obsessed to the last over his innocence for the charge decision, had already been recalled to London the previous January. Despite being disliked, most of the cavalry sided with him and felt he was badly handled. He was later exonerated and outlived Cardigan by twenty years and was promoted to Field Marshal in 1887, the year before his death.[5]

Cardigan got back to England before Lucan, ostensibly for reasons of ill health, benefitting from the huge public acclaim that came from Tennyson's epic poem. Hodge, still in the Crimea, heard 'Lord Cardigan has been received in triumph in England, and all the shops are full of prints of him jumping a gun, and sticking a Russian *en passant* in mid air.' He was not missed. 'I do not think that he ever intends returning here, and better that he should not.' In December 1856 Captain Somerset Calthorpe, one of Raglan's nephews and his ADC, wrote a series of letters highly critical of Cardigan and suggesting he did not even reach the Russian guns. A contentious legal action followed that dragged on, not appearing before the Queen's Bench until June 1863. Cardigan, meanwhile, was appointed Inspector General of Cavalry and Colonel of the 11th Hussars. The courts proved he reached the guns but the detail of the case revealed his complete indifference to his men, the neglect of his brigade and a callous lack of responsibility. His second marriage had also become a spectacular public scandal when his popularity bubble burst. Five years later he died in a fall from his horse, probably the result of a stroke.[6]

Nolan's body was never recovered from the hurriedly scraped ditch into which it was tumbled near redoubt 4. He was the last male family member of his line. The contemporary press coverage of his life and death was kinder than history, which has over dramatised his role. The *Illustrated London News* obituary commented 'the rash movement' of the charge 'was so opposed to his own published theory' on cavalry tactics, 'that he could never have willingly countenanced, much less directed it, even under an excess of zeal'. His fellow officers paid for a marble plaque to be erected in his memory on the wall of Holy Trinity Church in Maidstone, next to the place where the cavalry depot officers habitually sat. He was also honoured by the Army and Navy Club in London, alongside other members who fell in the charge, hardly the actions of men who considered him guilty of any offence.[7]

William Russell regarded Nolan a friend and 'God forbid I should cast a shade on the brightness of his honour'. Even so, he felt 'bound to state what I am told occurred when he reached his Lordship [Lucan]'. What he reported has been laboriously pored over since. Russell's sharp eye for a good story was to take him to record the Indian Mutiny in 1857, the American Civil War and the Austro-Prussian and Franco-Prussian wars. He is regarded as one of the first modern war correspondents and was knighted in 1895 and died in 1907.

Fanny Duberly returned to Ireland after the Crimea and accompanied her husband Henry when the 8th Hussars joined in the repression of the Indian mutiny. She covered 1,800 miles on horseback during the campaign, writing at age 29 on its conclusion 'my youth is gone and Henry is grievously changed'. They served on in England, Scotland and Ireland until Henry retired from the army, as a lieutenant colonel in 1881. He died in 1891 while she lived on at Cheltenham a further twelve years, passing away in January 1903 aged 71.

Lord George Paget, foreseeing no further action for the cavalry after Inkerman, returned to England to join his bride, left days after marriage in the spring of 1854. It had been a point of patriotic honour to accompany the expedition, because he had already announced his intention to leave the army. Nobody was surprised in the Crimea; they had seen enough death and a young bride promised life. But Paget 'was greatly snubbed at home' recalled an 8th Hussar subaltern: 'Everyone here thought him a most sensible man for leaving when he was tired of it; but the English people are such fools.'

Weight of public opinion forced Paget to return, but this time he took his young wife with him. He was reappointed to command the Light Brigade and completed the campaign, going on to become Inspector General of Cavalry and a Major General. His bride, Agnes, only lived for two years after the Crimea, and he married a second time in 1861 before dying unexpectedly in 1880.[8]

In September 1855 the first medals arrived in the Crimea and because the three clasps for the Alma, Balaclava and Inkerman looked like decanter labels, they were promptly christened 'Port', 'Sherry' and 'Claret'. Jemmy the terrier, who survived the charge and went on to India with the 8th Hussars, was presented with a dog collar with five medal clasps on return to England, including Sebastopol and Central India. The collar is still in the 8th Hussars Officer's mess today.[9]

Much less is known about the Russian participants at Balaclava after the events of these fateful 24 hours were over. General Liprandi was moved by the heroism of the Light Brigade, appreciating they were 'noble fellows' once he reconciled himself to accept they were probably not drunk. His force remained based around the village of Chorgun north-east of Balaclava, posing a continued threat to the Balaclava line of communication to the Sapoune Heights. He took part in the battles of Inkerman and led the attack on the Sardinians at Tchernaya in August 1855. Prince Obolensky's Don Battery, over-run by the Light Brigade at the end of the valley, was refitted nearby with replacements of men and horses. It was the first Russian battery to open fire at the Inkerman on 5 November. Crossing the Chernya River bridge once again, the battery formed part of a sixty-gun force supporting the Russian infantry attacks through dense fog. The action was 'fought with such ferocity,' one of its officers recalled, 'that gun crews had to be replaced three times' and 'losses in horses so great, that the batteries could not move out of their positions'.

Lieutenant Koribut Kubitovich's Composite Lancer Regiment was dissolved after the campaign. Artillery Lieutenant Stefan Kozhukhov and Ingermanland Hussar Yevgenii Arbuzov both survived the war to engage in a vociferous post-conflict literary debate in the 1870s, over the competence of the Russian cavalry that day. Arbuzov tended to support the inflated claims of Russian Major General Ryzhov's 1870 account of Balaclava. Kozhukhov always maintained Ryhzov's 'rabbit hunt' pursuit of the British from the guns was fiction. General Liprandi glossed over Ryzhov's shortcomings in his official dispatch to Prince Menshikov and the Tsar, but it was interesting to see Ryzhov only qualified for the Order of St Vladimir 2nd Class for his 'attack on the enemy park' during the Battle of Balaclava. His sideways appointment to command the 2nd Brigade of a Reserve Light Cavalry Division appears to implicitly reflect shortcomings not just voiced by Kozhukhov.[10]

The Turks got the blame for the setbacks at Balaclava and were accused of cowardice for abandoning the redoubts. They were treated appallingly for the rest of the campaign, routinely beaten, spat on and jeered by British troops. Their interpreter John Blunt watched British soldiers treat them like slaves, using them 'to carry them with their bundles on their backs across the pools and quagmires on the Balaclava road', as humorously portrayed in a *Punch* cartoon. Turkish troops were set to digging trenches or transporting heavy loads up the rutted Col track from Balaclava to the British trench lines on the plateau. 'No one seemed to care for them,' remembered an American commanding one of the ship transports. 'I have actually seen a mule and a Turk harnessed together in a cart, and a Frenchman riding upon it and whipping up the team.' Religion forbade them from eating most of the available British rations so their only recourse was to steal. If caught, their British masters flogged them, often well beyond the forty-five lashes allowed for British troops. Of the 4,000 Turkish soldiers that fought at Balaclava on 25 October, half were dead from malnutrition by the end of the year. The Russians were especially casual about burying Turkish dead, their Christian Orthodox faith applying the same pitiless indifference as their Christian Allied opponents.[11]

Private Albert Mitchell watched seventeen wounded horses paraded in the lines the day after the charge when all but one was shot. It survived the winter he remembered 'and was in the regiment when I left in 1862'. He became a police constable with the Kent County Constabulary and retired in 1887. Sergeant Timothy Gowing, the Royal Fusilier who had watched the entire action from the Sapoune Heights, went on to serve in India during the 1857 Mutiny. He completed twenty-two years' service, eighteen of them in India where he lost seven of eight children in a single day from cholera. On retirement he became a pastor for twenty-four years, married three times and had a further nineteen children, but only one had outlived him when he died in 1908, aged 74.

Private Christopher Fox with the 4th Light Dragoons received fifty lashes for absconding to join the charge. At the halfway point, when a new man with a fresh cat-of-nine-tails normally stepped in, the punishment paused. 'Hold!' his colonel ordered, 'I will forgive you the other 25.' Fox, a known hardcase, begged to differ, 'Oh, don't. Please Colonel, I don't want to be beholden to you for anything,' adding insolently, 'I'll take the other 25.' His punishment had not been popular in the ranks among the remnants of the 4th, and his colonel likely appreciated this. 'Silence, sir,' he admonished, and had him marched off to the hospital marquee. The balance was never given. Remarkably, he received another twenty-five lashes a year later for 'insolence to a superior officer'. Fox went on to serve in India and was discharged in 1872, by which time he had ironically accumulated five Good Conduct Badges. Doubtless as canny as he was independent minded, Fox's *News of the World* newspaper obituary on 14 October 1900 records that apart from riding in the charge, he had been a police inspector.[12]

The British military system was as uncompromising as it was unjust. Private James Wightman, after numerous adventures in Russian captivity, including a fist fight with his captors, was released after a year to the Royal Navy aboard HMS *Agamemnon*. Of twelve 17th Lancer men taken prisoner only three came back alive; all the wounded perished under the Russian surgeon's knife. 'A few days after rejoining,' he remembered, 'we three were tried by Court Martial for being absent without leave for 12 months.' This applied to all the repatriated thirty-seven prisoners returned to their regiments; twenty-one of fifty-eight had died in captivity. The onus was on the survivors to prove they had not been captured due to 'negligence'. Wightman and his comrades 'were honourably acquitted'. 'My comrades and I saw some tough scenes in the Indian mutiny,' Wightman later remembered and he discharged himself in 1868, by which time he had been promoted to ensign. He attended official charge commemorations with 'my two steadfast chums Marsh and Mustard' who settled near him. He can be seen in a commemorative group photograph in 1890. 'We three old comrades fight our battles o'er again, and thank God that we are alive to do so!' remembered Wightman, who died in February 1907.[13]

Tennyson's poem meant the spectacular success of Scarlett's Heavy Brigade charge was soon eclipsed in the public mind by the inspirational failure of the charge of the Light Brigade. The first major reunion was held twenty-one years after the event on

25 October 1875. Interestingly more than twice the total known to have survived turned up, so it appeared there were as many imposters as heroes seeking to celebrate the event. Annual reunion dinners continued beyond Queen Victoria's Golden Jubilee in 1887 and an 1890 photograph records thirty-six survivors present. Eleven charge survivors can be seen in a Buffalo Bill Wild West Show photograph in July 1891. A final Holborn Restaurant Dinner was held on 25 October 1913 attended by six survivors. Private Edwin Hughes from the 13th Light Dragoons outlived every other survivor, when he died in 1927 aged 96 years.

There was another aspect beyond the public adulation. Private Richard Palframan with the 8th Hussars survived the charge and was taken prisoner only to lose his leg in a threshing machine accident twenty-seven years later, which threatened destitution. The *Illustrated London News* commentary on the 21st reunion banquet reported that 'to a man they were dressed respectably' and 'seemed to be occupying comfortable positions'. Not all were there. Trumpeter William Perkins with the 11th Hussars, with several medals, was working as an attendant at a public London toilet. 'James the crossing sweeper' as he was called was an elderly gentleman who swept mud and horse manure while on crutches from a London street. He was Private James Watts from the 17th Lancers. He generally received a penny, halfpenny or farthing from pedestrians if he mentioned he had ridden the charge. His story mentioned his leg was amputated, after his horse was hit before reaching the guns. Although recorded 'severely wounded' at Balaclava, he went on to serve with the 17th Lancers in India, which he could not have done minus a leg. Such men at least managed a meagre income, others such as Troop Sergeant Major John Linkon with the 13th Light Dragoons, Private John Smith, 17th Lancers and Privates John Richardson and Richard Brown from the 11th Hussars, ended up in the workhouse.[14]

Richardson was interviewed by H. Yeo in 1890, the publisher of the popular penny *Spy* newspaper. He was 63 and destitute at the time. 'The gorgeous uniform of the noble 11th Hussars with its bright crested buttons' had been 'replaced by the workhouse cordways with their bright un-crested buttons,'Yeo wrote: 'Oh, Englishmen! Blush with shame! This man methought, is one of the Light Brigade whose heroism is lauded in every household in the land! There stood the old soldier paying deep respect to the workhouse master and to me.'

Lieutenant Percy Smith with the 13th Light Dragoons deliberately charged the guns with a completely maimed right hand. All he could usefully do was encourage his men. He survived virtually unscathed, and his horse was only one of two in the regiment that was unwounded. He subsequently married after selling his commission in 1858 and had one son. In 1913 he was one of only two officers still living who had ridden in the charge and passed away on 8 February 1917. He was buried five days later in Southampton cemetery completely unnoticed: the First World War was at its height and Smith's grave was sadly unmarked.

There is a petrol station at the intersection of the Balaclava–Yalta main road, which overlooks the position where the charge of the Light Brigade started, an incongruous setting for such an epic event. Given the right light and time of day, walking the line of the charge towards the Russian gun positions through present-day vineyards out of sight of the petrol station can resurrect ghosts. These appear on the shadowy outline of the Causeway Heights to the right and the Fedioukine Heights to the left. One cannot help but wonder what those fearful 664 men riding off 150 years ago must have been thinking.

NOTES

Chapter 1

1 Gowing, *A Voice from the Ranks*, pp. 28–9 and 42. Taylor, 27 Oct. 1854, *Letters from the Crimea*, p. 51.

2 Cathcart, Harris, *The Gallant Six Hundred*, p. 138. Gowing, p. 43. Taylor, 22 and 27 Oct., Taylor, p. 51.

3 Clifford, 24 Oct. 1854, *Henry Clifford VC: His Letters and Sketches from the Crimea*, pp.68–9. Taylor *p. 51*, Gowing, p. 28.

4 Townsend Wilson, Spilsbury, *The Thin Red Line*, pp. 132 and 130. Duberly, *Mrs Duberly's War*, p. 91. Russell, *The Crimean War*, pp. 101–2.

5 Russell on Raglan, and Clifford, Harris, pp. 142–3. Image, 16 and 17 Oct. 1854, *The Crimean Journal of John George Image*.

6 Hume, *Reminiscences of the Crimean Campaign*, pp. 49, 50 and 51. Russell, pp. 101–2. Gowing, p. 29. Sniper, Calthorpe, *Cadogan's Crimea*.

7 Dunkellin survived because he was titled and his father had been ambassador to Tsar Nicholas. *The History of the Present War with Russia*, p. 299. (Henceforth HOPWWR.)

8 Wilson, Spilsbury, p. 127.

9 Average trooper, Dutton, *Forgotten Heroes. The Charge of the Heavy Brigade*, p. 356. Mitchell, *Recollections of One of the Light Brigade*, p.18.

10 Maguire and truce, HOPWWR, p. 301. Townsend Wilson, Spilsbury, p. 133.

11 Temple Godman, 6 and 22 Oct. 1854, *Letters Home from the Crimea*, pp. 62 and 72–3. Watchfires, Scots Greys Officer letter, 21 Oct. 1854, Dawson, *Letters from the Light Brigade*, Russell, p. 102. Duberley, 25 Oct. 1854, p. 92.

12 Kubitovich, 'Recollections of the Balaklava Affair of 13 October, 1854', p. 153. Hodasevich, *A Voice from within the Walls of Sebastopol*, pp. 20 and 25.

13 Kozhukhov, 'Crimean Memoirs of the Last War', *Russkii Vestnik,* 1869, Vol. 7.

14 Arbuzov, 'Reminisences of the Campaign in the Crimean Peninsula in 1854 and 1855, *Voennyi Sbornik,* 1874, Vol. 96, No. 4.

15 Kubitovich and Khitrov, Kubitovich, p. 153.
16 Kozhukhov. Hodasevich, p. 20. Abuzov.

Chapter 2

1 RA Captain, Dawson, p. 72. Farquharson, Brighton, *Hell Riders*, pp. 73–4. Temple Godman, letter to father 6 Oct. 1854, *Letters Home from the Crimea*, p. 64. Mitchell, p. 47.
2 Mitchell, p. 47, Paget, Journal, 12 Oct. 1854. Stocks, Dutton, *Heavy Brigade*, p. 78. Wombwell, Brighton, p. 73. Wykeham Martin, ed. Fisher *Crimean Cavalry Letters*, p. 13. Highland soldier, Dawson, Letters, p. 69.
3 Vahey, Dutton, Forgotten Heroes: *The Charge of the Light Brigade*, p. 337.
4 Temple Godman, p. 39. Mitchell, p. 19. Calthorpe, *Cadogan's Crimea*, p. 9.
5 Lewis, letter 4 Aug. 1853, Dutton, Light Brigade, p. 253.
6 Mitchell, p. 34.
7 Wightman, *Nineteenth Century Magazine*, May 1892. pp. 850–1.
8 Hodge, letters 8 Aug. and 22 Oct. 1854, *Little Hodge*, p. 22 and 39. Henderson, Buttery, *Messenger of Death*, p. 31. Franks, *Messenger of Death*, p. 35.
9 Cartoon, Brighton, *Hell Riders*, pp.3–4.
10 Nolan, Journal, 23 Sep. 1854, *Expedition to the Crimea*, p. 65. Portal, Brighton, p. 56. Joke, Harris, *The Gallant Six Hundred*, p. 125.
11 'Showy' uniforms, *HOPWWR*, 1854, p. 306. *Times* reports 1840 and 22 Apr. 1854, Woodham-Smith, *The Reason Why*, pp. 62 and 137–8. Nolan, Buttery, p. 51. Heath, ed. V. Bonham-Carter, *Surgeon in the Crimea*, p. 87. Hunter, letter 27 Oct. 1854, Dutton, Heavy Brigade, p. 119.
12 Wykham Martin, letter 26 Jul 1854, ed. G. Fisher, *Crimean Cavalry Letters*, pp. 36 and 109. Yorke, Dutton, Heavy Brigade, p. 28.
13 Scot Hunter, Dawson, 22 Aug. 1854, p. 23. Sickness nos, Dawson, p. 13. Russell, ed. Lambert and Badsey, *The War Correspondents. The Crimean War*, pp. 90, 86, Varna 11 Aug., pp.31–2. Clifford, 27 Jul. 1854, p. 42.
14 Duberly, 4 Oct. 1854 p. 78, 25 Jun. p. 27, 11 Jul. pp. 33–4. Forest and Paget, Woodham-Smith, pp. 152 and 180.
15 Mitchell, p. 48. Sterling, *The Highland Brigade in the Crimea*, p. 48.
16 Calthorpe (Raglan's staff officer, nephew and ADC), Cardigan's Crimea, p. 51. Maude, Harris, p. 31.
17 Forrest, Woodham-Smith, p. 152.
18 Wolseley, Harris, p. 25. Staff College nos, Woodham-Smith, p. 170.
19 'Isle of Wight', Woodham-Smith, p. 159. Patullo and Adye, Harris, pp. 124 and 76.
20 Intelligence reports, Brighton, pp. 68 and 74–6.
21 Russell, Brighton, p. 77.
22 Mitchell, p. 46. Asst Surgeon, Dawson, letter 4 Oct. 1854, p. 62. Russell, report Sep. 1854, p. 76. Duberly, pp. 73–4. Eyewitness, UK writer *Illustrated London News* 10 Feb. 1855. B. Cooke, *The Grand Central Railway*, p. 35.

23 Temple Godman, letter to father, 12 Oct. 1854, p. 66. Clifford, p. 58. Sturtevant, letter 2 Nov. 1854, Dawson, p. 99.

24 Duberly, 10 Oct. 1854, p. 82. Lawson, *Surgeon in the Crimea*, p. 87.

25 Sterling, letter 22 Oct. 1854, pp. *vi* and 57.

Chapter 3

1 Hodasevich, pp. 101, 126, 148, 151, 156–7, 160 and 165.

2 Tolstoy, *The Sebastopol Sketches*, pp. 54–6. Hodasevich, p. 162.

3 Hodasevich, p. 155. Pavliuk, Thomas and Scollins, *The Russian Army of the Crimean War* 1854–56, p. 33.

4 Hodasevich, pp. 149–50 and 134–5. Tolstoy, pp. 47–8.

5 Hodasevich, pp. 134–5 and 164–5.

6 Kubitovich.

7 Officer, B.M. Kalinin, *Material for the History of the Don Artillery*, pp. 136–52.

8 Kozhukhov, pp. 381–4.

9 Yorke, letter 22 Oct. 1854, Dawson, p. 70. Farquharson and Smith, Brighton, p. 82.

10 Paget, *The Light Cavalry Brigade in the Crimea*, pp. 161–2.

Chapter 4

1 Blunt, Mawson, *The True Heroes of Balaclava*, p. 16.

2 Maude, P. Warner, *The Crimean War: A Reappraisal*, p. 87.

3 Wyekham Martin, letter 2 Aug. 1854, ed. Fisher, *Crimean Cavalry Letters*, p. 37. Clifford, letter 30 May 1854, p. 37.

4 Morley, 25 Jun. 1854, Dawson, pp. 15–16. Senior, 29 Jun. 1854, Dawson, pp. 17 and 19. Mitchell, pp. 50–1. Wykeham Martin, 2 Aug. 1854, Fisher, p. 38.

5 Kubitovich. Arbuzov.

6 Turkish soldier, Blunt account, Mawson, p. 16.

7 Maude, Baring Pemberton, *Battles of the Crimean War*, p. 81. Temple Godman, letter 26 Oct. 1854, Warner, p. 73.

8 Sterling, letter 22 Oct. 54, p. 60. Campbell, Harris, p. 157. Paget, Buttery, p. 166 and Brighton p. 87.

9 Gough, Barthorp, Heroes of the Crimea, p. 41. Temple Godman, Letter 26 Oct. 1854, Warner, p. 73. Yorke, letter 5 Dec. 1854, Dawson p. 111. Gough, letter 27 Oct., Dawson, p. 89. Cruse, Dutton, Hea*v*y Brigade, pp. 40–1.

10 Mitchell, pp. 52–3. Lucan, Selby, *The Thin Red Line*, p. 114.

11 Arbuzov. Kubitovich. Liprandi, Seaton, *The Crimean War*, p. 143. Hodasevich, p. 50. Krüdener, Fletcher and Ishchenko, *The Crimean War*, p. 165.

12 Temple Godman, letter 26 Oct. 1854, Warner, p. 73. Scots Greys Sergeant, anon letter 4 Nov. 1854, Dawson, p. 103. Mitchell, p. 53. Kubitovich, pp. 129–30. Azov casualties, Fletcher and Ishchenko, p. 166.

13 Gowing, pp. 29–30. Russell, 25 Oct. 1854, p. 106. Hume, pp. 56–7. Image, 24–25 Oct. 1854, p. 20.

14 Russell, p. 107.

15 *Ibid.*

16 Howell, Dutton, Heavy Brigade, p. 52. Morley, letter 25 Jun. 1854, Dawson p. 16. Mitchell, p. 53. Scott Hunter, letter 27 Oct. 1854, Dawson, p. 85. Forster letter, 2 Nov. 1854, *Dawson*, p. 96.

17 Calthorpe, *Cadogan's Crimea*, pp.70–1. Russell, p. 109.

18 Ryhzov, *Notes on the Battle of Balaclava, Russkii Vestnik*, Apr. 1870, Vol. 86, p. 464. Kalinin, pp. 136–52. Liprandi, *Report to Prince Menshikov's ADC, 26 Oct. 1854.* Arbuzov.

19 Mitchell, pp. 53–4. Blunt, Mawson, p. 16. Smith, Brighton, p. 85. Howell, Dutton, Heavy Brigade, p. 52.

20 Duberly, pp. 92–3.

21 *Himalaya* Officer, HOPWWR, p. 322. Sterling, p. 61.

22 Munro, Spilsbury, p. 145. Fisher-Rowe, letter 31 Oct. 1854, Fisher, p. 130.

23 Vahey and Fox, Dutton, Lig*ht Brigade*, pp. 337 and 36.

24 Russell, pp.109–10.

Chapter 5

1 Ryzhov, *Notes on the Battle of Balaclava*, Russkii Vestnik, Apr. 1870, Vol. 86.

2 Hodasevich, p. 128.

3 Russell, p. 110. Munro, Spilsbury, pp. 145–6. Sterling, p. 62. Duberly, p. 93. Howell and Forrest, Dutton, Heavy Brigade, p. 52 and 180. Godman, Warner, p. 75.

4 Cameron and Joiner, Dawson, p. 76. Munro, Spilsbury, pp. 146–7. 1st Dragoons Private, *Spilsbury,* 12 Dec. 1854, p. 113. 1st Royals, 26 Oct. 1854, p. 81. Higginson and Stotherd, Baring Pemberton, p. 87

5 Russian Hussar, Spilsbury, p. 147.

6 Gough, letter 27 Oct. 1854, Dawson, p. 89. Selkrig, *Dawson.*, 22 Dec. 1854, p. 115.

7 Clarke, Dutton, Heavy Brigade, p. 102. Smith, Brighton, p. 3. Handley, Dutton, Heavy Brigade, p. 115. Inniskilling private, letter 19 Nov. 1854, Dawson p. 106. Neville, Dutton, Heavy Brigade, p. 270. Hodge, diary entry 10 Jun. 1855, p. 112.

8 Khitrivo and Veselovskii, '*The Grand Duke of Saxe-Weimar's Hussar Regiment in the Crimean War'*. Arbuzov. Kozhukhov.

9 Russell, p. 110. Paget.

10 Mitchell, p. 55. Gowing, p. 30.

11 McGrigor, letter 2 Nov. 1854, Dawson, p. 98. Godman, Warner, 26 Oct. 1854, p. 75.

12 Inniskilling captain, letter 2 Nov. 1854, Dawson, p. 99. Kneath, letter 3 Nov. 1854, Dawson, p. 143.

13 De Brack, Aidkin, *The Waterloo Companion*, p. 224. Elliot witness, *New York Times* Account 21 May 1882, Dutton, Heavy Brigade, p. 21.

14 Inniskilling officer, letter 2 Nov. 1854, Dawson, p. 100. Scots Grey officer, 27 Oct. 1854, *Dawson*, p. 87. Scott Hunter, 27 Oct. 1854, *Dawson*, p. 85. Moodie, 27 Oct. 1854, Dawson, p. 86. McGrigor, 2 Nov. 1854, Dawson, p. 98.

15 Gibson, letter 9 Dec. 1854, Dawson, p. 112. Paget.

16 Ryzhov. Arbuzov.

17 Russian officer casualties were 43 per cent according to the Moscow main staff monthly report of Oct. 1854. Details of Russian casualties, Arbuzov; Genishta and Borisevich.

18 5th DG officer, 'WI', letter 27 Oct. 1854, Dawson, p. 91. Franks, Brighton, p. 94. Inniskilling trooper, letter 19 Nov., Dawson p. 105. Gowing, pp. 30–1.

19 Gough, letter 27 Oct., Dawson, p. 90. Taylor witness, Dutton, Heavy Brigade, p. 282. Abbot, Dutton, Heavy Brigade, p. 270.

20 Paget, The Light Cavalry Brigade, *Ibid*. Forrest, Massie, *The National Army Museum Book of the Crimean War*, p. 82. Dacres and Hodge, Hodge, pp. 47 and 44.

21 Stephenson, letter 3 Jan. 1855, Dawson, p. 120. Griffiths, *Hodge*, p. 49. Auchinloss, letter 27 Dec. 1854, Dawson, p. 118. Ryan witness, Dutton, *Heavy Brigade*, p. 213.

22 Howell, Dutton, *Heavy Brigade*, p. 52. 1st Dragoons Trooper, 'WP' letter 22 Nov. 1854, Dawson, p. 107.

23 Forster, letter 2 Nov., Dawson, p. 97. Paget, The Light Brigade *Ibid*. Gowing, p. 32.

Chapter 6

1 SG Officer, letter 27 Oct. 1854, Dawson, p. 87. Russell, p. 111.

2 Cardigan, Barthorp, p. 49. Mitchell, p. 55. According to Lt Col Calthorpe, *Cadogan's Crimea*, 'the men clamoured to be allowed to attack the enemy', p. 74. Wightman, '*One of the Six Hundred on Charge*', *Nineteenth Century Magazine*, May 1892, p. 851.

3 Paget, p. 177. 1st Royals NCO, letter 26 Oct., Dawson, p. 81. Mitchell, p. 55.

4 Temple Godman, p. 76. Duberly, p. 94. Moodie, letter 27 Oct. 1854, Dawson p. 97. Inniskillings officer, letter 2 Nov. 1854, Dawson, p. 87. Elliot, Dutton, *Heavy Brigade*, p. 24.

5 Bell, Massie, p. 83. Duberly, p. 94.

6 Hardinge, Dutton, Heavy Brigade, p. 11.

7 Vahey, *Dutton*, Heavy Brigade, p. 57 and Dutton, Light Brigade pp. 337–8.

8 Cathcart, Selby, p. 167.

9 Nolan, Journal, *Expedition to the Crimea*. Buttery, *Messenger of Death*, p. 38 and 64. Nolan conversation, Wightman, p. 852. Mitchell, p. 55.

10 Blunt, Brighton, *Hell Riders*, p. 106.

11 Russell, 'Notes from the Camp', *Times* newspaper, 2 Mar. 1855.

12 Shakespear, Dawson, 31 Mar. 1855, p. 154.

13 Cigar incident, Brighton, pp. 101–2.

14 Shakespear, Dawson, p. 154. Mitchell, p. 55.

15 Verbal exchanges orders, Brighton, p. 108. Williams, 7 Jan. 1855, Dawson, p. 153.

16 Wightman, p. 852. Seager, Brighton, p. 102, Richardson and Smith, Brighton, p. 110.

17 Woodham, Dutton, *Light Brigade*, p. 205.
18 Kubitovich. Ryzhov.
19 Farquharson, Pennington, Hutton and Richardson, Brighton, p. 111. Williams, 7 Jan. 1855, Dawson, p. 153.
20 Wightman, p. 852.

Chapter 7

1 Russell, before Sevastopol, 25 Oct. 1854, p. 114. Gowing, p. 34. Duberly, p. 94.
2 Conner, Dutton, *Light Brigade*, p. 23.
3 Russell, p. 114. Gowing, p. 34. Raglan, letter to Wykeham Martin, 2 Nov. 1854, Fisher, p. 48.
4 Wightman, p. 853.
5 Wroots, Dutton, *Light Brigade*, p. 206. Smith, Brighton, p. 115 and Dutton, *Light Brigade*, p. 197.
6 Mitchell, p. 56. Wightman, p. 854. Grant on Gowings, Dutton, *Light Brigade*, p. 38. Officer's remark, *HOPWWR*. 1854, p. 327. Smith, Brighton, p. 115.
7 Ryzhov. Don Battery officer, Kalinin.
8 Morley and Butler, Brighton, p. 125.
9 Kilvert and regimental casualty chart, Dutton, Light Brigade, pp. 170 and 120.
10 Paget. Pearson, 26 Oct. 1854, Dawson, p. 134. Doyle and 'Jenny', Dutton, *Light Brigade*, pp. 95 and 90.
11 Prince, 4 Nov. 1854, Dawson, pp. 103–4. 'WB', 22 Nov. 1854, Dawson. Yorke, letter to sister, 5 Dec. 1854, Dawson, p. 111; and Dutton, *Heavy Brigade*, pp. 88–9. Selkrig, 22 Dec. 1854, Dawson, p. 115.
12 Royal's Trooper 'WP', 22 Nov. 1854, Dawson, p. 107. Walker, Dutton, Heavy Brigade, p. 17.
13 Clifford, 27 Oct. 1854, p. 73.
14 Baker, 7 Nov. 1854, Dawson, p. 144. Wombell and Morley, Brighton, pp. 126–7.
15 Don Battery officer, Kalinin. Morley, Brighton, p. 130.
16 Paget.
17 Wightman, p. 854. Sergeant 13th Light Dragoons, 7 Nov. 1854, Dawson, p. 146. Williams, 7 Jan. 1854, *Dawson,* p. 153. Dudley, 18 Dec. 1854, *Dawson,* p. 151.
18 Maxse, Baring Pemberton, pp. 106–7. Walker, 18 Nov. 1854, Dawson, p. 149, Wroots, Dutton, Light Brigade, p. 206.
19 Anon 8th Hussar trooper, Brighton p. 121. Tremayne, Baring-Pemberton, p. 107.
20 Nicholson, Dutton, Light Brigade, p. 254. Phillips, Fisher, p. 255. Williamson, Massie, p. 87.
21 Mitchell, p. 56. Dudley, 18 Dec. 1854, Dawson, p. 151. Gordon, Brighton, p. 137. Morgan, Dutton, Light Brigade, p. 313. Grigg, Lawrence, Mammoth Book of *Eyewitness Battles*, p. 298. Vahey, Dutton, Light Brigade, p. 338.
22 Morgan, Dutton, Light Brigade, p. 313. Berryman, Brighton, p. 135. Mitchell, p. 56.
23 Morley, Brighton, p. 139. Wightman, p. 855.

Chapter 8

1 Cardigan, Brighton, p. 138. Wightman and Maxse, Wightman, p. 855.
2 8th Hussar trooper, M. Barthorp, *Heroes of the Crimea*, p. 53. Vahey, Dutton, Light Brigade, p. 338. Woodham, *Dutton*, Light Brigade, p. 205.
3 Grigg, Lawrence, p. 298. Dudley, 18 Dec. 1854, Dawson, p. 151. Olley, Dutton, Light Brigade, p. 60. Spring, Dutton, Light Brigade, p. 191.
4 Low, Baring-Pemberton, p. 111. Low, eyewitness, Bath newspaper letter, Dutton, Light Brigade, p. 54. Grant, Dutton, Light Brigade, p. 38.
5 Buckton, Dutton, Light Brigade, p. 146. Smith, Dutton, Light Brigade, p. 264.
6 Anonymous Don Battery officer, Kalinin.
7 Kubitovich and Kozhukhov, Brighton, pp. 151–2.
8 Vahey, Dutton, Light Brigade, p. 338. Morris, *Dutton*, Light Brigade, p. 316.
9 Vahey, Dutton, Light Brigade, p. 338. Grigg, *Lawrence,* p. 229.
10 Ivanovich, David, *The Homicidal Earl,* p. 409. Kubitovich, Brighton p. 152. Kozhukhov. Smith, Brighton, p. 155.
11 Russell, report 25 Oct. 1854, p. 114. Kozhukhov, Brighton, p. 163. Gowing, pp. 34–5.
12 Paget. Mitchell, p. 57.
13 Smith, Brighton, pp. 160–1. Anonymouse 17th officer, Dawson, p. 141.
14 Firkins, Massie, p. 87. Wightman, p. 856.
15 Pennington, Dutton, Light Brigade, p. 181. Lazell, *Dutton*, Light Brigade, p. 150. Wightman, p. 857.
16 Arbuzov, pp. 389–410. Reilly, Harris, p. 240.
17 Pennington, Brighton, p. 165; and Harris, p. 241. Seager, Massie, pp. 88–9.
18 Kubitovich. Paget. Herbert, Dutton, Light Brigade, p. 45.
19 Woodham, Dutton, Light Brigade, p. 205. Phillips, letter to father, 27 Oct. 1854. Fisher, p. 256. Hutton, Dutton, *Light Brigade*, p. 47.
20 Mitchell, pp. 57–8. Chamberlayne, Dutton, *Light Brigade*, p. 215.
21 Duberly, p. 94. Witness, Harris, pp. 246–7.
22 Donoghue, Dutton, *Light Brigade*, p. 92. Smith, Brighton, p. 187. Lucan and Cardigan, David, pp. 412–13.
23 Trooper's response, David, p. 413. Wombwell, Brighton, p. 188.

Chapter 9

1 Russell, p. 114 and 116. Anonymous 17th officer, 10 Feb. 1855, Dawson, p. 140.
2 Lucan, Brighton, pp. 183–4. Russell, S. David, p. 414. Nolan's grave and Lucan, Buttery, pp. 143–4.
3 Figures, Brighton p. 293, David, p. 415 and Buttery, pp. 145–6.
4 Duke, Dutton, Light Brigade, p. 220. Terrot, Buttery, p. 146.
5 Seager, Massie, p. 90. Mitchell, p. 58. Smith, Brighton, p. 186.
6 Bandsman, Oct. 1854, Dawson, pp. 94–5. Duberly, pp. 95 and 274.
7 Fox, Dutton, Light Brigade, p. 36. Sheridan and Pardoe, Brighton, pp. 196–7. Vahey, Dutton, *Light Brigade*, p. 339.

8 Scots Greys officer, 27 Oct. 1854, Dawson, p. 92. Kozhukhov. Bandsman, Oct. 1854, p. 95. Russell, p. 117.

9 Dryden, Dutton, p. 153. Clowes, Massie, p. 91.

10 Wightman, pp. 857–8.

11 Mitchell, p. 59. Cameron, Bancroft, *The Way to Glory*, p. 14 Surgeon Scott, Dawson, p. 156. Yorke, 27 Oct. 1854, Dawson.

12 Russell, 25 Oct. 1854, despatch, p. 117. Sterling, 27 Oct. 1854, p. 63.

13 Kozhukhov. Kubitovich.

14 Paget. Lucan, Hibbert, *The Destruction of Lord Raglan*, pp. 151–2.

15 Paget, evening Oct. 25 1854. Hodge, pp. 51–2. Nunnerly, Brighton, p. 188.

16 Mitchell, p. 60. Gray, 12 Nov. 1854, Dawson, p. 148. Williams, 7 Jan. 1855, Dawson, p. 153. Wightman, pp. 858–9.

17 Duberly, pp. 96–7 and 274.

18 Gowing, p. 38.

Beyond 24 Hours

1 Paget, Harris, p. 264.

2 *Times* newspaper, Brighton, p. 230. *Morning Chronicle, HOPWWR,* pp. 307–8.

3 Walker, Dutton, Heavy Brigade, p. 17.

4 Forest, Buttery, p. 150. Auchinloss, 27 Dec. 1854, Dawson, p. 119.

5 Raglan, Woodham-Smith, *The Reason Why*, p. 268. Hodge, 29 Jan. 1855, p. 116.

6 Hodge, 29 Jan. 1855, p. 83.

7 Nolan, Buttery, pp. 161–2.

8 Subaltern, *Hodge*, p. 59. Paget, Dutton, *Light Brigade*, p. 61.

9 Jemmy, Dutton, *Light Brigade*, p. 90; Brighton, p. 221.

10 Don Battery Officer, Kalinin, pp. 136–52. Liprandi. Additional material from Kubitovich, Arbuzov, Kozhukhov and Ryzhov.

11 US Ship Captain, Mawson, p. 9.

12 Fox, Dutton, *Light Brigade*, p. 36.

13 Wightman, Dutton, *Light Brigade*, pp. 344–5; and Wightman, p. 863.

14 Down and out details, Brighton, pp. 227–8 and Bancroft, pp. 12–13.

BIBLIOGRAPHY

GENERAL PUBLISHED SOURCES

Adkin, M., *The Charge* (Pimlico 1996)

Adkin, M., *The Waterloo Companion* (Stackpole Books, 2001)

Bancroft, J.W., *The Way to Glory: Men of the North West who rode in the Charge of the Light Brigade* (private publication Neil Richardson 1988)

Baring Pemberton, W., *Battles of the Crimean War* (Pan 1962)

Barthorp, M., *Heroes of the Crimea* (Blandford 1991)

Brighton, T., *Hell Riders* (Penguin 2005)

Buttery, D., *Messenger of Death* (Pen & Sword 2008)

Cooke, B., *The Grand Crimean Central Railway* (Cavalier House 1990–1997)

David, S., *The Homicidal Earl* (Abacus 1998)

Figes, O., *Crimea* (Penguin 2011)

Fletcher, I. and Ishchenko, N., *The Crimean War: A Clash of Empires* (Spellmount 2004)

Harris, J., *The Gallant Six Hundred* (Hutchinson 1973)

Hibbert, C., *The Destruction of Lord Raglan* (Penguin 1985)

James, L., *Crimea 1854–56: The War with Russia from Contemporary Photographs* (Van Nostrand Reinhold Co. 1981)

Lawrence, R.R. (ed.), *The Mammoth Book of Eyewitness Battles* (Carroll & Graf 2002)

Lewis Stempel, J. (ed.), *The Autobiography of the British Soldier* (Headline Review 2007)

Massie, A., *The National Army Museum Book of the Crimean War* (Sidgwick & Jackson 2004)

Selby, J., *The Thin Red Line* (Hamish Hamilton 1970)

Shavshin, V., *The Valley of Death* (Sevastopol Kiev 2005)

Spilsbury, J., *The Thin Red Line* (Weidenfeld & Nicolson 2005)

Thomas, R.H.G. and Scollins, R., *The Russian Army of the Crimean War 1854–6* (Osprey 1991)

Warner, P., *The Crimean War: A Reappraisal* (Wordsworth 2001)
Windrow, M. and Wilkinson, F. (ed.), *The Universal Soldier* (Guiness Superlatives Ltd 1971)
Woodham-Smith, C., *The Reason Why* (Penguin 1958)

NINETEENTH-CENTURY PUBLISHED MEMOIRS AND PERSONAL ACCOUNTS

Barnstone, W. and R., *Letters from the Crimea and India* (Herald Printers 1998)
Calthorpe, S.J., Lt Col, *Cadogan's Crimea*, Letters from Headquarters 1856 (Atheneum 1980)
Clifford, H., *Henry Clifford VC: His Letters and Sketches from the Crimea* (Michael Joseph 1956)
Dawson, A., *Letters from the Light Brigade* (Pen & Sword 2014)
Duberly, F. (ed. Kelly, C.), *Mrs Duberley's War* (Oxford University Press 2007)
Dutton, R., *Forgotten Heroes: The Charge of the Heavy Brigade* (Info Dial Ltd 2008)
—— *Forgotten Heroes: The Charge of the Light Brigade* (Info Dial Ltd 2007)
Fisher, G. (ed.), *Crimean Cavalry Letters* (Army Records Society Pub, Vol. 31, 2011)
Gowing, T. (ed. Fenwick, K.), *A Voice from the Ranks* (London Folio Society 1954)
Hodge, E. (ed. Marquess of Anglesey), *Little Hodge: His Letters and Diaries of the Crimean War* (Military Book Society 1971)
Hume, J.R., Lt, *Reminiscences of the Crimean Campaign with the 55th Regiment* (Unwin Brothers 1894)
Image, J., Lt (ed. Ross, D.), *The Crimean Journal of John George Image* (Manitoba Museum of Men and Nature, Manitoba Canada 1971)
Kerr, P., *The Crimean War* (Channel Four Book 1997)
Lawson, G. (ed. Bonham-Carter, V.), *Surgeon in the Crimea* (History Book Club 1968)
Lluellen, R., Lt, *The Murder of a Regiment: Winter Sketches from the Crimea 1854–1855* (Withycut House 1994)
Mitchell, A., *Recollections of One of the Light Brigade 1888* (Crimean War Research Society Special Pub No. 31)
Nolan, L.E., Journal, (eds Guy, A.J. and Massie, A.), *Expedition to the Crimea* (NAM 2010)
Paget, G. Col, *The Light Cavalry Brigade in the Crimea* (John Murray 1881, accessed on VictorianWeb.org)
Russell, W., (eds Lambert, A. and Badsey, S.), *The War Correspondents: The Crimean War* (Bramley Books 1997)
Sterling, A., Lt Col, *The Highland Brigade in the Crimea* (Absinthe Press 1895/1995)

Warner, P. (ed.), *Letters Home from the Crimea* (Windrush Press 1999)

Wightman, J., 'One of the Six Hundred on the Balaclava Charge', *Nineteenth Century Magazine*, May 1892, pp. 850–863

ARCHIVE SOURCES

The History of the Present War with Russia (London Printing & Publishing Co. 1854)

Elphinstone, H.C. Capt., *Journal of the Operations Conducted by the Corps of Royal Engineers* (Eyre & Spottiswoode London 1859)

RUSSIAN ACCOUNTS

Arbuzov, Y., 'Reminiscences of the Campaign in the Crimean Peninsula in 1854 and 1855', *Voennyi Sboronik*, 1874, Vol. 96, No. 4, pp. 389–410, (trans. Conrad, M.)

Genishta, V.I. and Borisevich, A.T., 'The Grand Duke of Saxe-Weimar's Hussar Regiment in the Crimean War', *Istoriya 3-go dragunskago Ingermanlandskago polka 1704-1904* (St Petersburg 1904) (trans. M. Conrad)

Hodasevich, R.A., *A Voice from within the Walls of Sebastopol* (John Murray London 1856)

Kalinin, B.M., *Material for the History of the Don Artillery*, (Novocherkassk 1907), (trans. Conrad, M.)

Kozhukhov, S., 'Crimean Memoirs of the Last War', *Russkii Arkhiv*, 1869, Vol. 7, pp. 381–4, (trans. Conrad, M.)

Kubitovich, K., Lt, (ed. Dubrovnin, N.F.), 'Recollections of the Balaklava Affair of 13 October, 1854', St Petersburg 1871–72, Personal Account, *Voennyi Sbornik,* 1859, No. 2 (trans. Conrad, M., 1999)

Liprandi, I., Lt Gen, Official Report to General Prince Menshikov 26 October 1854

Ryzhov, Iv., Lt Gen, *On the Battle of Balaclava*, *Russkii Vestnik,* Apr. 1870, vol. 86, pp. 463–69, (trans. Conrad, M., 1999)

Seaton, A., *The Crimean War: A Russian Chronicle* (Batsford 1977)

Smirnov, Ya., Staff-Capt, *The Moscow Infantry Regiment in the Crimean War*, Istoriya 65-go pekhotnago Moskovskago Ego Imperatorskago Vysochestva Gosudarya Naslednika Tsesarevicha polka 1642–1700–1890 (Warsaw 1890)

PERIODICALS

Gates, D., 'Coalition Warfare and Multinational Operations in the Crimean War' (RUSI Aug. 1994)

Jones, D.R., *An Illustrated Guide to the Battlefield of Balaclava* (Crimean War Research Society Special Pub. No. 42)

Mawson, M.H., *The True Heroes of Balaclava* (Crimean War Research Society Special Pub. No. 14)

Mercer, P., 'Sebastopol' (*Military History Monthly*, No. 54, Mar. 2015)

Niderost, E., 'Into the Valley of Death' (Military Heritage US, Feb. 2004)

Sewell, A., 'Taken by the Russians: The Light Brigade Prisoners of Balaclava' (Crimean War Research Society, Special Pub. No. 11)

—— 'Casualties in the Light Brigade at Balaclava' (Crimean War Research Society, Special Pub. 10)

Taylor, A.H., 'Letters from the Crimea: Assistant Surgeon Arthur Henry Taylor' (RUSI Aug. 1994)

RADIO AND TV

Bragg, M., *In our Time, The Charge of the Light Brigade* (Radio 4, 10 Jan. 2008)

Farren, J.K. (prod.), *The Charge of the Light Brigade* (SMG TV Productions)

Morgan, M. and Melman, R. (prod.), *The Crimean War* (NAM and History Channel 2003)

Wason, D., *Battlefield Detectives: Balaclava 1854* (Granada TV 2003)

INDEX

Note: *italicised* page numbers indicate illustrations.

You may also enjoy …

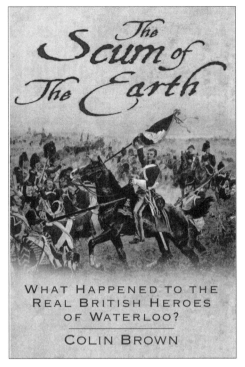

978 0 7509 8917 6

The Scum Of The Earth follows common soldiers – those whom Wellington angrily condemned as 'scum' for their looting at Vitoria – from victory at Waterloo to a Britain at war with itself. Colin Brown skilfully dismantles the myth that the defeat of Napoleon ended the threat of revolution spreading from France and presents a new view of Regency Britain.

You may also enjoy …

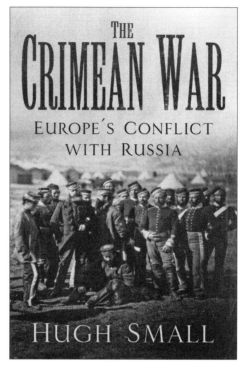

978 0 7509 8587 1

Hugh Small, whose biography of
Florence Nightingale first exposed
the truth about her wartime hospital,
now shows how the history of the
Crimean War was manipulated to
conceal Britain and Europe's failure.